*Marianne Moore,*

*Elizabeth Bishop,*

*and*

*May Swenson*

*Marianne Moore,* The

*Elizabeth Bishop,* Feminist Poetics

*and* of

*May Swenson* Self-Restraint

KIRSTIN HOTELLING ZONA

ANN ARBOR

THE UNIVERSITY OF MICHIGAN PRESS

2005   2004   2003   2002      4   3   2   1

*A CIP catalog record for this book is available from the British Library.*

Library of Congress Cataloging-in-Publication Data

Zona, Kirstin Hotelling, 1968–
    Marianne Moore, Elizabeth Bishop, and May Swenson : the feminist
  poetics of self-restraint / Kirstin Hotelling Zona.
       p.      cm.
    Includes bibliographical references and index.
    ISBN 0-472-11304-6 (Cloth : alk. paper)
    1. American poetry—Women authors—History and criticism.
  2. Feminism and literature—United States—History—20th century.
  3. Women and literature—United States—History—20th century.
  4. American poetry—20th century—History and criticism.   5. Moore,
  Marianne, 1887–1972—Criticism and interpretation.   6. Bishop,
  Elizabeth, 1911–1979—Criticism and interpretation.   7. Swenson,
  May—Criticism and interpretation.   8. Feminist poetry—History and
  criticism.   9. Self-control in literature.   I. Title.
  PS310.F45 Z66   2003
  811'.50809287—dc21                                         2002008277

*For Thomas,*

*and for Ella*

# Acknowledgments

While I am grateful to the many people who helped bring this book into being, I would like to thank those whose support has been essential. James Longenbach provided generous and invaluable guidance; without his astonishing acumen and ear for elegance this would be a different—undoubtedly lesser—book. Bette London offered incisive readings at every stage of composition, particularly in reference to my feminist framework. Cristanne Miller's excellent work on Moore has been an inspiration to me, and her careful attention to this manuscript sparked crucial revisions. I owe many thanks to Rozanne Knudson for her big-hearted enthusiasm and helpful insights concerning May Swenson's life and work. The curators of Special Collections at Amherst College, Vassar College, Washington University, and the Rosenbach Museum & Library have been gracious in their assistance with archival materials. I would especially like to thank Dr. Evelyn Feldman, former Keeper of the Marianne Moore Papers at the Rosenbach, and Anne Posega, former Curator of the May Swenson Papers at Washington University; both were enormously generous to me during various research visits. LeAnn Fields, Editor at the University of Michigan Press, has been indefatigable in her assistance. Several institutions and foundations helped fund my research and writing, and to them I am indebted: the Rush Rhees endowment at the University of Rochester; the Department of English at the University of Rochester; the Susan B. Anthony Institute for Gender and Women's Studies at the University of Rochester; and Illinois State University.

The following friends and family members also deserve special thanks: Heidi Julavits and Jill Goldman Leviton for their vitality and loyalty; Alexandra Schultheis for her keen intellect and no-nonsense advice; and Martha O'Connor and Kittie MacMahon for their sensitive guidance and creativity. My parents, Rebecca Riter Hotelling and David Rawson Hotelling, instilled in me the love of language and passion for justice that underpins this project, and my sister, Kimberly Hotelling-O'Connor, embodies more than anyone I know the attitude of wonder so integral to the life of a poet. My baby daughter Ella, whose birth coincided with the contracting of this book, brought calm and confidence to my writing when it was needed most. Finally, I owe more than I can possibly say to Thomas Allen Zona, who continues to honor and amaze me as both my best reader and my best friend.

I would like to acknowledge the following publications in which portions of this book originally appeared: *Modernism/Modernity* 5, no. 1 (1996); *Twentieth Century Literature* 44, no. 2 (1998); *"In Worcester Massachusetts": Essays on Elizabeth Bishop*, ed. Laura Jehn Menides and Angela Dorenkamp (New York: Peter Lang, 1999); and *Dear Elizabeth: Five Poems and Three Letters to Elizabeth Bishop*, by May Swenson (Logan: Utah State University Press, 2000). Permission for the quotations from the unpublished letters of Marianne Moore and Mary Warner Moore and from an unpublished manuscript by Marianne Moore is granted by Marianne Craig Moore, Literary Executor for the Estate of Marianne Moore. All rights reserved. Reprinted by permission of Farrar, Straus, & Giroux, LLC: Excerpts from *The Collected Prose* by Elizabeth Bishop. Copyright © 1984 by Alice Helen Methfessel. Excerpts from *The Complete Poems 1927–1979* by Elizabeth Bishop. Copyright © 1979, 1983 by Helen Methfessel. Excerpts from *Unpublished Letters* by Elizabeth Bishop. Copyright © by Alice Helen Methfessel. Permission for the quotations from the unpublished letters and manuscripts of May Swenson and to reprint the poem "Her Early Work" is granted by Rozanne Knudson, Literary Executor for the Estate of May Swenson. I am grateful to the Rosenbach Museum & Library, Philadelphia, for permission to quote from materials housed in the Marianne Moore Collection, and to Special Collections, Vassar College Libraries in Poughkeepsie, New York, for permission to quote from the Elizabeth Bishop Papers.

# Contents

# Abbreviations

ELIZABETH BISHOP

CP      *The Collected Poems.* New York: Farrar, Straus and Giroux, 1969.

Prose    *The Collected Prose.* Ed. Robert Giroux. New York: Farrar, Straus and Giroux, 1984.

OA      *One Art: Letters.* Ed. Robert Giroux. New York: Farrar, Straus and Giroux, 1994.


MARIANNE MOORE

AN      "Archaically New." In *Trial Balances,* ed. Ann Winslow. New York: Macmillan, 1935.

CP      *The Complete Poems of Marianne Moore.* New York: Macmillan/Viking, 1982.

ME      "A Modest Expert." *The Nation,* September 28, 1946, 354.

MMC   Marianne Moore Collection, Rosenbach Museum & Library, Philadelphia.

O       *Observations.* New York: Dial Press, 1924.

Poems   *Poems.* New York: Egoist Press, 1921.

SL      *The Selected Letters of Marianne Moore.* Ed. Bonnie Costello, Cristanne Miller, and Celeste Goodridge. New York: Knopf, 1997.


MAY SWENSON

HS      *Half Sun Half Sleep.* New York: Scribner's, 1967.

IOW    *In Other Words.* New York: Knopf, 1982.

LP      *The Love Poems of May Swenson.* Boston: Houghton Mifflin, 1991.

MSP    May Swenson Papers, Olin Library Special Collections, Washington University, St. Louis.

MWW   *Made with Words.* Ed. Gardner McFall. Ann Arbor: University of Michigan Press, 1998.

N       *Nature: Poems Old and New.* Boston: Houghton Mifflin, 1994.

# Introduction: Feminism and the Poetics of Self-Restraint

T he self does not realize itself most fully when self-realization is its most constant aim.[1] Had this aphorism of Marianne Moore's first appeared as part of "Marriage" or "A Grave," it would have helped clarify the feminist design so central to each poem. Like the young women at Barnard to whom these words were delivered, Moore was the product of a selective women's college, an environment she credited with refining her notorious restraint in tandem with her feminist convictions.[2] For Moore, humility was not simply a moral stance, but a sign of her distrust of the claims of self-expression. Unearthing the overlap between Moore's moral insistence and her poetic reserve is central to understanding her feminism—to seeing, that is, why an admonition against self-absorption is an appeal to self-awareness, an urging of her audience toward revelation, not retreat.

While Moore's paradoxically insistent reserve both compelled and perplexed Elizabeth Bishop, the younger poet never questioned Moore's feminist commitment. In a critique of those who read Moore's restraint as feminine whimsy, Bishop turns to the poem "Marriage" and wonders, understandably, "how much of Marianne's poetry the feminist critics have read" (*Prose*, 144). Like Moore, Bishop was a feminist who never saw self-affirmation as a conduit to revelation; as a result, she did not have to choose restraint at the expense of social vision. Nevertheless, Bishop struggled throughout her life to reconcile Moore's aversion to self-indulgence with her penchant for strict admonitions (to which Bishop herself was occasionally subject). Subsequently, Bishop would be the first to commend Moore's feminist prowess even as she described her as "what some people might call 'prudish'" (*Prose*, 130).

Interestingly, while Bishop positioned herself as rebellious protégé in relation to Moore, she adopted a remarkably Moore-like temperament in her extensive correspondence with May Swenson. Swenson labored over the contingency in Bishop's writing between revelation and reserve, especially as it shaped Bishop's depictions of lesbian desire. But as their letters reveal, Swenson's frustrations with Bishop's self-restraint had as much to do with her own emerging poetic as they did with her friend's. In order to come to terms with Bishop's reserve, Swenson first needed to examine her conflicted draw to what she once called the "physical" realm (*MWW*, 224–28). In doing so, she would refine the poetic elements that shaped her own fraught relations with feminist critics: a ripe sensual immediacy that questions the claims of sexual authenticity or bodily truth.

These overlaps among Moore, Bishop, and Swenson invite not only an articulation of the feminist potentials of self-restraint, but an account of the lingering conventions that posit such an equation as unlikely. All three of these poets wrote with a certain reserve—precisely the motive against which most feminist poets and critics of the last thirty years have established themselves. In response to the largely male-dominated field of poetry and criticism in America through the 1960s, many feminist poets sought the establishment of an alternative female tradition, the central goal of which has been, in Alicia Ostriker's words, the "quest for autonomous self-definition."[3] The premise of this project, Paula Bennett explains, is that the "acceptance of the self, whatever that self is, is the base upon which the woman poet must work, the source of her greatest authority and strength."[4] Ostriker calls this tradition "gynocentric," for as her readings suggest, when "defining a personal identity, women tend to begin with their bodies."[5] In the wake of this critical reclamation, female poets as different as H.D. and Millay are praised for what Bennett describes as a "readiness to look unflinchingly at themselves as women," to "release their power fully and base their craft upon their sex."[6]

By locating feminist purpose in self-expression, and self-expression in sexual frankness, this narrative of feminist poetry can account only partially for the poets who make up this project. Though Moore, Bishop, and Swenson differ in dramatic ways, their writings converge around a common tension: a thirst for accurate observation underscored by a wariness of objective truth. While this tension signals modernist poetry in general, these three poets were distinct in their embrace of its implications—the surrender of ultimate authority that authorship can seem to confer. Such surrender, however, is anathema to a search for autonomous self-definition.

The source of this disjunction has less to do with degree of feminist commitment than the conceptions of self that underpin one's poetry. In recent years a handful of Moore and Bishop critics have focused our attentions on the strategic potentials of self-restraint, and to them my project is indebted.[7] Bonnie Costello and Cristanne Miller, for instance, have shown that for Moore and Bishop, self-reserve signals a skepticism of the essential, coherent subject, that presence which is often assumed in overtly autobiographical verse. Such readings enable us to rethink the premium feminist poetry has often placed on self-expression, and to argue, as Miller does, for a wider understanding of what feminist poetry might be.[8] Nevertheless, with the exception of Miller's instructive book on Moore, a gap is growing between feminist repossessions of Moore and Bishop and recent readings of their antiessentialist poetics. On the one hand, these poets are appearing more frequently in the feminist canon, but the price of this inclusion is usually the suppression of their strategies of self-restraint. On the other hand, critics have focused recently on the ways in which reserve signals a wariness of the coherent, confessional self, but these readings do not suggest the feminist potential of such poetics. My analysis builds on the banks of this critical divide in an effort to help bridge it. In the following pages I suggest that Moore, Bishop, and Swenson expressed their commitment to feminism by exposing its most treasured assumptions: not only do they challenge the ideal of autonomy, but they contest the integrity of a sensual or sexual authenticity by which that ideal is measured.

While a partnership between feminism and antiessentialism is commonplace within studies of fiction and feminist theory, it has been less welcome in the world of poetry. This critical gap is the inspiration behind *Feminist Measures: Soundings in Poetry and Theory,* edited by Cristanne Miller and Lynn Keller.[9] This important collection offers evidence that the distance between current feminist theory and discussions of poetry is narrowing, just as the genre of feminist poetry is becoming more varied and complex. But because the editors' goal is to account for the current range of these "feminist measures," they are more concerned with the continuities among various perspectives than with the differences between them:

> Feminist theory and criticism are cumulative as well as developing fields. Kinds of inquiry particularly central in earlier decades—

explorations of female traditions and influence, retrieval and reval-
uation of lost female writers or of typically female genres—have
not been abandoned but instead continue, often incorporated into
other currently more urgent kinds of inquiry. (9–10)

Clearly, Keller and Miller trace this genealogy in an effort to under-
score the diversity of feminist approaches available to us today. Never-
theless, this gesture of inclusion inadvertently displaces those feminist
practices that *have* abandoned the kinds of inquiry so central to earlier
decades—namely, those strategies that are deeply skeptical of the
rhetoric of "retrieval" and "female tradition." That several of the essays
in *Feminist Measures* do, in fact, take this skepticism for granted points
up the deep degree to which the project of feminist poetry in this coun-
try is wed to the language of self-affirmation.

Such tenacious devotion to an ideal of authenticity signals a broader
trend within American poetry since midcentury. James Longenbach
has observed that the "breakthrough" narrative dramatized by Robert
Lowell's *Life Studies* lingers in a certain preoccupation with form; while
the privileging of personal confession is not as widespread today as it
was twenty years ago, "its assumptions are perpetuated by many poets
and critics who, whatever their differences, agree that a great deal of
cultural weight depends upon the choice of poetic form." Thus, "an
easy confluence of formal and social vision is assumed, and almost any
new development in American poetry is heralded at the expense of a
previous 'breakthrough,' now seen to be either too timid or too
severe."[10] It is no coincidence that Bishop is the one poet my book has
in common with Longenbach's; within feminist criticism, the "break-
through" narrative is fueled by the privileging of sexual frankness over
sexual reserve, in the belief that female agency is contingent upon the
shedding of a sexual repression to which all women are subject. Such
an account sees Bishop's cagey love poems as "stillborn," Moore's lack
of intimate expression as asexual and unfeminine, and Swenson as
irrefutably "Sapphic."[11] Despite the useful questions such readings
may raise, they foreclose an analysis of the strategies of self-restraint.
Consequently, the fact that these poets contest the plausibility of an
authentic, unmediated sexuality (the presumption by which they are so
often read) remains overlooked.

In order to articulate the feminist potential of such poetry we need a
critical discourse that questions the conventions of self-expression, just

as it strives for what Moore called "self-realization." Recent work by Kaja Silverman and Judith Butler is especially useful in this regard. Despite their differences, Silverman and Butler meet in their mutual efforts to challenge the "dominant fiction" by using its narratives in unorthodox ways.[12] For example, in the now classic *Gender Trouble* Butler applies Foucault's critique of the repressive hypothesis to Freud's version of the Oedipus scenario, showing that its "success" depends upon a primary taboo against homosexuality. In the process, she appropriates elements of Freudian analysis in order to critique its heterosexist premise. In complementary fashion, Silverman maintains Lacan's insistence that subjectivity is engendered through the acquisition of language in order to turn the patriarchal presumption of dominant culture against itself. Her most recent book, *The Threshold of the Visible World*, runs counter to more traditional trends within feminist and psychoanalytic film theory by suggesting that the processes of identification—that series of psychic maneuvers through which we come to "know ourselves" within normative terms—can be employed as an agent of social change.

Butler and Silverman stand out because of their abilities to craft unlikely allegiances, as does Donna Haraway, another theorist whose presence is palpable in the following pages.[13] Like the poets at the heart of this book, these writers craft agency from impurities and have no use for innocence. Haraway articulates this perspective in her notion of "situated knowledges," wherein "partiality and not universality is the condition of being heard to make rational claims" (173). She asserts the feminist potential of the particular, arguing that "feminist objectivity" is not enabled by a search for identity. Because identity is always an unfinished, imperfect process, we must emphasize the slippages, the failures—what Butler calls the "weakness in the norm." In the process we may refigure that norm, forging overlaps and exchanges where oppositions traditionally triumph.

Haraway's articulation of the subversive potential of "partiality" helps to complicate Moore's asexual reputation. In chapter 1 I draw a parallel between Moore's supposed prudishness and her antiessentialist poetic. At the heart of this reading is what I call Moore's "strategic selfhood," a style of authorship by which self-restraint enables an interrogation of subjectivity without recourse to self-promotion. Exploring the feminist implications of Moore's strategic selfhood, the discussion shows how her poetry deconstructs the lyric "I" along with the sexed body through which this "I" is made to seem a priori. Consequently, we are able to see that Moore, though reserved, was not asexual; on the contrary, she was fascinated with the discursive practices that instruct "sex." Moore's interest in embodiment takes us to the heart of her relations with feminist critics. Although Bishop and Swenson share Moore's aversion to self-indulgent poetry, it is Moore's unmatched ability to proffer moral standards without recourse to a fleshy, lyric "I" that has made her, for feminists, the most difficult and diversely read poet of this century. Grounding feminist principle in autonomous selfhood, and the autonomous self in female sexuality, the most vocal feminist critics of the past thirty years have contributed largely to what Taffy Martin terms the "myth" of Marianne Moore:[14] the popular conception of a self-protective, well-mannered eccentric who flirted coyly with her peers, went dutifully to church, and wrote reticent poems with what Louise Bogan called "her delightful innocence of approach."[15] In some ways, of course, Moore was all of these things. However, in search of autobiography, political purpose, and sexual frankness, the majority of feminist critics through the mid-1980s glossed over the intricate and often paradoxical ways in which Moore was also none of these things at all. As Bishop once wryly reminisced, Moore "was rather contradictory, you know, illogical sometimes. . . . You could never tell what she was going to like, or dislike."[16]

In the last ten years, several critics have sought to complicate this portrait of Moore, but it lingers tenaciously.[17] Undoubtedly its persistence is due in part to Moore's own complicity in fostering this persona within the public spotlight of her later life. Miller notes that this stereotype of Moore was so firmly entrenched by midcentury that even Bishop seems to have encouraged it, at least in part. Bishop's memoir "Efforts of Affection" *(Prose)* and especially her poem "Invitation to Miss Marianne Moore" frequently construct an "image of the poet as quaintly harmless."[18] At the same time, as I discuss in chapter 2, recent feminist scholarship on Bishop often endorses the image of Moore as archaically prim and private in an effort to position Bishop as a different—namely autobiographical—poet.

And indeed, while feminist reclamations of Moore have been slow in coming, such readings of Bishop have flourished in recent years. Adrienne Rich offered the first revision of this sort in her 1983 review of Bishop's *Complete Poems,* and her words set the tone for the interpretations to follow. Conceding that Bishop's poetry "now seems . . . remarkably honest and courageous," she simultaneously mourns the fact that "attention was paid to [Bishop's] triumphs . . . not to her struggles for self-definition and sense of difference."[19] As if in response to Rich's regret, recent critics have focused largely on the details of Bishop's biography (her lesbianism, her alcoholism and asthma, and her emotional hardships), culling evidence from her later poetry in particular in an effort to emphasize coded sexual longings and the unfolding of an autobiographical bent.[20] These timely studies have helped cultivate a fast-growing interest in Bishop's poetic restraint, pointing out, as Rich goes on to do, that Bishop's reserve is inextricable from her identity as a lesbian. But while such efforts grant Bishop a place in the feminist canon, they do not alter the logic of the earlier readings that kept her out. Such reclamations often assume a notion of selfhood—progressive, stable, authentic—that Bishop's poems routinely call into question. As a result, this body of writing champions Bishop's later, ostensibly more personal poetry at the expense of her early work. The new feminist Bishop is achieved in exchange for the old, more ambivalent one, while her self-restraint remains a mark of misfortune, a silent plea for sympathy.[21]

In chapter 3 I suggest that Bishop's reserve is more than a protective guard: it expresses her distrust of the confessional lyric speaker, that presence so often preserved in the poetics of sexual masking. Moreover, I posit that in her most personal poems Bishop offers her keenest challenge to the notion of coherent selfhood that the term *autobiography* often assumes. Bishop's later turn to her own history is inextricable from her lifelong focus on *otherness;* for Bishop, exploring one's self is dependent upon exploring one's notion of difference, so that the pursuit of one will always come on the heels of pursuing the other. Juxtaposing Bishop's early poems about fantastical others with her poems about race and class, I maintain that the constant negotiation of the abject and ideal within her poetry provides the possibility of Silverman's "productive look," a conscious, though always limited, determination to reidentify with what one initially finds repulsive or merely other.

In many ways the story of Swenson's career encompasses and exaggerates the disjunction that emerges in recent studies of Bishop and Moore. Effusive and unabashedly erotic, Swenson's poetry has enjoyed spare but steady approval from some feminist critics. But Swenson's poetry also thrives on the enigmatic—it revels in riddles and puzzles and the rewards of holding back. Because Swenson is so much more exuberant than Moore or Bishop, her reserve seems more labored, and the provocative tension between her generosity and her restraint more bizarre; indeed, the relative critical silence surrounding Swenson implies that perhaps this tension has appeared to some the mark of a more careless, less mature poet.[22] This book suggests otherwise. While Swenson was fiercely independent, uncomfortable with the idea of influences in general, her letters reveal the deep, particular kinship she felt with Bishop and Moore. In chapter 5 I focus largely on Swenson's love poems in order to show how she disrupts the notion of female sexuality by which she is so often read. By appropriating heterosexual tropes, Swenson rewrites the terms of desire and broadens the scope of possible pleasures in her poems. In this vein my concluding chapter insists on the generative, productive power of language, the element that ultimately underpins the feminist poetics of these three poets.

Interlacing the three chapters on Moore, Bishop, and Swenson are two that explore the extensive correspondence they shared. I approach these poets' letters in much the same way I do their poems; that is, as carefully constructed texts, replete with their own strategies of self-restraint and revelation. As I examine the interrelations of these poets in chapters 2 and 4, my aim is not to establish a particular tradition among them, but to learn how our readings of their poems might be enlightened by their readings of each other and the relationships they shared. At stake in their own often fraught interpretations is the issue at the heart this study: the complex powers of a calculated self-restraint.

Thus, in chapter 2, "Marianne Moore and Elizabeth Bishop," we see how each poet's attempt to understand the other was both fueled and frustrated by the paradox at the heart of Moore's poetry: an adamant moral urgency combined with a persistent admonition against self-assertion. In turn, I highlight the ways in which our own readings of Moore and Bishop often assume the simplified portraits left in the wake of their relationship. I conclude that reconciling Moore's feminist vision with her moral stance means understanding that her wariness of self-absorption goes hand in hand with her ethical urgency—that the two are one and the same.

Although the correspondence between Moore and Bishop is well known within American poetry circles, the relationship between Swenson and Bishop has yet to be explored in critical depth. Between their first meeting in 1950 and Bishop's death in 1979, Bishop and Swenson

exchanged 268 letters (making Swenson one of Bishop's primary corre-
spondents, along with Moore and Robert Lowell). Chapter 4 provides a
detailed analysis of this correspondence, along with discussion of the
four poems Swenson wrote to Bishop. Swenson's playful and incisive
readings of Bishop's work afford a richer view of what she once called
Bishop's "cagey" love poems, granting Bishop's poetry a conscious
agency, and hence respect, that she is sometimes denied. While Bishop
clearly struggled against the confines of heterosexist culture, her
restraint is not merely the product of repression or self-protection. On
the contrary, Swenson helps us see that Bishop's silences were often
strategic, in the service of unearthing assumptions instead of giving
answers.

Moore, Bishop, and Swenson were never convinced that truth is some-
thing a poem could unearth. Rather, meaning for these poets is pro-
duced in the *process* of recording one's observations; representation is
not secondary to that which it depicts. To some degree any poet strug-
gles with this sense, but the poets to whom this study is devoted did
not resist their understanding, for they never saw it as a reason for
despair. And this commonality yields another, no less notable feature
of their poems: a palpable lack of self-pity that does not sacrifice an
ounce of acumen. Moore, Bishop, and Swenson did not narrate an inti-
mate identity or an explicit sexuality because they were more interested
in exposing the illusions such narratives uphold. As the poems at the
heart of this study suggest, we may profit by shifting our focus from the
contours of selfhood to the connections through which our selves are
made real. After autonomy, feminist poetry may find sustenance in
self-restraint.

# 1  Marianne Moore's Strategic Selfhood

T he myth of Marianne Moore as modest eccentric perseveres both innocently and insidiously in readings that emphasize her observational prowess at the expense of her moral and political integrity, or in analyses that describe her difficult technique as self-protective armor, a "shield that [Moore] constantly hides behind."[1] Moore's poems *are* marked by stunning concrete descriptions and a shifting, restless, even reticent "I," but to dismiss or praise her work as masked or object-oriented is to ignore the biting satire and subversive coils of language that make her work so radical, as both modernist and feminist. The power of Moore's observations cannot be grasped in isolation from her refusal of the stable lyric "I," for, as May Swenson once asked, who "of us is able to be such an acute instrument for the objectification of sensual perceptions and states of mind as she, without emphasizing *self* as subject?"[2]

Swenson's question implies that it is exactly the tension created by Moore's remarkably precise observations and her simultaneous undermining of the "I" from which they emanate that defines Moore's most puzzling, and rewarding, poetic. That poetic, with its vital relevance to the currently shifting parameters of American feminist criticism, is the focus of this chapter. Exploring the implications of Moore's strategic selfhood, we shall see how her poetry deconstructs the lyric "I," and even more radically, the "sexed" body through which this "I" is made to seem essential. Like the glacial octopod in "An Octopus," Moore's restless eye is discernible only at moments of intricately palpable existence, the slippery but tenacious tentacles of sensual connection. As we are led through layer after layer of material detail in Moore's poems, we are taken farther astray from any a priori or ontological perspective: "Completing a circle, / you have been deceived into thinking that you have pro- / gressed" (CP, 71). In marking subjectivity by sensual response rather than sexual convention, Moore asks that we loosen sen-

11

sual experience from the dictates of sexuality, and in doing so, refor-
mulate what it means to have both a sex and a self.

Although Moore's later work suggests that she never fit completely the
mythic guise of the modest eccentric, personal records of her early
years leave no doubt that Moore's vision of herself was anything but
hesitant or selfless. In January 1908, when Moore was a junior at Bryn
Mawr, her mother, Mary Warner Moore, cautioned her:

> You may not know that you are very strongly self-centered. . . .
> Now, there are advantages connected with self-analysis, and self-
> regard: one is well-mannered, and well-dressed; and is possessed
> too, of good taste and delicate sensibility,—brings forth from his
> resources that which will make the individual pleasing to those
> whom he wishes to please. But there are also disadvantages con-
> nected with being self-centered. He may put forth his best and
> those he attracts may expect his best yet to develop, and be accord-
> ingly disappointed when they find that back of that bright promise
> there is a good deal of colorless material.[3]

What is especially revealing about this excerpt is the way in which Mrs.
Moore hints at the self as a kind of design, or tool—an aperture to be
sized for different scenes by self-awareness; one's "I" is an entity over
which we have at least some conscious control, not something fixed or
given. Mrs. Moore's conception of the self was largely shaped by her
Presbyterian conviction that selfishness is blindness, a mantra we hear
throughout Moore's work. But like her daughter, Mrs. Moore was
never meek or selfless. A professional woman and single mother at the
turn of the century, Mary Warner Moore had strong opinions and a dri-
ving sense of justice to which she dedicated much energy and time.
Writing to her son from a suffrage convention, Mrs. Moore provides a
portrait of herself quite different from the one to which we are accus-
tomed:

> Our cars had great banners on them with the legend on them
> "Votes For Women." As I lay on my tum-tum—fastened a huge
> banner of this description from the 2nd story front window of the
> courthouse—a child looked up and read, "Vote For Women?—No!

Me? I'd rather vote for men." Everybody who passed gaped, so we got what we wanted—attention. But I dropped my glasses so I paid dear. I knew at first it would cost and went forth solemnly! But I am not afraid! Bunny Belong![4]

Hardly a retiring model of Victorian femininity, Mrs. Moore exerted strong influence over both her children, with whom she remained extremely close until her death in 1947. Though somewhat less devout than her mother, Moore also incorporated the basic Presbyterian mandates of self-tempering within her life and work.[5] At the same time, as her mother's letter suggests, Moore struggled with her tendency toward impatience and selfishness. An avid athlete who once declared after a game of lacrosse that she "felt like the trademark inside Sir Knight's iron pants,"[6] the young Moore wrote home often with her many judgments and opinions. One such excerpt explains how Moore, upon arriving one fall at Bryn Mawr, found a friend had been stuck with a "vilely" trying roommate, a young woman who would surely drive Moore to "murder the girl and commit suicide after being with her half a day."[7] In another passage, Moore tells her family how after a conversation concerning suffrage with an unsympathetic friend, she "could have beat her with a book."[8] Moore's letters gush with stylistic observations in a flaired and breathless hand, often ending without inquiry into the lives of those to whom she's writing. The young persona that emerges from Moore's early correspondence has more in common with the spirited "Helena Morely" of Bishop's 1957 translation than with the fantastical feminine Moore in graying braids and a tricorne hat.[9] As Cristanne Miller has observed, "Moore's stance seems . . . more belligerent than modest."[10]

Moore's correspondence is also marked by moments of deep reflection and tolerance, as many readers have noted. But it is the tension between her self-indulgence and self-reserve that interests me most, because this tension occupies such a central place in her poetry. Insatiably drawn to poetry as a profession, Moore was also her mother's daughter and wary of the inevitable egoism writing entails. As early as 1908, three months after she received her mother's words of warning quoted above and before she had come in contact with any contemporary writers, Moore wrote her family from college with the following announcement:

> Writing is all I care for, or for what I care most, and writing is such a puling profession, if it is not a great one, that I occasionally give it up—You ought I think to be didactic like Ibsen poetic like "Sheats," or pathetic like Barrie or witty like Meredith to justify your embarking as self confidently as the concentrated young egoist who is a writer, must—writing is moreover a selfish profession and a wearing (on the investigator himself). (*SL*, 45–46)

As a junior at Bryn Mawr, Moore was acutely cognizant of her writing as a "profession," of the egoism of that profession, and of the struggle she would face throughout her life as a person who simultaneously believed that "what you are comes out in what you write."[11] Bonnie Costello has artfully written that to impose "the self and its accumulated structures on the world is to narrow the world and trap the self, a self-defeating gesture."[12] But rather than despair at this paradox, Moore reveled in the challenges it posed:

> If you will tell me why the fen
> appears impassable, I then
> will tell you why I think that I
> can get across it if I try.
>                    (*CP*, 178)

In response to what might seem like an impossible impasse, Moore developed her famous "armor," a key component of her strategic selfhood, in the shape of eclectic quotations, riddled verse, and an elusive, shifting narrative presence—what many have taken to be the poet's self-protective mask. But as Costello insists, the "abnegation of the self ultimately satisfies the self, for it widens the sphere of response, the self being continually discovered through response to the external world."[13] To armor oneself is to enter the world, not shy away from it, as when Moore thanks T. S. Eliot for his introduction to her *Selected Poems*, claiming that she is "grateful for the armor afforded me by your introduction to my book."[14] It is for this reason that, as Richard Howard has said, Moore's "was the most personal poetry ever written."[15] As on her famous pangolin, whom "simpletons thought a living fable," "who endures / exhausting solitary trips through unfamiliar ground at night," Moore's "Armor seems extra." After all, the pangolin has a "grit-equipped gizzard" and is "the night miniature artist engineer . . . of whom we seldom hear." But the "impressive" self of "the armored / ant-eater" is nurtured by his "closing ear-ridge" and "contracting nose and eye apertures"; his "armor" is what lets him meet the "driver-ant" and "not turn back"—it fosters courage, and thus enables curiosity. An integral aspect of the pangolin's identity, his armor is also adjustable—he can contract, be "[s]erpentined," or rolled into a ball that has the "power to defy all effort to unroll it." Indeed, as Moore writes, to "explain grace requires / a curious hand" (*CP*, 117–18).

Moore's discomfort with the lyric "I" was, of course, a concern of many of her modernist contemporaries as well. Michael Levenson has explained eloquently that the advent of scientific empiricism in the mid-1800s challenged belief in divine order, resulting in a tension between external standards and individualistic self-consciousness that, in turn, engendered early modernism as a movement.[16] Reacting to what seemed a Romantic excess, as well as to the threatened guarantee of transcendental promise, Ezra Pound, Williams Carlos Williams, H.D., Mina Loy, Gertrude Stein, and in some senses Moore and Eliot, attempted in a variety of ways to strike a balance between the individualistic thrust to "make it new" and a growing wariness of universal truths. A turn to "objective" experience—Williams's "no ideas but in things," Pound's "the natural object is always the adequate symbol," Eliot's "objective correlative"—spawned a curiously nonautobiographical yet egoistic movement in the arts at the start of this century, one of which Moore was always critical yet deeply a part. Though akin, for example, to Pound and Williams in their quests for exactitude and fresh observation, Moore never condoned Pound's pride or Williams's conviction that "the poet must use anything at hand to assert himself."[17]

At the same time, as Sandra Gilbert and Susan Gubar have argued, the modernist milieu in which Moore forged her literary career was marked by an anxiety over sex and gender; in the wake of the women's movement, scientific challenges to biological determinism, suffrage, and the wartime imperative for women's public work, gender roles were fundamentally questioned.[18] It would be absurd to suggest that Moore was not conscious of the sexism in her professional climate; a cursory glance through the first few pages of *Poems* (1921), where we encounter "Pedantic Literalist" and "To a Steam Roller," or a look at slightly later poems like "Sojourn in the Whale," "A Grave," and "Marriage" (*Observations*, 1924), reveals otherwise. But it would be just as erroneous to conclude that Moore considered herself a mere satellite to the largely male group of her modernist peers. Though never granted, or interested in, the status of an Eliot or Pound, Moore was, as several critics have noted, at the fore of the new poetry movement, involved in close friendships with Pound, Williams, and later Eliot and Stevens in which each poet sought the promotion of the other.[19]

Nevertheless, "experience attests," wrote Moore in 1923, "that men have power / and sometimes one is made to feel it" (*CP*, 67). Given all the ways in which Moore resembles her contemporaries, she remains unequaled in her ability to distinguish, and distance, poetic innovation and observation from self-affirming presence. Always aware of the dueling drives of authorship and reticence, Moore never attempted to soften the disjunction between keen modernist observation and her deep distrust of the lyric "I." Though the poetry of Moore's peers also turns on this inherent paradox (Eliot and Stevens perhaps most of all), no one embraced it with a joy or gusto matching Moore's. Indeed, whereas other modernists sometimes saw this paradox as a problem to be solved, Moore unceremoniously marshaled it as the goal of her poetic.

In keeping with the perception of Moore as modestly mannered, readers tend to agree that as the poet matured, poems like "A Grave" gave way to less assertive, more self-conscious work. Regarding the often judgmental, declarative tenor of Moore's early verse as the expression of youthful egoism, critics often view her later voice as a reaction to the emphatic confidence of her younger years. Margaret Holley gives the best articulation of this argument: in Moore's "mature poems . . . the private self is now perceived as one more objective item out there in the public world, while that public world outside the self turns out to be thoroughly permeated with the subjectivities of others' limited points of view, superstitions, and fabulous stories."[20] Holley's reading is based on her premise that the "early poetic voice that responds personally by expressing the views and feelings of the self gives way . . . to the poet as an artificer who records, designs and textualizes the materials of the culture in a poetic way" (83). However, examination of some of Moore's first poems reveals that her practice was always inextricable from her acute analysis of selfhood; that Moore's earliest poems, opinionated and raw as they may be, are the products of a subversive architect (indeed, an "artificer") committed to displacing the Romantic lyric "I."

One such piece, "He Made This Screen," initially titled "To a Screen Maker," is ostensibly a poem about the power—presumably an artist's, perhaps God as artist—to create life and the world in which we live it. The final three stanzas appear as follows:

Here, he introduced a sea
Uniform like tapestry;

Here a fig-tree; there a face;
There a dragon circling space—

Designating here, a bower;
There, a pointed passion flower.[21]

But in one of Moore's earliest drafts of the poem, written in a letter to her family in 1908, it appeared in two parts, its biblical references much less pronounced and its object of description more enigmatic (which, under the eagle eye of Mrs. Moore, may be why it was revised):[22]

1. *To an Artificer*
Not of silver nor of coral,
But of weather-beaten laurel.
Carve it out.

II
Make a body long and thin
And carve hairs upon the skin
Make a snout.

III
On the order of a tower
Faintly wrinkled like a flower
On the paws

IV
Carve out heavy feline toes
Make each claw an eagle's nose.
Carve out great jaws.

2. *To a Screen-Maker*
Not of silver nor of coral,
But of weather-beaten laurel
Carve it out.

II
Carve out here and there a face
Flying a symbol out in space
Of grim doubt.

III
Represent a branching tree
Uniform like tapestry
And no sky.

IV
And devise a rustic bower
And a pointed passion flower
Hanging high.

The first part of the poem, "To an Artificer," suggests an agent, an inventor who carves a literal life that parallels the making of the poem itself. Part 2, "To a Screen-Maker," also addresses an inventor, one who works with the same common material—"weather-beaten laurel"—as opposed to the more difficult to procure "silver" or "coral." But the screen-maker's product is one of surroundings, of context, perhaps that in which the artificer's claw-toed body might live. Whereas the artificer's ordered efforts forge a single material creature, contained and local, the screen-maker's impart intellection, a "symbol" of "grim doubt" emanating from a dappled haze of bodiless heads. Furthermore, it is the ambiguity afforded by this abstract doubt that precipitates a radical shift in the agent's work. Unlike the artificer, who seems to enjoy a direct and unmediated relationship to its artifact, the screen-maker, surrounded by the intellectualizations of its own making, now merely "[r]epresent[s]" a "branching tree," "a rustic bower," and a "pointed passion flower" in its efforts. In devising its skyless surroundings, the screen-maker produces a screen between its own agency and its craft; what started as an ordered procedure of cause and effect turns into a highly mediated artistic endeavor, much like the scenario enacted between the artist and his subject in John Ashbery's poem "The Painter."[23] Indeed, it is precisely the screen-maker's power to construct this world of thought (the screen-maker's own intellect, projected) that accounts for the loss of innocence this part of the poem invites. Thus, the world becomes a screen, a "symbol" of itself, crafted by the screen-maker and, in turn, screening the screen-maker's relation to it. The Romantic relation of the speaker to her subject, in which the artist emerges as conduit to the real, is refigured in this version of the poem, the real and the artist becoming interlaced threads of a "weather-beaten" screen, letting in light while blocking it out.

From this perspective, the ostensible opposition between the first and second parts of the poem also becomes blurred. What seemed at first to be the contrast between unmediated artistic vision and the frustration of artistic struggle becomes instead a contingency, as we realize that the creature of the first stanza is, in fact, no more real than the "branching tree" and "rustic bower" of the second. As the artificer carves out the "body long and thin," a picture immediately starts to form; however, the totality hinted at by the assertive tenor of the poem's first stanza begins to crumble under the weight of disconnected body parts and a series of incongruous images: wrinkled flower, eagle's nose, a snout, and great jaws. The break in meter in the last line of the poem, enacted through the flattening addition of "out," further belies whatever sense of completeness the beginning of the poem suggests. Subsequently, the artificer's artifact is no more actual than the screen-maker's, and neither artist's agency transcends its crafted scene. Just as the creature of the first stanza eludes our visualization, so the artists themselves seem to fold into the space of their creations.

The actions of both the artificer and screen-maker become the body of this poem, establishing a parallel between their roles and the poet's. Like the inventors in "To an Artificer/To a Screen Maker," Moore has crafted an artifact in which she is, strategically, both implicated and evaded. The egoism of artistry is announced in the self-referential title of the poem and then displaced in the schism between artistic intent— "Carve it out"—and its sketchy results. Though other relatively early poems such as "I May, I Might, I Must" (1909), "To a Steamroller" (1915), "Pedantic Literalist" (1916), "Sojourn in the Whale" (1917), and certainly "Marriage" (1923) may be gleaned for their more obvious feminist nuances, the mechanisms at work in this poem provide a more suggestive example of why Moore poses such a problem—and promises so much—for feminist critics and fellow poets: foreshadowing later and more accomplished poems like "Black Earth" and "Those Various Scalpels" (to which I will later turn), "To an Artificer/To a Screen Maker" finds no possibility for autonomous self-definition because coherent autonomy is precisely the illusion that the poem disperses with its screening vision. Constantly announced by the imperative commands of the narrative voice, the artist is at once literally brought to life by her craft and undermined by it as well.

Moore's poems are perhaps most recognizable by their acutely descriptive observations, a point made manifest in the large amount of critical work devoted to this aspect of her poetry. In a conversation with Taffy Martin, Kenneth Burke said that on "occasion . . . [Moore] would be nearly overcome by the visual stimuli in a museum."[24] Eliot described her poetic eye as akin to a "high-powered microscope," while Bishop once referred to Moore as "The World's Greatest Observer." Moore's letters to friends and family are suffused with visual details about artwork, architecture, clothing, style, and plant and animal life. Indeed, in the words of Jean Garrigue, might "we not attribute to [Moore] what she did to Henry James: 'a rapture of observation'? For who has held up to inspection more 'skeined, stained veined variety'?"[25]

Miller suggests that Moore's love of science, and particularly her fascination with physics' recently popularized quantum theory, helps explain Moore's angle on vision. "According to quantum theory, an object manifests itself differently according to the context of the experiment in which it is seen," so that for Moore redefining "clarity . . . dovetails with redefining authority, both positive values for Moore but only to the extent that clarity does not entail transparency and authority does not rest on inflexible notions of identity and truth."[26] As an avid biology student at Bryn Mawr, Moore contemplated a major in science but settled on history and political science instead. Like Swenson, Moore was devoted to scientific precision throughout her life, a commitment expressed in her poems as well as her prose: "Do the poet and scientist not work analogously?" asked Moore in an interview with Donald Hall. "Each is attentive to clues, each must narrow the choice, must strive for precision. . . . [S]cience is the process of discovering. In any case, it's not a thing established once and for all, it's evolving."[27]

Of course fascination with scientific perspective and analysis was not unique to Moore; Pound used metaphors of scientific method to elucidate his "new" poetics, as Eliot did after him.[28] The early imagists, led by Pound, Richard Aldington, and H.D., unsuccessfully sought Moore's membership, urged by what seemed a mutual affinity for "[d]irect treatment of the thing." Like her modernist contemporaries', Moore's allegiance to empirical acuity was in tension with a skepticism of objective vision. But as I've suggested, this tension served, for Moore, as something different. The object of her observation "means just as much or just as little as it is understood to / mean by the observer" (*Poems*, 17), or, in Wallace Stevens's words, "no individual fact is a universe in itself."[29] The experience of observing was consonant with writing poetry; Moore's "I" was precise in its efforts to delineate its debts, as her extensive notes and habits of quotation suggest.

Moore's passion for partial vision finds a fitting explication in Donna Haraway's notion of "situated knowledge," a "practice of objectivity that privileges contestation, deconstruction, passionate construction, webbed connections, and hope for transformation of systems of knowledge and ways of seeing," where "partiality and not universality is the condition of being heard to make rational claims."[30] A feminist historian of science, Haraway takes to task standard claims to scientific objectivity *and* popular attempts to discount the necessity of some such effort, warning, "For political people, social constructionism cannot be allowed to decay into the radiant emanations of cynicism" (184). Mirroring Moore's distaste for movements, Haraway cautions against the temptation to replace one doctrine of transcendence—scientific knowledge—with another: Marxism, psychoanalysis, "feminist empiricism" (186), or, Moore might add, the autonomous lyric "I":

[M]y problem and "our" problem is how to have *simultaneously* an account of radical historical contingency for all knowledge claims and knowing subjects, a critical practice for recognizing our own "semiotic technologies" for making meanings, *and* a no-nonsense commitment to faithful accounts of a "real" world. . . . Feminists don't need a doctrine of objectivity that promises transcendence, a story that loses track of its mediations just where someone might be held responsible for something. (187)

For Haraway "feminist objectivity" is opposed to the search for identity and an understanding of the self as whole, since "only partial perspective promises objective vision."[31] Because "the knowing self is partial in all its guises"[32]—because, as Moore's "gossamer-like"[33] associations suggest—we are constantly being constructed through our interactions with the world, we are always "stitched together imperfectly, and *therefore* able to join with another, to see together without claiming to be another."[34] Thus it is at the very nexus of accurate description ("the objectification of sensual perceptions and states of mind") and acknowledgment of that description as partial and contingent ("without emphasizing *self* as subject") that what Haraway terms accountability, or what Moore might call moral responsibility, is made possible. Transforming the world in which we live, a goal Moore never would have expressed as such but one to which her ambitious sense of fairness and duty is akin, is achieved not by transcendence, but through "conscious fastidiousness" (*CP*, 38) combined with "armor's undermining honesty" (*CP*, 151). "The only way to find a larger vision," asserts Haraway, "is to be somewhere in particular."[35]

Haraway is instructive when it comes to Moore's poetry because she makes clear the potential of partiality, the possibilities of the particular. Moore's "messages," in other words, are contingent upon her method: "We do not seek partiality for its own sake, but for the sake of the connections and unexpected openings situated knowledges make possible."[36] I cannot think of a more apt theoretical paradigm for the workings of Moore's poetic. Her sentences and stanzas, like the sea creatures in "The Fish," "slide each on the other,"

> with spotlight swift-
> ness
> into the crevices—
> in and out, illuminating

the limits to which we are accustomed by repeatedly citing and then blurring them, creating bridges out of boundaries.[37] What at first seems a "defiant edifice," the limit of one's understanding carved out by human "burns and hatchet strokes," is shown to harbor teeming life, a "sea" of sensibilities that has in turn transformed the edifice that may seem "dead":

Repeated
evidence has proved that it can
    live
    on what cannot revive
its youth.
                  *(Poems,* 15)

By recalling Foucault's explication of knowledge as produced rather than foreclosed by prohibition, we may better understand Moore's "edifice," the "chasm side" (*Poems,* 15) of which seems dead, as the shape of our assumptions.[38] Apparently static and immovable, "defiant" in its authority, the lifeless edifice appears to both predate and outlive the sea; in its very inorganicness it seems to claim omniscience and thus a kind of a priori realness. But the incessant, wavelike motion of the poem disrupts this vision of impermeability, as Moore's highly constructed "edifice" is seen to embrace the sea, which "grows old in it" (15). Collapsing the distance between title and poem, beginning and end, the rippling stanzas *become* the wave of the poem, driving a

    wedge
    of iron through the iron edge
of the cliff, whereupon the stars,

pink
rice grains, ink-
    bespattered jelly-fish, crabs like
        green
        lilies and submarine
toadstools, slide each on the other.
                  (15)

The tide of the poem, the motion of the speaker's vision, erodes the stability of the edifice by introducing, then interlacing, the particularities of its inhabitants. Consequently, the "defiance" of the edifice becomes a life-giving embrace. The juxtaposition of rocklike cliff and life-drenched sea is confounded as each becomes the agent of the other. Importantly, the sea "cannot revive" the cliff's "youth," and vice versa—innocence is lost in the wake of unfinished, as opposed to ontological, meaning. No lyric "I" transcends this poem, and as we come to understand the cliff's mutability, we also learn that Moore's "objective," partial vision is most promising in its exposure of our own.

It is crucial to focus on the transformative potential of Moore's partiality and situated knowledge because this method of observation has been misunderstood as apolitical, superficial, or distancing. Various readers, feminist and otherwise, have interpreted Moore's observational verse as deflective, with its dazzling surface sheen warding off connection. Echoed by Moore's eclectic vocabulary, weblike network of notes and quotations, unconventional rhymes, midword enjambments, and fastidious manipulations of form, this characteristic has seemed to many the hallmark of a self-protective distancing. Moore, however, is after just the opposite. By offering a remarkably precise vision of her surroundings and a concomitant ungrounding of the "I" that frames the environment, she proffers poetry as an ongoing process in which meaning is made through interaction with an audience, rather than simply presented. (In this light perhaps we can better understand Moore's almost unmatched dedication to revision.) Just as Moore's poems displace the static lyric "I," so they reveal the extent to which the poet is implicated by her strategy of selfhood. Moore's poems are often followed with notes that, unlike Eliot's, do not direct the reader to a fuller understanding of the poem by way of broader contextualization, but rather point one outward, toward an ever widening pool of associations that may or may not add discernible "meanings" to the poem. In this case the poem emerges as a starting point, an occasion for interaction with the world around us, rather than a conclusion garnered from the roamings of a poet's "I."

All of this means that Moore expects her readers to *work*. At the same time, we can rest assured that the energy we put into enjoying her poems is surpassed by that which she gave them herself: "the most difficult thing for me," Moore confessed, "is to be satisfactorily lucid, yet have enough *implication* in it to suit myself."[39] What may seem to be an abstruse foreclosure is in fact Moore's attempt to connect the reader with a challenge—what she calls "implication." A lover of riddles from a very young age (as was Swenson), Moore often found explicitness disrespectful.[40] For this reason Moore felt that Williams's "uncompromising conscientiousness sometimes seems misplaced; he is at times almost insultingly unevasive."[41] Miller puts it nicely:

Moore does not see the "self" as a refuge against a hostile outer world and therefore does not imagine her most essential "armor" as that which protects her from others; the difficult surface of her poetry is not meant to keep a reader out or to protect a vulnerable poet but to promote "inquisitive intensity" and hence enable perception.[42]

Moore is after the act of revelation, and, as she knows, a mapped epiphany is a contradiction in terms. For Moore complexity, not transparency, yields clarity.

No poem of Moore's says this better than "In the Days of Prismatic Color" (1919), in which the speaker famously declares that "complexity is not a crime."[43] Leading up to this proclamation, however, is a sketch of the time when Adam

was alone; when there was no smoke and color was
fine, not with the fineness of
        early civilization art but by virtue
of its originality, with nothing to modify it but the

mist that went up.
                                        (O, 49)

Composed of a series of overlapping descriptions, this initial stanza builds to a final observation: in the Adamic days of "prismatic color," "obliqueness was a varia- / tion of the perpendicular, plain to see and / to account for" (49). The voice shifts abruptly as the speaker announces that today, presumably in the days of Adam *and* Eve, things aren't so simple:

it [obliqueness] is no
        longer that; nor did the blue red yellow band
of incandescence that was color, keep its stripe: it also is one
                                                                of

those things into which much that is peculiar can be
        read.
                                        (49)

Here, almost in the middle of the poem, the speaker defends the ostensible transition from clarity to complexity by describing the latter as "not a crime." But just as the speaker tolerates complexity, she cautions against its extreme:

>           carry
>   it to the point of murki-
>           ness and nothing is plain. A complexity
>   moreover, that has been committed to darkness, instead of
>           granting it-
>
>   self to be the pestilence that it is, moves all a-
>           bout as if to bewilder with the dismal
>   fallacy that insistence
>           is the measure of achievement and that all
>   truth must be dark.
>
>                                                          (49)

On one level Moore is clarifying the perpetually thorny issue of implication, showing that, when "not a crime," complexity is achieved with precarious balance: it harbors "much that is peculiar" (and therefore much of the material of Moore's verse), while simultaneously avoiding "murkiness," "insistence," and the fallacy that "truth must be dark." Complexity must allow itself to be the "pestilence that it is." Clearly, complexity here is a challenge, even a burden, to be confronted and perhaps even cured; when something is a pestilence it nags, begging for attention, whether as an itch or an unsolved problem. Complexity becomes a crime, though, when it shuts people out, when it attempts to bewilder and makes grandiose claims about truth being dark. Though the Adamic days of "prismatic color" were free from murkiness, they were also void of the difference that engenders complexity—both kinds. And as Moore's poetry repeatedly suggests, the risk of murkiness is better than no risk at all.

Introduced as a kind of fairy-tale ideal of clarity, Adam's Eveless Eden thus emerges as rather a bore—an opinion whose complicated profits are manifested four years later in the brilliant achievement of "Marriage." In a reading diary from which Moore worked when composing "Prismatic Color," she copied down a passage from Baudelaire's prose poem "Any Where Out of the World" that may further explain this sense of transparency as tedium. In Baudelaire's poem, the speaker is talking to his enervated, unresponsive soul about new places to live, expressing his insatiable desire to be wherever he is not. After a series of unsuccessful attempts at provocation, he exclaims, "Let us set our camp at the Pole! There the sun strikes the earth obliquely and the slow alteration of light and night suppresses variety and increases monotony—that better half of nothing." At this, his soul finally breaks forth and "wisely" cries: "No matter where, no matter where, so long as it is out of the world!"[44] Given the reference to antipodes in the penultimate stanza of "In the Days of Prismatic Color" and obliqueness in the second, the connection between Moore's poem and this passage is likely. Furthermore, Moore uses the word *oblique* in the same way that Baudelaire does—not as the popularized term for "indirection" or "deviousness," but to delineate a sloping angle, a "varia- / tion of the perpendicular" (*O*, 49). But what is, in Moore's poem, "plain to see and / account for" is, in Baudelaire, that which "suppresses variety," causing "prolonged baths of shadow." The difference here lies between Baudelaire's grounding in this world of complexity (to which his soul's cry attests) and Moore's grounding in the Adamic land of fantastical clarity; obliqueness can only seem "plain" when the word *plain* itself has no meaning—when, in other words, there is nothing but more plainness with which to compare it.

Miller suggests that the ideal days of clarity and color in Moore's poem are an illusion, that truth for Moore is found in the region of "negation, contradiction, and modification, all verbal characteristics in distinct contrast to Adamic language or Lacan's symbolic, with its representation in the law."[45] I agree with Miller that the progress of Moore's poem subverts the ideality with which it ostensibly opens; after all, what "is more precise than precision" but "Illusion"? (*CP*, 151). But what is so clever about this poem is the way in which Moore subtly insists that this illusion is a product of our own complexities.

Reviewing the first stanza of the poem, we can see that the "fineness" of the "days of prismatic color," recognizable as such "with nothing to modify" it, is in fact modified constantly—more clearly than any other element of the poem—by the series of qualifications in which it is couched. Indeed, our vision of this unmodified "fineness" is actually produced by a succession of modifications: it is the fineness "not in the days of Adam and Eve but when Adam / was alone" (*O*, 49), "not . . . the fineness / of early civilization art" but fine in its "originality." Moore's

method of description thus contests the possibility of the "days of pris-
matic color" just as she writes it into the poem. At the same time, the
halting effect of the first stanza's numerous modifications is recalled in
the "short-legged, fit- / ful advance, the gurgling and all the minutiae"
(49) of the penultimate stanza, so that Adamic "clarity" becomes, in
review, the double of complexity—not the good kind, but the bad. Like-
wise, as the speaker moves from "clarity" to "complexity" in the third
stanza, the mood becomes decidedly more declarative; phrases become
shorter, no-nonsense: "it is no / longer that" "complexity is not a
crime," "it is also one of // those things" (49). Ironically, what seemed
so "plain" and up-front is the epitome of obliquity after all.

At the end of the fourth stanza, Moore presents "sophistication,"
presumably in contrast to the earlier days of color and clarity, as that
which is

> . . . as
> it al-
>
> ways has been—at the antipodes from the init-
> ial great truths.

(O, 49)

Juxtaposed with the apparent evolution from clarity to complexity—an
evolution that is, by this point in the poem, undermined by its own
"insistence"—sophistication, in its age-old sameness, seems to be what
has been there all along. This is a stunning assertion on Moore's part,
given the "initial great truths" that open the poem—the story of Adam
and Eve and the Fall. Sophistication, then, is the result of complexity,
while "the initial great truths" are an illusion. But in the process of dif-
ferentiating sophistication from prismatic plainness, the distance
between "the initial great truths" that open the poem and the illusion of
"clarity" is elided: in search of clarity, we construct "initial great
truths" that claim, tautologically, they are the key to their own con-
struction. But in reality—the version of "truth" that ends the poem by
assuring us, as sophistication might, "I shall be there when the wave
has gone by" (*O,* 50)—there is no such thing as clarity, and to claim oth-
erwise is to be duped into believing that there once were days of only
"fine" prismatic color.

Moore is making a parallel between the illusory nature of our "initial great truths" and the story of Eve's Fall. In light of Moore's religious convictions this may seem unlikely, but given her love of complexity and challenge, combined with an unmistakable—if sometimes subtle— distaste for masculinist presumption, it is actually quite apt. Moore is not only contesting the authority or "plainness" of this mythic truth, but redeploying its very terms, constructing a different truth, one that quietly but confidently ends the poem by asserting its endurance. According to the story of the Fall, Eve's introduction to the Garden of Eden summoned the end of innocence; by eating the forbidden apple, Eve ushered in the world of knowledge and, hence, enslavement and mortality. But Moore's poem mocks the innocence, the "clarity," that the Adamic "days of prismatic color" purport to have offered. As in her later poem "Marriage," when Adam

> stumbles over marriage,
> "a very trivial object indeed"
> to have destroyed the attitude
> in which he stood—
> the ease of the philosopher
> unfathered by a woman,
>              (CP, 65)

Moore rejects nostalgia and celebrates complexity, the passion of knowledge, and thus, Eve's Fall. Having chosen the myth of her native culture most squarely concerned with heterosexual difference, Moore's revisionist version should be read accordingly: it is the advent of women in the poem that enables the complexity of which the poem itself is an example. Clearly, the genesis of sexual difference and its relationship to our "initial great truths" are at the core of Moore's thoughts in "In the Days of Prismatic Color." However, it is crucial to remember that Moore is most interested here in *complexity,* not women, and according to the script of this poem, complexity would not exist in an Adamless Eden any more than it would in an Eveless one. Most importantly, if "the days of prismatic color" are indeed an illusion of our own making, a making precipitated by the interaction of women and men, then nobody is innocent—least of all Moore.

Understanding Moore's commitment to complexity as an invitation to participate in the process of her poems is key to comprehending the feminist tenor of her work. All poetry functions to a certain extent by allowing readers to confront the limited terms of their selves, but Moore invites a participation quite unlike that of her peers. In refusing the parallel positions of either omniscience or innocence, Moore's strategic selfhood imparts a remarkable *agency* to her readers. Within her poems this sense of agency is most evident in the way Moore privileges the animals, plants, objects, and scenes of which she writes rather than her own perspective on them. Nevertheless, Moore has no truck with a nostalgic view of nature; the world she observes is wholly contingent upon her framing of it. Again we are led to the tension between Moore's partial "I" and her intensely detailed observations. Haraway can help us understand this methodology: "Situated knowledges require that the object of knowledge be pictured as an actor or agent, not a screen or a ground or a resource, never finally as slave to the master that closes off the dialectic in his unique agency and authorship of 'objective' knowledge" (198). Simultaneously, "Accounts of a 'real' world do not . . . depend on a logic of 'discovery,' but on a power-charged social relation of 'conversation.' The world neither speaks itself nor disappears in favor of a master decoder. The codes of the world are not still, waiting only to be read" (198).

The implications of this perspective on one's understanding of bodily existence are particularly profound for feminism; if neither one's own knowledge nor the outside world from which that knowledge is gleaned has authority over the other, the distance between the two—one's sense of inner and outer—is displaced. (It is amusing to note at this point that in 1906 Moore wrote home announcing she'd failed a biology quiz for giving an external diagram of the grasshopper and lobster instead of an internal one.)[46] From this vantage point one's body becomes inextricably wed to its surroundings; fish are buoyed by the sea in which they live, a chameleon feeds upon the light that paints its skin. Moore's explorations of embodiment find current expression in Haraway's cyborg, a fusion of human, animal, and machine, a being "wary of holism, but needy for connection," who has an "intimate experience of boundaries, their construction and deconstruction."[47] In the cyborg world, "Nature and culture are reworked; the one can no longer be the resource for appropriation or incorporation by the other. The relationships for forming wholes from parts, including those of polarity and hierarchical domination, are at issue in the cyborg world."[48]

"Black Earth" offers an early and telling confrontation of these issues that lie at the heart of Moore's poetry—perhaps too telling, for Moore never republished it again after the poem appeared as "Melancthon" in her *Collected Poems* of 1951.[49] Melancthon ("black earth" in Greek) is the Protestant reformer Philip Melancthon, famous for his distaste for theological dogmatism and subsequent importation of humanism to the German Reformation. (Moore had a wind-up toy elephant named "Melancthon" as well.) In light of this later title, Martin has written that "Melancthon addresses quite specifically the difficult and yet obvious necessity of acknowledging another's perspective while remaining oneself."[50] To this I would add that Moore also asks what it means to *be* a self in relation to another's perspective. Moreover, the most striking characteristic of "Black Earth" is its sensual immediacy; as in "A Jellyfish" (1909), "My Senses Do Not Deceive Me" (1910), and the later "An Octopus" (1924), questions of identity are very clearly questions of embodiment throughout this poem.

The relationship between the lyric "I" and material existence is announced assertively in the first two stanzas:

Openly, yes,
with the naturalness
        of the hippopotamus or the alligator
        when it climbs out on the bank to experience the

sun, I do these
things which I do, which please
        no one but myself. Now I breathe and now I am sub-
        merged

                                        (*Poems*, 10)

This speaker, one of the most unabashedly self-indulgent of Moore's repertoire, "openly" declares its love of sensuous experience: "Now I breathe and now I am sub- / merged." The rhythm of the speaker's voice is mesmerizing, so that we too are lulled into the languid pleasures of sensual immersion. Indeed, the "I" with which this poem so emphatically begins is only known to us through its bodily contact with the world it inhabits:

        The sediment of the river which
encrust my joints, makes me very gray but I am used

to it, it may
remain there; do away
     with it and I am myself done away with, for the
     patina of circumstance can but enrich what was

there to begin
with.

                                       (*Poems*, 10)

Although the speaker suggests an essence that has been "there to begin / with," somehow preexisting the "patina of circumstance" that encrusts its joints, the fusion of riverbed and body undermines any such possibility—were one to "do away / with [the sediment of river,] I [would be] done away with" (10). Suitably, the speaker's body is figured as its map: "This elephant skin / which I inhabit, . . . is a manual for the peanut-tongued and the / hairy toed" (10)—literally a guide to *itself*. "[F]ibred over like the shell of / the coco-nut," "cut into checkers by rut / upon rut of unpreventable experience" (10), the elephant's skin bears the history of its experience, that which has engendered its very being. Surroundings and selfhood, inner and outer, are collapsed, and the utterance of "I" appears as "natural" as the alligator's swagger.

But even cursory familiarity with Moore asks that we examine such self-indulgence; when we look closely it becomes clear that the hippopotamus and alligator are exemplars of "naturalness" (10) because they are not aware of themselves as such. In contrast, the speaker's "I" is drenched in self-consciousness, and its attempt at "naturalness" ("I do these / things which I do") becomes a parody of its own self-confidence. Indeed, as the poem progresses, the comfortable "I" of the first few stanzas becomes increasingly unstable; as soon as the speaker specifies its body as an elephant's, the narrative voice shifts from an unmediated first- to a strangely detached third-person voice, referring to itself no longer as "I" but as one of the generic "peanut-tongued and . . . / hairy-toed." The elephant/speaker's easy existence is interrupted as it begins to question its own assertions:

    Black
but beautiful, my back
        is full of the history of power. Of power? What

is powerful and what is not?
(10)

Whether or not Moore intended here to invoke an understanding of bodies as racially marked, her interrogation of embodied subjectivity certainly demands it. "[C]ut / into checkers by rut / upon rut of unpreventable experience," one is, of course, constructed *as* a body, mapping not only one's self, but also the "history of power." The ecstasy of sensuous experience that opens the poem is thus tempered, as the body itself is "checker[ed]" by experience; the elephant, by stanza 9, is now "on [its] guard."[51]

The second half of the poem (at seventeen stanzas, this is the longest poem Moore had written by the time of its 1918 publication) enacts a different approach than the first, turning upon the relationship between embodiment and intellection. Exactly halfway through the poem, the elephant tells us that

> through-
> out childhood to the present time, the unity of
> life and death has been expressed by the circumference
>
> described by my
> trunk.
>                                          (10)

Nevertheless, it "perceives feats of strength to be inexplicable after / all" (10). As the elephant becomes conscious of its embodied vision (its partial perspective), the easy union of body and speaking "I" turns elastic, more interactive than fused. Simultaneously, the unity of the poem and the lyric "I" begins to crumble when selfhood becomes an object of contemplation, a potential strategy rather than a foundation for expression. Immersion in one's self gives way to observation—

> external poise, it
> has its centre
> well nurtured—we know
>         where—in pride, but spiritual poise, it has its centre
>                                          where?
>                                          (10–11)

—then judgment: "I see / and I hear" (11), says the elephant. This hearing, though, is not like "the / wandlike body of which one hears so much, which was made / to see and not to see; made to hear and not to hear" (11). Contemplating the contingency between identity and observation (Moore's primary concern), the speaker compares the "wandlike" human, the bearer of "external poise," to its

> spiritual
> brother . . . the coral
> plant, absorbed into which, the equable sapphire light
> becomes a nebulous green
>
> (11)

and assertively concludes that the "I of each is to // the I of each, / a kind of fretful speech / which sets a limit on itself" (11). Egoism, or "pride" (11), does not enhance one's reach, but truncates it.

Technically, the "I of each"—the "pride" behind "external poise"—refers to the human and coral, and not the elephant/speaker. But the close repetition of I's within the speaker's warning cannot help but recall the emphatic "I" of the elephant that so heavily marked the poem until now. Moreover, as if to contest the limit of this insistent "I," the narrative voice again immediately shifts to third person, asking ironically what "the elephant is" (11). The final three stanzas of the poem are a labyrinthine answer to this question; the speaker is no longer distinct as elephant, human, coral plant, or omniscient "I," but exists as a fleeting interaction of them all:

> It is to that
> phenomenon
> the above formation,
> translucent like the atmosphere—a cortex merely—
> that on which darts cannot strike decisively the first
>
> time, a substance
> needful as an instance
> of the indestructibility of matter; it
> has looked at the electricity and at the earth-
>
> quake and is still
> here; the name means thick. Will

depth be depth, thick skin be thick, to one who can see
no

beautiful element of unreason under it?

(11)

The "it," the subject of this sentence, seems to be at once the elephant, and thus the speaker, while at the same time, "It is to that // phenom-enon / the above formation." But *what* above formation? A "kind of fretful speech"? The "spiritual / brother" to the "coral / plant"? A "tree trunk without / roots"? (11). As if to assure us that there is an answer to this question, that there is sense—literally—in this concluding grid of metonymic metaphors, we are told that "it / . . . is still / here; the name means thick." But as it happens, the key to understanding lies in this confusion, in what Moore would call "complexity": depth is depth, thick skin is thick, only to those who see unreason under it. In other words, truth is more likely to be found in the messy "patina of circum-stance" than in "the days of prismatic color."

The emphatic "I" that begins "Black Earth," unmediated and whole, gives way by the end to a radically unfixed voice no longer linked to a self. Judith Butler's work on language and embodiment is helpful in understanding this juncture in Moore's poetry between body and self, as well as its implications for notions of subjectivity. Arguing the cul-turally mediated "nature" of our bodies, Butler comments,

> "Inner" and "outer" make sense only with reference to a mediating boundary that strives for stability. And this stability, this coher-ence, is determined in large part by cultural orders that sanction the subject and compel its differentiation from the abject. Hence, "inner" and "outer" constitute a binary distinction that stabilizes and consolidates the coherent subject. When that subject is chal-lenged, the meaning and necessity of the terms are subject to dis-placement. If the "inner world" no longer designates a topos, then the internal fixity of the self, and, indeed, the internal locale of gen-der identity, become similarly suspect.[52]

Given the blatant collapse between environment and inner self that begins "Black Earth," we can understand the progressively troubled lyric "I" of the poem as entirely logical. Concurrently, the "I" of the opening stanzas, brazen in its collapse of environment and self, may be read retrospectively as anything but natural; the speaker's inability to gesture toward a "self" so surely seems almost comically self-conscious, akin to those unenlightened who cannot see the "element of beautiful unreason under it."

This is, of course, another instance of Moore's strategic selfhood, another angle of her situated knowledge. The most provocative aspect of both Butler's formulation and Moore's "Black Earth," though, is the troubled place the body occupies in terms of the unfixed lyric "I." As both Butler and Moore suggest, the illusion of autonomous selfhood is literally grounded in, or naturalized in regard to, the actual body. The speaker of Moore's poem announces itself "openly," with all the "naturalness" in the world, through the contours of its flesh: "Now I breathe and now I am sub- / merged." Moore's poem, however, is a warning against the limitations of that wallowing "I." Hence, the body as a foundation for that "I" is also questioned. By the end of the poem, the speaker floats among myriad metaphors of bodily existence: "translucent like the atmosphere—a cortex merely / that on which darts cannot strike decisively." Materiality still exists—"substance" "is still / here"—but, unleashed from a "fretful" dialectic with the declarative "I," its reach is significantly extended. The trade-off, as I have suggested, is the "I" that is lost at the end of the poem. Butler explains that "coherence is . . . an effect of corporeal signification. . . . [A]cts, gestures, and desire produce the effect of an internal core or substance, but produce this *on the surface* of the body, through the play of signifying absences that suggest, but never reveal, the organizing principle of identity as a cause."[53] Which is to say that one's physical experience, though it is always from one's perspective, is not any less mediated or any more innocent than the "self" that grounds itself there.

From such a vantage point, the body, like Haraway's cyborg, cannot be understood as contained or passive. Instead, much like Moore's poems, it is a continual process, marked but not moored in its contingency with the world it inhabits. The hierarchical relationship between body and spirit is undermined: selfhood depends upon the sensual perceptions of the body, but at the same time it cannot take refuge in, or find legitimization through, the mutating dimensions of the flesh. In this way we have come full circle. What began for Moore as a strategy of selfhood has become a strategy of embodiment. Though Moore constantly insists on the primacy of sensual experience within her poems, she also shows perception to be a highly mediated means to knowledge. The notion of a stable materiality, then, is not prior to the perceptions it enables, but is, in fact, like the screen-maker's or Melancthon's, a product of one's own desire to ground one's "self."[54]

This insight is both disturbing and exciting, and lies at the heart of Moore's discomfort with sexually explicit and gender-specific poetry. For if Moore's poetic asserts a mistrust of bodily "truth," than it simultaneously contests the sexed body as a viable foundation for political *or* aesthetic agency. This conviction is etched ferociously into the stylized portraiture of "Those Various Scalpels," a poem Moore published in 1917, one year before "Black Earth." The speaker of this poem itemizes with a majestic violence the various body parts of a fantastic, ornately dressed woman, emphatically drawing our attention to the constructed nature of her materiality.[55] Several critics read this poem as an analysis of the tension between a whole and its parts. Holley, for instance, maintains that the portrait both diminishes and expands its subject:

On the one hand, the poem is a condemnation by systemic reduction of an outlandish person to a pile of non-human objects. On the other hand, it makes this individual embody a whole chain of being. She is animal, vegetable, and mineral, wild and cultivated; she is a work of art.[56]

At the same time, though, I would argue that "systemic reduction" is in line with Moore's unnostalgic view of self and artistic vision—that it echoes the screen-maker's early revelations. Like Jeanne Heuving, I believe that "Moore's brilliance in the poem is that the figure is not merely depicted by bodily parts, but by the depictions that depict it."[57]

Indeed, we should not overlook the fact that Moore's portrait is produced by a poem whose stylistic structures draw as much attention to their own constructedness as they do to the lady herself. Like the various parts of the woman, the stanzas of the poem are highly irregular in shape, yet, as is almost always the case with Moore's work, they are "consistently" so, emphasizing the connection between artifice and "autonomy," or repetition and construction. For "construction," maintains Butler, is neither a subject nor its act, but a process of reiteration by which both "subjects" and "acts" come to appear at all. . . . Crucially, then, construction is neither a single act nor a causal process initiated by a subject and culminating in a set of fixed effects. Construction not only takes place in time, but is itself a temporal process which operates through the reiteration of norms; [the] sex[ed body] is both produced and destabilized in the course of this reiteration.[58]

Appropriating the Renaissance convention of portraying a female beloved through an itemization of body parts, Moore fantastically exaggerates her own descriptions in an attempt to expose the "inflection"—the gaps between Butler's "reiterations"—that is usually disguised by such conventional poetics. In doing so, Moore's material reductions call attention to the sexed body as a process of inscription.

The poem wields "those various scalpels," whose "sounds [are] consistently indistinct, like intermingled / echoes / struck from thin glass successively at random." The sharp, metallic clash of the speaker's descriptions—a series of hard *c*s, piercing *s*s, stony *d*s and *t*s—"echoes" the sound of scalpel on scalpel, steel on steel. These sounds are clearly punctuated by stanzaic breaks, halting enjambments, and lines ending midword, so that each echo is unraveled from the other, even as each sound is rendered emphatically distinct. This effect is mirrored by the dissection the poem enacts: each body part is lavishly described through a metaphor that shares no continuity with the next, a metaphor so elaborate in its associations that moving from one to the other is like leaving behind an unfinished story in order to start another. As we are led from "fighting-cocks" to "the cordage of disabled / ships" to "emeralds from / Persia," we are introduced to a body whose only mark of coherence is her "hard majesty of . . . sophistication," that which is "su- / perior to opportunity"—her steely powers of deflection. Unlike conventional poems of this sort, there is no recourse to totality through either a final image of integrity or the grounding of a lover's lyric "I." Instead, the poem's own "surgery," though clearly not "tentative," is no less "ambiguous" in its discovery than the woman's raised hand; are "they weapons or scalpels?" Does this dissection yield a more precise understanding of an interior state, or does it ward off closer inspection?

Given the title and the weaponlike feel of the poem's imagery, this question is (typically) misleading. The tools of dissection—the speaker's gaze, the dialectic of subject/object through which identity is formed—are scalpels and weapons; they produce and destabilize the woman's embodiment. Thus, her ornate, larger-than-life appearance is "uniform / and at the same time, diverse." As Heuving has implied, the emphasis here is on the process, not the product, of construction. In effect, the speaker dissects its own actions just as it depicts the woman; for this reason the poem, despite its efforts, cannot provide a coherent image. Similarly, its final turn, the question upon which the poem closes, must be read as ironic:

> why dissect destiny with instruments
> > which
> are more highly specialized than the tissues of destiny
> > itself?
>
> > > (*Poems*, 7)

The parallel positions in the poem of "destiny" and the woman's body (both are objects of dissection) suggest that they are one and same, that the woman's destiny is traced by her anatomy. In light of the use of the word "tissues" instead of Moore's later revision to "components of destiny" (*CP*, 52), this reading seems all the more accurate. But as this poem elaborately reiterates, the woman's body is both created and dislodged through the speaker's address; hence, an embodied destiny is "less highly specialized" than the "instruments" by which its shaped, precisely because in its promise of ontological plenitude such "destiny" is an illusion, a wry commentary expressed suitably without recourse to a single gendered pronoun. Appropriately, the metaphors through which the woman's body is established do not coalesce into some kind of intractable casing but, rather, deliver her beyond corporeal limits and national borders, to Persia, Florence, "French chateaux," and shipwreck sites. At the same time, it is her weaponlike body—her hair like "fighting-cocks" or "scimitars," her eyes like "flowers of ice," her cheeks "rosettes / of blood," her hand a "bundle of lances"—that resists feminization, deflecting the speaker's gaze back to itself, ultimately blurring the distinction between subject and object, gazed and gazed-upon. Throughout the poem, as with the whole of Moore's oeuvre, it is the speaker's "self" that has been "consistently indistinct."

In *Bodies That Matter* (1993), Butler explores the consequences for feminism of an antifoundational view of bodily materiality, observing, as Moore did nearly ninety years ago, that though "sexual difference is often invoked as an issue of material differences," it "is never simply a function of material differences which are not in some way both marked and formed by discursive practices."[59] Often criticized as asexual, Moore has been largely misunderstood. Moore was, on the contrary, fascinated by the "discursive practices" and cultural markings that make up sex to begin with: the notions of bodily truth and the autonomous self that roots itself there. By refusing the material irreducibility of the sexed body, her poetry undermines the popular distinction between gender and sex, suggesting that the latter is a product of the former, and not its antecedent: if "gender is the social construction of sex," explains Butler, "and if there is no access to this 'sex' except by means of its construction, then it appears not only that sex is absorbed by gender, but that 'sex' becomes something like a fiction, perhaps a fantasy, retroactively installed at a prelinguistic site to which there is no direct access" (5). For Moore, to ground one's politics, one's "self," or one's poetry within something called female sexuality or female experience is to have been "deceived into thinking that you have progressed." At the same time, Moore's lifestyle makes it clear that an antifoundational approach to issues of sexuality and selfhood does not foreclose the possibility of committed political action. Moore was an avid suffragist throughout her years in college and in Carlisle, Pennsylvania, and continued to advocate women's rights throughout her life. Nevertheless, by radically rejecting the sexed body as a password, stamp of authenticity, or site of truth, Moore asks us to review the very ground upon which feminist poetics have traditionally been built.

## 2   Marianne Moore and Elizabeth Bishop

An examination of Moore's poetics of selfhood in the last chapter helped explain why over the years her poetry has proved so difficult for feminist critics: Moore's interrogations of subjectivity undermine the assumptions that fortify much feminist work, so accounting for the feminist consciousness throughout Moore's poems demands that we either reject or revise these assumptions. But while Moore's poems do not, of course, exist in isolation from her politics, this explanation falls short as a reason for the lingering reluctance among critics to explore Moore's feminist commitment.[1]

Though this characteristic of Moore criticism is especially remarkable since the opening of Moore's archives, it was no less so thirty years ago to those who knew her well. Elizabeth Bishop was the first of Moore's readers to remark on the incongruity between feminist critiques of the older poet's work and the feminist sensibility she knew Moore possessed. In her memoir of Moore, "Efforts of Affection," Bishop became indignant as she witnessed this critical approach to Moore taking root:

> Do they know that Marianne Moore was a feminist in her day? Or that she paraded with the suffragettes, led by Inez Milholland on her white horse, down Fifth Avenue? Once, Marianne told me, she "climbed a lamppost" in a demonstration for votes for women. What she did up there, what speech she delivered, if any, I don't know, but climb she did in long skirt and petticoats and large hat. . . . Now that everything can be said, and done, have we anyone who can compare with Marianne Moore, who was at her best when she made up her own rules and when they were strictest—the reverse of "freedom"? (*Prose*, 144–45)

Bishop's exasperation—"one wonders how much of Marianne's poetry the feminist critics have read" (*Prose*, 144)—is no doubt sincere, and the sharp tone with which she chastises these "feminist writers" stands out within the essay's otherwise mild-tempered stream of recollections. Yet Bishop's defensiveness signals more than sheer frustration with the feminists who couldn't, or wouldn't, see Moore as one of themselves; after all, only pages earlier it is Bishop who writes that "Mrs. Moore and her daughter were what some people might call 'prudish'" (*Prose*, 130). Indeed, the essay as a whole presents an otherworldly poet who appears, despite her independence, undoubtedly old-fashioned. Of course, "prudishness" does not preclude a feminist mind-set, but the word summons a host of tropes that often do. The frustration Bishop faced in reconciling these aspects of Moore seems displaced here upon those who were misled by the same incongruities that she herself struggled to understand.

And a struggle it certainly was, as a number of scholars have made clear.[2] In her person as in her poetry, Moore was notorious for bridging the most unlikely interests and perspectives; we may recall Bishop's claim that Moore "was rather contradictory, you know, illogical sometimes . . . you could never tell what she was going to like, or dislike."[3] Bishop's memoir of Moore strains against its own uncertainty, its "efforts" to decipher not only the mentor she admired but more importantly, her own lifelong confusion in the face of Moore's paradoxical nature. Though "Efforts of Affection" does not produce any answers for the author who is clearly attempting to understand her relationship by mining her memories of it (which is probably why the manuscript was found unfinished at the time of Bishop's death), Bishop does arrive in the last paragraph at an articulation of what it is that puzzles her most about Moore:

> I find it impossible to draw conclusions or even to summarize.
> When I try to, I become foolishly bemused: I have a sort of subliminal glimpse of the capital letter *M* multiplying. I am turning the pages of an illuminated manuscript and seeing that initial letter again and again: Marianne's monogram; mother; manners; morals; and I catch myself murmuring, "Manners and morals; manners *as* morals? Or is it morals *as* manners?" Since like Alice, "in a dreamy sort of way," I can't answer either question, it doesn't much matter which way I put it; it *seems* to be making sense. (*Prose*, 156)

What makes sense to Bishop is her "subliminal" apprehension of Moore's morality as that which feels at once most familiar and foreign, as that dimension of Moore which somehow holds the key to what she can't possess of Moore's persona. Moore's morality, or more precisely, Bishop's view of it, is also what underpins the strange contingency between Bishop's tribute to Moore's feminism and her depiction of Moore as "prudish"; it is in large part Moore's sense of propriety that leaves Bishop with the "mental or moral bends" when leaving Moore's apartment (*Prose*, 137), just as it accounts for the feminist poet "who was at her best when she made up her own rules and when they were strictest." Given Bishop's final confession that her inability to "draw conclusions" about Moore is somehow tangled up with her failed efforts to chart the nuances of Moore's morals, we may better understand the vehemence with which she reproaches those "feminist writers" as evidence of Bishop's own frustrated "efforts" at "making sense" of her mentor.

That Bishop was the first writer to express exasperation over feminist misreadings of Moore is both appropriate and ironic; appropriate because Bishop herself once received similar treatment, and ironic because it is within the field of contemporary Bishop scholarship that these readings of Moore appear most often.[4] Throughout this chapter I am concerned with the relationship between Bishop and Moore and how their lifelong efforts to understand each other shaped not only the poetry they left us, but the ways in which we have come to read those poems. As this brief exploration of Bishop's memoir is meant to suggest, current portraits of Moore capitalize upon the images that Bishop herself provided, and we shall see that the inverse is true as well: it is common practice today to speak of Moore the moralist in contrast to Bishop the "unbeliever."[5] But I will argue that this oppositional reading is complicated by an undercurrent of "subliminal glimpses," those recurring moments throughout their public and private exchanges where frustration marks a deeper if less defined desire to probe the limits of one's self. In the process of exploring these instances we will come to understand not only what was at stake for each poet in her sometimes reductive accounts of the other, but perhaps more importantly, what we may gain by rethinking the stakes of our own simplifications.

As the well-rehearsed story has it, Moore and Bishop met outside the door to the reading room of the New York Public Library in the spring of 1934. It is fitting that these two women met in front of a door, a passageway that both separates and bridges a collection of books and its readers. Doorways invite movement and direct it, they signal boundaries and the need to cross them, they witness comings and goings. They mark inside from outside, and frame the familiar by opening onto what's not. Doorways enable *exchange*. The relationship between Bishop and Moore began in the midst of thresholds both metaphoric and real, and as the years went by, this context came to determine the pulse of the friendship it spawned.

In their personal lives as well as their poems, Bishop and Moore thrived on the liminal place, on probing connections and the conclusions they often maintain. Like Moore, Bishop did not fit easily into any recognizable niche: she was not of the waning Millay, Wylie, or Teasdale school, and her poetry was, as she once put it to Moore, too "old-fashioned" to catalog as obvious heir to the make-it-new modernists.[6] Though Bishop was acutely aware of the post-Depression imperative to make one's art accountable to a social or political purpose, she, like Moore, saw such a goal as potentially averse to fresh perspective and thus, to meaningful art. And while both Bishop and Moore admired the grace with which Eliot questioned Romantic ideals of transcendent selfhood, they never shared his ensuing sense of loss. At issue among this chart of likes and dislikes is the defining tenet of post-Romantic poetry: the shaping and expression of identity in selfhood and the role that writing should—or shouldn't—appear to play in the process. The shifting and often tenuous distinctions that delineate Romantics from modernists, political poets from aestheticians, or feminist writers from masculinist ones, all turn in part upon the script of the speaking "I," and like all memorable writers, Bishop and Moore troubled these distinctions by taking this knowledge for granted.

Both writers were especially sensitive to that "awful core of ego" that the act of writing can seem to assume, and the friendship they forged was based largely on a joint wariness of self-promotion.[7] But as the insistent query at the end of Bishop's memoir implies, their friendship was also fueled by the struggles it sparked—struggles to comprehend their differences and, perhaps the more difficult challenge, struggles to articulate their commonalities. In essays and reviews and even poems about each other their words encompass dual attempts at identification and differentiation, a demand both complicated and urged by the historical moment in which their exchanges unfolded. Driving these efforts is the desire to define one's self in relation to one's work, so that ironically, yet typically, we come full circle: just as Moore and Bishop bonded over their distaste for self-indulgent verse, their relationship necessitated a constant and careful rethinking of the sort of selves they knew their writings would reveal.

It is for this reason that Bishop was attracted from the beginning to the conundrum posed by Moore's moral stance, an attraction sustained as much by her inability to explain it as by her desire to do so. From her first essay on Moore to her last, Bishop always introduced Moore's moral character in one way or another, affirming the central place it plays in defining Moore's poetic. But these introductions are sand-wiched by uncertainty, a persistent, analytical puzzlement that under-mines the integrity of the portrait she's ostensibly painting. Well into their relationship Bishop began to make her confusion explicit: Moore's "meticulous system of ethics could be baffling," admitted Bishop in "Efforts of Affection" (*Prose*, 155). While Moore's mystery continued to lure her friend's curious mind, Bishop had by this time refined her grasp on just where that mystery emerged—at the sticky space that dis-tinguishes "manners" from "morals," where Moore's "meticulous sys-tem of ethics" distinguishes self-consciousness from self-assertion.

Bishop sheds some light on this difficult distinction and her attempts to process it in "A Sentimental Tribute," her 1962 review of *A Marianne Moore Reader*. Describing the "bushel-baskets-full" of discarded drafts that go into the making of Moore's poems, Bishop hones in on the incongruity between Moore's attempts at clarity and her often compli-cated results:

> [Moore] admits the hard work: "I never knew anyone who had a passion for words who had as much difficulty in saying things as I do and I know I'm trying." In spite of her wish to be clear and sim-ple, this last phrase brings up the question that always baffles us with great artists of Miss Moore's kind: the supremely original, nevertheless unpretentious, small-scale ones. . . . Just how deep does their self-consciousness go? I certainly cannot measure it, and there is always the perfectly agreeable (to me) possibility that I am being teased a little on purpose.[8]

Bishop calls our attention here to Moore's rather astonishing ability to break with staid conventions while deflecting attention away from her-self, to her "supremely original" though "unpretentious" persona. But what baffles Bishop most is what Moore herself makes of this unlikely juncture, how "self-conscious" she is of the portrait she presents through her work. When Moore asserts that she's "trying," are we to assume that the combination of elements that makes her verse so original happens despite her efforts, that like the rest of us, Moore is "trying" above all else to clarify that complicated impulse that drives her to write? If not, then what do we make of that "I" which is trying so hard to articulate her thoughts—that "I" which throws bushel-baskets of drafts away before a poem may be published—and the "unpretentious," "small-scale" presence that same "I" assumes in the final product? Indeed, how deep *does* Moore's self-consciousness go? It is no wonder that after thirty years Bishop "felt teased a little on purpose" by Moore, for the better she got to know her (having been, for instance, allowed to see those bushel-baskets) the more pronounced Moore's paradoxical nature became.

But Bishop did not always find Moore's complicated persona—what she often referred to as Moore's "contradictory" ways—to be "perfectly agreeable." The "bafflement" that Bishop cheerily admits of in "A Sentimental Tribute" appears in a more exasperated tone in "Efforts of Affection," where, we may remember, Bishop claims that Moore's "ethics could be baffling." The use of this word in both of these contexts underlines the contingency between Moore's moral stance and her take on subjectivity, between the issue of "self-consciousness" and Moore's "meticulous system of ethics." Understanding the interdependence of these elements in Moore means grasping the relationship between manners and morals, between Moore's ethical aversion to self-absorption and her simultaneous insistence on holding others up to the standards defined by *her* moral stance. As Moore's protégé, Bishop felt this conflict intensely since she herself was subject to these standards throughout the years.

Despite—or perhaps because of—the personal impact Moore's standards had on Bishop, the younger poet zeroed in on Moore's "contradictory" nature early on. Bishop's earliest piece on Moore, "As We Like It" (1948), does not display the degree of understanding that we find in her later pieces, but it is full of those incisive "subliminal glimpses" that fascinated her from the start.[9] "As far as I know," asserts Bishop, "Miss Marianne Moore is The World's Greatest Living Observer" (129). This dramatic introduction calls Moore's definitive trait to the fore with a confidence that the essay goes on to complicate. After comparing Moore's descriptive prowess to Hopkins's and Shakespeare's, Bishop coyly claims that while she herself does "not understand the nature of the satisfaction a completely accurate description or imitation of anything at all can give," she does see that such description "must be brief, or compact, and have at least the effect of being spontaneous" (130–31). It is this *effect* that intrigues Bishop most, Moore's ability to produce observations that are so sharp, so startlingly *true*, that the source from which they emanate is virtually eliminated in the "immediacy of identification" between reader and poem (131): "Does it come simply from her gift of being able to give herself up entirely to the object under contemplation, to feel in all sincerity how it is to be *it?*" (131). Foreshadowing her later and more explicit interrogation of Moore's "self-consciousness," Bishop wonders what happens to Moore's subjective eye in the process of crafting such seemingly objective descriptions. How does Moore's *effort*—that stamp of a distinctive, unique perspective that lurks behind any poem—give way "entirely to the object under contemplation"? This is, of course, a question generated by all art produced with a precision that makes it appear effortless, but Bishop sensed something else in Moore's work that made this quality especially complicated and therefore alluring.

This "something else" is cloaked in the next paragraph, where the essay takes a telling turn. Continuing her consideration of Moore's descriptive prowess, Bishop notes that sometimes in Moore's "poetry such instances 'go on' so that there seems almost to be a compulsion to this kind of imitation. The poems seem to say, 'These things exist to be loved and honored and we *must*,' and perhaps the sense of duty shows through a little plainly" (131). As a way of summarizing her point, Bishop then quotes the following lines from Shakespeare's *As You Like It:* "Did he not moralize this spectacle? / O Yes, into a thousand similes." In one swift shift Bishop has moved from Moore's trademark self-erasure to her characteristic moral urgency, and she has done so with that same sort of serpentine, discomforting ease that marks the best of Moore's work. Though Bishop does not refer explicitly to the incongruity of this juncture, the strangely abrupt yet fluid transition implies it. The restless intensity with which Bishop probes Moore's "gift of giving herself up entirely" becomes more understandable when we encounter Moore's *must* in the very next breath. How, this contingency begs, can a poet be at once so stunningly "unpretentious" and so full of insistent opinion?

Bishop invokes Poe in order to praise Moore for her infrequent recourse to metaphor, and in the process commends the older poet for precisely that which she complained of two paragraphs ago:

> In Poe's "Philosophy of Composition" he points out that it is not until the last two stanzas of "The Raven" that he permits himself the use of any metaphorical expression . . . and then says that such expressions "dispose the mind to seek a moral in all that has been previously narrated." He has already stressed the importance of avoiding "the excess of the suggested meaning," and said that metaphor is a device that must be very carefully employed. Miss Moore does employ it carefully and it is one of the qualities that gives her poetry its steady aura of both reserve and having possibly more meanings, in reserve. (132)

So while Moore's poetry tends to "go on" at times with a transparent "sense of duty," it also succeeds in avoiding "the excess of the suggested meaning." But Bishop was much too savvy and self-conscious a thinker to surrender to this potential conflict, and indeed, a closer look at the passage reveals one of those "subliminal glimpses" at work. Bishop's double play on the word *reserve* brings us back to the issue underlying her essay: what Bishop senses as Moore's contradictory approach to the self. Echoing Eliot's claim that good writing demands a "continual surrender of [the poet] as he is at the moment to something which is more valuable,"[10] Bishop describes Moore's verse as having "a steady aura" of "reserve," of personality withheld, an impression that is ironically the result of Moore's ability to "give herself up entirely to the object under contemplation." As I have argued, Moore (like Eliot) is often read as reserved, or impersonal, for just this reason. But Bishop swerves from this reading through her concomitant claim that this aura also implies a store of "more meanings, in reserve." With this twist Moore the person is pulled back into focus as we are asked to imagine a plotting poet who parcels out her perceptions, bit by bit (to "tease a little on purpose"?), a person much like Moore's "Student," who "is too reclusive / for some things to seem to touch / him; not because he / has no feeling but because he has so much" (*CP*, 101–2).

This abundance of feeling in Moore's work has been sacrificed by readers who describe her as morally stiff and impersonal. As Bishop knew, Moore's thirsty embrace of life's quirks and conundrums marked a poet who was anything but reticent or removed. Nevertheless, Bishop was also aware of the ways in which Moore's poetry urged self-restraint over self-indulgence, and examining her attempts to make sense of these dual dimensions enables us to better explain our own efforts to do so. What begins for Bishop as a perplexing play between Moore's moral urgency and her unprecedented lack of pretension gives way consistently to an image of the older poet's pervasive *presence*, an intimation of a personality that threatens to overwhelm its context: the end of "Efforts" is contested by a capital *M* that multiplies Moore into a multitude of faces, a force that strains against the literal limit that a conclusion inevitably offers. In a similar fashion, Bishop concludes "As We Like It" with a portrait of the poet who "may be somewhat embarrassed by her own precocity and sensibilities," a genius whose "rhyme schemes and syllabic logarithms are all a form of apology," a sort of "self-imposed taxation to keep everything 'fair' in the world of poetry."[11] While the former image highlights Moore's impact on Bishop, the latter hints at Moore's view of herself, a view that mirrors Moore's early need to feed her fiery will while avoiding the self-centeredness that her family warned against.

In the previous chapter we learned that Moore's letters home from college depict an electrified lover of life who often apologizes for "losing herself" in lengthy descriptions before asking after family or friends. As a close correspondent of Moore's, Bishop was intimately familiar with this characteristic of her older friend, since the letters she received from Moore indulge in a similar sort of abandon. In the first years of their friendship, their correspondence followed a fairly regular pattern in which Bishop would write keen descriptions of her travels to Moore, often accompanied by exotic or idiosyncratic gifts, to which Moore would respond with expansive, detailed elaborations. In one such instance, Bishop sent her friend a selection of fruit (she often sent fruit to the health-conscious Moore), which inspired the following response:

> The pear is another epic. We decided to engross these wonders,—
> not engage in doubtful generalities—and the pear, we (principally
> I), are eating, a slice a day, or maybe two slices and never wearying
> of its sumptuousness—the patent leather skin and the neat surface
> left by the seed at the inner edge—the color should make a painter
> of anyone,—the pure Chinese apple green without a flaw, beside

the cream yellow—lending into it I should say. So do not imagine, dear Elizabeth, that the "point" of the present centered most in the sending! We have been all a-quiver over this episode and over the hoarded rarities.[12]

Characterized by a kind of carefree indulgence in the pleasures of her own descriptive talents, this letter is typical of the kind that Bishop often engendered. In her published work, however, Moore was far more self-conscious. It is no wonder, then, that Bishop was at times annoyed by Moore's moralizing, when it may well have appeared to her that Moore's advocacy of restraint contradicted a concomitant penchant for self-centeredness.

Allowing for this aspect of Moore's character enables us to piece together the somewhat disparate images of the poet that Bishop presents: Moore's moral stance was born of a deep aversion to self-indulgence, an aversion turned urgent in the face of a conflicting need to share her observations. Though the conclusion to Bishop's memoir claims that her "bemused" ruminations don't lead to the answers she seeks, it does shed light on the dilemma with which this chapter began: the discrepancy between Moore's feminist politics and the standard critiques that feminists often give her. Bishop's "subliminal glimpses" open our eyes to the frequency with which critics stress Moore's morality while either ignoring or discounting her feminist characteristics, as if the one opposed the other; while the feminist Moore is still scarcely known, the "Protestant poet of morals and manners" is widely recognizable.[13] But Bishop also shows us that the problem is more complicated than a mere opposition, that there is something especially peculiar about *Moore's* morality that makes it difficult to comprehend and thus easy to oversimplify: "Marianne never gave away the whole show. The volubility, the wit, the self-deprecating laugh, never really clarified those quick decisions of hers—or decisive intuitions, rather—as to good and bad, right and wrong" (*Prose*, 155). Bishop's description of Moore recalls the paradox upon which the previous chapter is focused: while Moore's verse is adamantly principled, it rejects absolutes. Throughout her poetry Moore contests egocentricity, but she does so with such consistent fervor—such "moral" urgency—that her sense of conviction seems perpetually at odds with the selflessness she prescribes. The brilliance of Moore's work, however, lies in the fact that this tension nurtures her writing and never overwhelms it. Moore's morality is the *product* of incongruous alliances, it exists *as* paradox, not alongside it. Recognizing that Moore's moral code aims to decenter the self, and that this destabilization is not at odds with her confident voice, is the key to comprehending how Moore the feminist can also be Moore the moralist. However, to allow that such a stance might be feminism's ally means that autonomous self-definition may not always be a useful aim.

In 1936 Moore wrote a small introduction to Bishop's work called "Archaically New." This essay was the first critical piece to be published on Bishop's poetry, and in it Moore admits of those perplexing poetic standards that Bishop would henceforth struggle with while shaping her own: "One asks a great deal of an author—that he should not be haphazard but considered in his mechanics, that he should not induce you to be interested in what is restrictedly private but that there should be the self-portrait: that he should pierce you to the marrow without revolting you" (*AN*, 83). Moore's demands reveal the focus that her fascination with Bishop would take in the years to come: that difficult dance between self-assertion and self-consciousness that also drew Bishop to Moore. On the one hand, a poet must attend to the mechanics of her craft, and on the other, she must "pierce" the reader with poetic content; bridging these complementary edicts is Moore's mandate that a poem avoid the "restrictedly private" while divulging the "self-portrait." Indeed, Moore does ask a lot of an author, but no more than she asks of herself—that one's writing admit of the perspective that binds it while maintaining a commitment to self-restraint. Understanding that Moore's ethical code is rooted in this approach to subjectivity, that it stems directly from what I call her "strategic self-hood," enables us to better understand the tone of moral urgency in the passage above. Moore was passionately committed to her belief that poetry should "subterraneously change the observer so that afterward his critical apparatus seemed different" (*SL*, 365). But there is a difference between inspiring that change and dictating it, or, as Moore puts it at the end of "Archaically New," "a good which is communicated and not purveyed" (*AN*, 83). This difference hinges upon that self-consciousness in Moore which both pleased and perplexed her younger friend, the insistent intuition that "you're not free / until you've been made captive by supreme belief" (*CP*, 113).

It is this embrace of "supreme belief" that distinguishes Bishop from

Moore most definitively in recent criticism. Bonnie Costello inspires such a view when she writes that "Moore is the poet of ethics and aesthetics," while "Bishop is the poet of epistemology and ontology, asking what we can know and who we are rather than what we should do and what we should admire or condemn."[14] But this distinction elides the complex concern with selfhood that determines Moore's "ethics and aesthetics" and thus, what it is that bonds these dimensions of Moore's poetry most. Moore was, without question, more concerned than Bishop about doing what the latter called the "the right thing,"[15] but this moral consistency does not preclude an intensely inquisitive, self-questioning poetic. As a junior in college Moore was already thinking seriously about the contiguity between "ethics" and "epistemology" that would come to distinguish her work, as this letter home reveals:

> You are emotionally drifting when you feast the eye on a landscape or beautiful object—you lose your sense of what "is." . . . If then you get to disassociating yourself habitually from the practical and material, your sense of proportions grows warped—art for art's sake makes fools of people—robs them of their efficacy—a certain amount of aestheticism is of course essential. . . . When you get to looking at yourself in a disassociated way, you lose your power as a factor in society—you stop to "see how to do it" instead of "doing it."[16]

For Moore, maintaining one's "power as a factor in society" depends upon one's ability to be immersed in the "practical and material," to remain rooted in the world so that one's *own perspective*—one's "sense of proportions"—does not become "warped." While this passage bears the unmistakable stamp of Moore's moral stance, it also displays a deep-rooted concern with the relationship between one's self and one's society from which that stance takes it stand. In later years Moore would give greater voice to the ways in which "seeing how" to do it informs one's ability to "do it" better, but she always maintained an instructive awareness of "egocentricity / and its propensity to bisect, / mis-state, misunderstand / and obliterate continuity" (*CP*, 231).

Surely Moore is reacting to her own propensity for "feasting" on landscapes and beautiful objects, her "habitual" way of seeing that apparently runs the risk of "disassociation." It is because Moore was acutely aware of her own self-centeredness, of her capacity for being overwhelmed with *feeling*, that she adopts such an adamant tone. Bishop alludes to this proclivity of Moore's in "Efforts of Affection":

Marianne was intensely interested in the techniques of things— how camellias are grown; how the quartz prisms work in crystal clocks; how the pangolin can close up his ear, nose, and eye aper- tures and walk on the outside edges of his hands "and save the claws / for digging"; how to drive a car; how the best pitchers throw a baseball; how to make a figurehead for her nephew's sail- boat. The exact way in which anything was done, or made, or func- tioned, was poetry to her. (*Prose,* 149)

This firsthand knowledge of "feasting" fortifies Moore's famous quip in "Archaically New" that some "authors do not muse within them- selves; they 'think'—like the vegetable-shredder which cuts into the life of a thing" (*AN,* 82). Moore managed to avoid such unchecked abandon in her work, but not without great effort. Once again, her letters to Bishop reveal an almost comical disjunction between her public restraint and her private inclination toward what she called "disassoci- ated" drifting. In response to a shipment of papayas from Bishop, Moore writes:

I was fascinated by the seeds, first of all by the distribution and amethyst color, and then by the necks, so that they stood up like seed-pearls set on stiff silk. I got a magnifying glass to examine the seed proper, which reminded me of those little squares called 'Sem- Sems' that drug stores used to sell in tiny little envelopes like miniature seed packets? [*sic*] (*SL,* 423)

Surely Moore's reproach against cutting "into the life of a thing" was, at least in part, a projection of her own disposition for doing so. In con- trast, Moore admires (and maybe envies) Bishop's "ungrudged self- expenditure" that is as "automatic apparently, as part of the nature" (*AN,* 83). Such "expenditure" signals "self-respect" instead of selfish- ness because it is exists alongside a "rational considering quality. . . assisted by unwordiness, uncontorted intentionalness, the flicker of impudence, the natural unforced ending" (82). According to Moore, Bishop achieves these qualities in her writing because she is sensitive to the line between self and other, between the act of musing "within" and "the life" of the thing about which one muses: "We are willing to be apprised of a secret—indeed glad to be," writes Moore, "but technique must be cold, sober, conscious of self-justifying ability" (82).

In her first essay on Bishop Moore returns again and again to this distinction between self-assertion and self-consciousness, but she does so with a moral diction that's often read at the expense of this complexity: "The specific is *judiciously* interspersed with generality"; "the *permitted* clue to idiosyncrasy has a *becoming* evasiveness"; one "notices the *deferences* and *vigilances* in Miss Bishop's writing" (*AN*, 82–83; emphases added), and so on. Ten years later we find that Moore's phrasing has ripened: "A Modest Expert" begins with Moore's assertion that "Elizabeth Bishop is spectacular in being unspectacular" (*ME*, 354) and goes on to praise her for a "verisimilitude that avoids embarrassingly direct description" (354). Moreover, Moore finds fault with the younger poet in terms that seem especially prim: "Miss Bishop does not avoid 'fearful pleasantries,' and in 'The Fish,' as in the subject of the poem, one is not glad of the creature's every prerequisite" (354).

It would be a mistake to discount Moore's mannered propriety, or to deny the proximity between her poems and this aspect of her persona. Nevertheless, we forsake much more if we fail to understand the link between Moore's morality and her interrogation of self-consciousness—how it is that she can both bristle at the "embarrassingly direct" description and enumerate the rewards of an "[a]rt which 'cuts its facets from within'" (*ME*, 354). Moore took it for granted that "Art . . . / is always actually personal" (*CP*, 192), that poetry is the product of a distinct personality, so that to assert this in one's writing is to overstate the already obvious. In this light we may read Moore's embarrassment at the too-direct description as akin to her claim, quoted earlier, that "Williams' uncompromising conscientiousness sometimes seems misplaced; he is at times insultingly unevasive." At the same time, achieving self-restraint in one's writing does not always come naturally, precisely because art *is* so personal; one must constantly check one's propensity for overdivulgence through an ever-awake self-consciousness, a cautious yet committed effort to keep the "restrictedly private" distinct from the "self-portrait."

Moore saw in Bishop a rare and perhaps enviable talent for maintaining this division. In "A Modest Expert" Moore once again lauds Bishop's "mechanics of presentation," describing them as "underlying knowledges" that reduce "critical cold blood to cautious self-inquiry" (*ME*, 354). This is a telling confession on Moore's part, one that is often overlooked by readings that stress the essay's mannered reserve. In the face of Bishop's poetry Moore is prompted to question herself—*she* is turned inward, her confident tone gives way to self-questioning. This is not praise from a woman who disdains self-analysis, but from one who "habitually" thrives on it. Moreover, it is crucial that we see the continuity between this statement and the one that precedes it—Moore's opening applause of the "Modest Expert's" "unspectacular" spectacularity. "Modesty" should be read here as much more than feminine deference; Bishop's reserve is the symptom of "underlying knowledges" that enable that tenuous balance between self and other, between "critical cold blood" and "cautious self-inquiry." Moore is not advocating a poetic primness or lack of emotional passion. On the contrary, she believes that restraint *presumes* a passion that needs reigning in so that the reader's own resources may be brought to the fore.

This interpretation is buttressed by the fact that Moore chose the following lines from *North & South* to introduce Bishop's work: " 'icebergs behoove the soul,' 'being self-made from elements least visible . . . fleshed, fair, erected indivisible' " (*ME*, 354). These snippets from "The Imaginary Iceberg" recall a poem that is centrally concerned with the issue of self-consciousness, a poem that stresses the relationship between one's sense of self and one's place among others. "We'd rather have the iceberg than the ship," begins Bishop's poem, "although it meant the end of travel" (*CP*, 4). Immediately the speaker establishes an opposition between the ship upon which she sails and the iceberg, whose "glassy pinnacles / correct elliptics in the sky" (4). The ship is a vehicle for travel, a means by which its passengers crack open their perspectives by encountering a world outside of their everyday lives. By comparison, the iceberg is static, stable—"fleshed, fair, erected indivisible" (4). It is triumphant in its isolated self-satisfaction:

> The wits of these white peaks
> spar with the sun. Its weight the iceberg dares
> upon a shifting stage and stands and stares.

> This iceberg cuts its facets from within.
> Like jewelry from a grave
> it saves itself perpetually and adorns

only itself, perhaps the snows
which so surprise us lying in the sea.
                    (4)

But of course the speaker cannot give up her ship, and like all expedi-
tions, this one must come to an end: "Good-bye, we say, good-bye, the
ship steers off / where waves give into one another's waves / and
clouds run in a warmer sky" (4). As our attentions are returned to the
ship, we are drawn, along with the speaker, back to the space where
subjectivities do not exist in isolation from each other, "where waves
give into one another's waves." Unlike the world in which the iceberg
"takes repose," this ship is inhabited by many faces and various histo-
ries; it represents that "warmer," messier world back home where bod-
ies mingle and minds are interdependent—the condition of self-con-
scious, human life.

Bishop is exploring the strange seductions of self-enclosure, of
autonomous self-definition: the promise of utter security and absolute
independence. Though such icebergs do not exist (they are imaginary,
after all), they nevertheless "behoove the soul . . . to see them so" (*CP*, 4).
This poem admits of our need to believe in a completely coherent self-
hood, a need made no less real in the face of its impossibility. In the next
chapter I explore in detail this defining aspect of Bishop's poetry, but
what interests me here is the position this poem occupies in Moore's
final review of Bishop's work. Interestingly, when Moore confesses that
Bishop's writing "reduces critical cold blood to cautious self-inquiry,"
she situates herself in the place of the poem's speaker, thereby putting
Bishop in the place of the poem: like the traveler whose initial awe of the
iceberg's chilly composure eventually surrenders to the tug of the tem-
perate *real*, Moore's determined attempt at outward critique gives way
to a "cautious" self-questioning. Not only is Moore applauding Bishop
for making her think twice, but she's done so in a way that both marks
and contests the adamant moral tone that Bishop knew all too well.

It makes sense, then, that Moore chose to make her point with a
poem that centers on that aspect of Bishop's writing that initially trou-
bled her most. In a key letter of 1938 Moore outlined these concerns as
clearly as she ever would:

> I feel that although large-scale "substance" runs the risk of inconse-
> quence through aesthetic impotence, and am one of those who

despise clamor about substance—I can't help wishing you would
sometime in some way, risk some unprotected profundity of expe-
rience; or since no one admits profundity of experience, some char-
acteristic private defiance of the significantly detestable . . . I do feel
that tentativeness and interiorizing are your danger as well as your
strength. (*SL*, 391)

This passage recalls Moore's commitment to "doing what's right" while
revealing the extent to which she judged Bishop accordingly. Much has
been made of this dimension of their relationship, with the overall result
that Moore has emerged as the moralizing mentor while Bishop is often
read as the less conclusive, thus more profound thinker. But as we have
seen, Moore's sense of moral duty has everything to do with her analy-
sis of subjectivity, an ongoing investment in "self-inquiry" that is any-
thing but static. It was Bishop's propensity for "interiorizing" that trou-
bled Moore, that made her fear for the younger poet what she feared for
herself: losing one's "sense of what 'is,'" "disassociating" oneself
"habitually from the practical and material" so that one's "sense of pro-
portions grows warped." For Moore, the act of asserting a "private char-
acteristic defiance" means that one has triumphed over the seductions
of self-immersion; the two go hand in hand.

Bishop was well aware of her "interiorizing" nature; she often pon-
dered this dimension of her character and its impact on her writing in
journals and letters. These recorded ruminations appear most fre-
quently during the early years of her friendship with Moore, and are
articulated thoughtfully in letters to the older poet:

I scarcely know why I persist at all—it is really fantastic to place so
much on the fact that I have written a half-dozen *phrases* that I can
still bear to re-read without too much embarrassment. But I have
that continuous uncomfortable feeling of "things" in the head, like
icebergs or rocks or awkwardly-shaped pieces of furniture. It's as if
all the nouns are there but the verbs are lacking—if you know what
I mean. And I can't help having the theory that if they are jiggled
around hard enough and long enough some kind of electricity will
occur, just by friction, that will arrange everything—But you
remember how Mallarmé said that poetry was made of words, not
ideas—and sometimes I am terribly afraid I am approaching, or try-
ing to approach it all from the wrong track. (*OA*, 94)

Bishop's disclosures suggest the deeply personal relevance of the issues explored in "The Imaginary Iceberg." Whereas the speaker in the poem seems to long for the illusionary security she sees reflected in the iceberg's self-enclosed angles, the author of this letter speaks from *within* that interiorized space, rendering it cramped, "uncomfortable," and literally frozen from movement ("the nouns are there but the verbs are lacking" [*CP*, 4]). At the same time, though, it is precisely this discomfort that eventually leads to the "kind of electricity" that "will arrange everything," that will produce the poems that Bishop always felt to be too slow in coming. The parallel between this passage and the poem it echoes suggests that for the young Bishop, "interiorizing" was both inevitable and necessary for the production of her work, *and* something that made her "uncomfortable," that led her to wonder if she was, after all, on "the wrong track." That Bishop was constantly negotiating these dual impulses is what made it possible, indeed unavoidable, for her to achieve that balance between "ungrudged self-expenditure" and a technique that is "conscious of self-justifying ability."

But it took Moore some time to accept that Bishop's brand of interiorizing was, as Kalstone put it, the mark of a "poet whose *method* was her message,"[17] a message that was, moreover, much like Moore's despite the difference in their approaches. While Moore praised Bishop early on for her "rational considering quality" and her "ungrudged self-expenditure," she also prodded the younger poet to assert herself in a style more akin to her own:

> When I set out to find fault with you, there are so many excellences in your mechanics that I seem to be commending you instead, and I wish to say, above all, that I am sure good treatment is a handicap unless along with it, significant values come out with an essential baldness. (*SL*, 384)

Though Moore recognized in Bishop the sort of liberating self-restraint she strove after herself, she had yet to commend what she would ten years later: Bishop's "much instructed persuasiveness . . . emphasized by uninsistence" (*ME*, 354).

It is not until Moore seriously questions herself that she is able to rethink her critique of Bishop. We may see, then, that Moore's decision to frame "A Modest Expert" with "The Imaginary Iceberg" reveals an intellectual progression that is often elided by readings that stress the essay's old-fashioned restraint. This growth was largely the result of an avid exchange between Bishop and Moore during what Lynn Keller has termed their "apprenticeship" period, those years between 1934 and 1940 when their correspondence was most intense.[18] This phase of the relationship culminated in their divergence over Bishop's poem "Roosters," in a passionate exchange that brought their differences— and their similarities—to a head. This exchange enriched Moore's understanding of Bishop's poetry (as well as her own), an evolution Moore admits to by fleshing out "A Modest Expert" with her praise of "Roosters." Thus, it is all the more ironic that their exchange over this poem has come to signify Moore's interpretive limits. As we have learned, each woman recognized in the other a poetics of selfhood that was inspiring in its familiarity while discomforting in its difference. But it is just at the slippery space where the different determines what's known that self-consciousness breeds, and thus, where their relationship took root.

In October 1940 Bishop made a trip to New York from Key West, where she was living at the time. Along with her she brought a new poem called "Roosters" (CP, 35), a piece she considered her most ambitious yet and one with which she hoped to win Moore's approval. Throughout the past few years, Moore had been Bishop's most cherished source of critical and professional advice, and Moore's response to "Roosters" is indicative of just how intense this aspect of their relationship had become: the day after Moore received the poem by mail, she called Bishop on the telephone to tell her—and perhaps warn her—that she and her mother had stayed up well into the night writing their own revision. Bishop received Moore's version, along with a dense letter of mingled praise and criticism, the next day.

Readers have commented at length on the refined, moralizing nature of Moore's revision as opposed to the brasher, less certain tenor of Bishop's original, a reading for which there is ample evidence.[19] While the cries of Bishop's roosters echo with "horrible insistence," grating "like a wet match / from the broccoli patch" (CP, 35), the "crow" of Moore's cock is less distressing as "an immediate echo." Whereas Bishop's birds have "cruel feet" and "stupid eyes" (CP, 35), Moore's creatures are merely "unseeing."[20] Moreover, Bishop's roosters usher in an aura of chaotic, mounting frenzy that permeates the first half of her poem, enacting a "displacement in perspective" that Moore neatens by naming it: "Confusion multiplies," she informs us rather flatly. In contrast, Bishop's narrator is too caught up in the roosters' insistent "screaming" to achieve this critical distance, and rests instead with the interrogative only—"Roosters, what are you projecting?" (*CP*, 36). Such attempts to shift Bishop's poignant, unresolved exploration of human error and forgiveness into a more assertive commentary culminate in Moore's insistence that "'Deny deny deny' / is not now as it was, the roosters' cry." Bishop had allowed the more ambiguous "'Deny deny deny' / is not all the roosters cry" (*CP*, 38), a difference, as Kalstone points out, that conjures a "sense of perpetual re-enactment," an "unavoidable mixture of self-assertion and a more benign consciousness" that is so central to Bishop's poem.[21]

Many more comparisons of this kind may be made, but the most notorious aspect of Moore's rewriting concerns what Bishop called her "sordidities," those explicitly graphic words or phrases that Moore either replaced or excised altogether.[22] The most irritating of these to Moore—and according to Kalstone, what sparked an argument over the phone—was Bishop's portrait of the "Cries galore" that emanated from the "water-closet door" and "from the dropping-plastered henhouse floor." Indeed, half of Moore's letter to Bishop was devoted to her conviction that these phrases and others like them should be removed from the final version. "Regarding the water-closet," explained Moore, "Dylan Thomas, W.C. Williams, E.E. Cummings, and others, feel that they are avoiding a duty if they balk at anything like unprudishness, but I say to them, 'I don't care about all things equally, I have a major effect to produce, and the heroisms of abstinence are as great as the heroisms of courage, and so are the rewards.'"

David Kalstone established the critical response to the "Roosters" exchange when he claimed that Moore's "rewriting insistently purges the poem of a Bishop that Moore clearly doesn't recognize."[23] He goes on to explain that it was "precisely [Bishop's] interiorizing element that Moore attempted to ignore in rewriting 'Roosters'" (82). As a result, her version is "less psychological, less human" (84). Though Kalstone's reading is respectful of Moore in many ways, it depicts the older poet as a less daring thinker than Bishop, whereas the latter triumphs as a "survivor" (85), a more troubled and therefore more far-reaching philosopher of our times. At the same time, Moore is presented as somewhat slow to catch on to the psychological drama of Bishop's craft, while we are left to assume that Bishop, on the contrary, grasped Moore's (rather obvious) meaning from the start.

Needless to say, the "Roosters" exchange has enjoyed a wide circulation among Bishop/Moore scholars and is often invoked as evidence of their deeply divergent ways. But once again, this oppositional reading overlooks a thorough understanding of Moore's moral stance, assuming from the start a rather one-dimensional reading of the relationship between her assertive tone and her poetics of restraint. This interpretation is guided largely by Bishop's oft-cited response to Moore, in which she carefully addresses Moore's changes, one by one:

> I cherish my "water-closet" and the other sordidities because I want to emphasize the essential baseness of militarism. In the 1st part I was thinking of Key West, and also of those aerial views of dismal little towns in Finland and Norway, when the Germans took over, and their atmosphere of poverty. . . . It has been so hard to decide what to do, and I know that aesthetically you are quite right, but I can't bring myself to sacrifice what (I think) is a very important "violence" of tone.

Though Bishop provides thoughtful explanations of her opinions at every juncture, she does so without directly addressing Moore's own lengthy explication. Instead, she catalogs Moore's critique as "aesthetically" admirable, implying a subtle but distinct line of differentiation between Moore's mechanics and her own more purposeful content.

This is an ironic distinction for Bishop to make, given Moore's urging over the years that she "risk some characteristic private defiance of the significantly detestable." Indeed, "Roosters" comes as close as Bishop ever would to meeting this sort of demand, and more likely than not, Bishop must have felt that Moore *didn't* "recognize" her attempts to produce the kind of poem she'd been asking for all this time. David Bromwich provides a subtle reading of this schism; rather than simplify Moore's reaction to the poem, he argues that during the 1930s and 1940s Moore "was withdrawing from a style of polemical irony which had been vital to her early poems."[24] For this reason Moore was unable or unwilling to appreciate Bishop's "defiance" because "'Roosters' was calculated to remind her of a part of her imagination that she wanted to be finished with" (76). While Bromwich restores a degree of sophistication to Moore's response to "Roosters," his reading still elides what I see as the most subversive, if subtle, characteristic of Moore's poetic at this time: the contingency for Moore between "subterraneously chang[ing] the observer" and "the heroisms of abstinence."

That critical accounts of this exchange have largely bypassed this kernel of Moore's correspondence suggests that sympathetic readings of Bishop increasingly come at the cost of simplified readings of Moore. But Moore's October 16, 1940, letter to Bishop reveals a poet who was anything but oblivious to Bishop's motives, however archly she defended her own:

> I think it is to your credit, Elizabeth, that when I say you are not to say "water-closet," you go on saying it a little . . . and it is calculated to make me wonder if I haven't mistaken a cosmetic patch for a touch of lamp-black, but I think not. The trouble is, people are not depersonalized enough to accept the picture rather than the thought. You see with what gusto I acclaimed "the mermaid's pap" in Christopher S. but few of us, it seems to me, are fundamentally rude enough to enrich our work in such ways without cost.

Though Moore's concerns here may seem somewhat exaggerated to contemporary audiences, her critique cannot be dismissed adequately as reactionary or prudish. Fearing that Bishop's "sordidities" will carry tropes too burdensome for the poetic "picture" to overcome, Moore worries that the poem's meaning will be marred or mistaken as a result. People are not "depersonalized" enough—they are too immersed within their own perspectives—to step outside of their conditioned associations in the face of such laden phrasing. Whether we agree or not with Moore's critique, we need to acknowledge its analytical nature. It seems to me that Moore is zeroing in on the issue of "interiorizing," a characteristic, as we have seen, that she was keenly aware of when it came to Bishop's work. If Moore believes people are "not depersonalized" enough, it is because they are too self-involved. For Moore, rewriting the uncertainty out of Bishop's poem goes hand in hand with excising the "sordidities" because both are means by which the temptation to withdrawal, or "interiorizing," is checked. Moore was not avoiding the internalized atmosphere of Bishop's work; she was contesting it in the manner she had been for years.

Nevertheless, I do not want to argue that Moore's version of "Roosters" honors those aspects of Bishop's poem that have come to define her poetic over the years—her unsettling ability to hover in that liminal space between inside and out, self and other, complicity and criticism. Discomfort with this dimension of Bishop is different, however, from not sensing it at all. Allowing ourselves to see the complexity of Moore's response to Bishop also enables us to account for the rather radical aspects of "The Cock," those portions of Bishop's poem that Moore left *untouched*. As many have pointed out, "Roosters" offers, among other things, a scathing commentary on masculine egoism, what Bishop refers to as the "baseness of militarism." Her roosters know no boundaries, they are territorial, abrasive, with "Deep . . . protruding chests / in green-gold medals dressed." While "from their beaks . . . rise . . . uncontrolled, traditional cries," they attempt to "command and terrorize" their "many wives / who lead hens' lives of being courted and despised" (*CP*, 35). Though Moore omits the word "traditional" from this passage, her version keeps the thrust of this image perfectly intact. Furthermore, Moore's poem is less forgiving than Bishop's, which takes a turn toward the end as the speaker becomes somewhat complicit with the portrait she's painted:

> In the morning
> a low light is floating
> in the backyard and gilding
>
> from underneath
> the broccoli, leaf by leaf;
> how could the night have come to grief?
>
> gilding the tiny
> floating swallow's belly
> and lines of pink cloud in the sky,
>
> the day's preamble
> like wandering lines in marble.
> The cocks are now almost inaudible.
>
> The sun climbs in,
> following "to see the end,"
> faithful as enemy, or friend.
>
> (*CP*, 39)

The poem that opened at "four o'clock" on the dot in the steely "gun-metal blue dark" concludes in a bath of hazy morning sun, a meandering light that slinks back through the poem's sinews to link not only broccoli and bird, but the speaker's ambiguous grief and the rooster's invasive antics. Dwarfed by the world in which they live, a world that like the "admir[ing] wives" cannot be entirely absolved of its part in the "picture," the once-inescapable cocks are now nearly indistinct.

In contrast, Moore's speaker is both less implicated and less forgiving:

> In the morning
> a low light is floating
>
> From underneath
> the broccoli stems, leaf by leaf,
> gilding the lines of pink in the sky,
>
> the day's preamble
> like wandering lines in marble;
>
> and climbing in to see the end,
> The faithful sun is here,
> as enemy, or friend.

Compared to Bishop's speaker, Moore's maintains a calculated distance until the end of the poem—she divulges little that would bring her presence to the fore, that would enmesh her in the sticky threads connecting fault and forgiveness at the crux of the poem. At the same time, though, Moore grants less leeway to the creatures that bear the brunt of her critique. While she returns us to the start of the poem by way of the broccoli patch, she does so without recalling the roosters, and in doing so Moore forecloses the possibility of recasting them in the gentler, more welcoming light. In this way "The Cock" consistently risks a "defiance of the significantly detestable," what Moore tellingly saw as an "unprotected profundity of experience"—or in other words, she personalizes her poem by risking an opinion.

Moore's speaker does not, however, maintain a pure, unsullied distance from the psychological explorations of this poem, and that she steps into the foray when she does reveals at least as much about her motives as do those instances of standing back. "Roosters" interrogates our compulsion to selfishness and cruelty, our propensity for mistaken judgment and regret, and the process of forgiveness that is elemental to the transition between them. At issue in Bishop's contemplation is that strange and inevitable condition of human consciousness, the realization that we are always somehow a part of that which we condemn. "Roosters" dramatizes this realization by pairing the speaker's scorching satire of masculinist presumption with the biblical story of Peter's betrayal of Christ, two narratives in which roosters play a central role. The speaker's transition from a position of seething disgust to a perspective of possible forgiveness is catalyzed by the roosters' metamorphosis at midpoem: the stupid-eyed barnyard bullies that begin the first stanza become, two pages later, the victims of a senseless cockfight.

> Now in mid-air
> by twos they fight each other.
> Down comes a first flame-feather,
>
> and one is flying,
> with raging heroism defying
> even the sensation of dying.
>
> And one has fallen,
> but still above the town
> his torn-out, bloodied feathers drift down;
>
> and what he sung
> no matter. He is flung
> on the gray ash-heap, lies in dung
>
> with his dead wives
> with open, bloody eyes,
> while those metallic feathers oxidize.
>
> (CP, 37)

Though this fate feels somewhat like just deserts for the birds who "command and terrorize," it also broadens the locus of blame beyond the roosters themselves to the human context in which they have been prompted, like enemies at war, to self-destructive displays of violent offense. Bishop's speaker underlines this awareness by addressing the roosters as "You, whom the Greeks elected / to shoot at on a post, who struggled / when sacrificed, you whom they labeled // 'Very combative . . .'" (*CP*, 36). But Moore subtly revises this portion of the poem in a way that emphasizes the dimension of human complicity (and therefore the speaker's) to an even greater degree: Moore's poem describes the "Greek sacrificial cocks / tied to a post to struggle, / whom we label // fighting-cocks." Her "we" implicates the speaker in the labeling, here clearly revealed, whereas Bishop's speaker inserts a curious distance at this point between herself and a more removed "they." This aspect of Moore's version is made even more remarkable when we realize the parallel for which it prepares us: the transition from the speaker's initial anger to the possibility of forgiveness is completed by the roosters' eventual resurrection:

>    outside the Lateran
>
>  there would always be
>  a bronze cock of the porphyry
>  pillar so the people and the Pope might see
>
>  that even the Prince
>  of the Apostles long since
>  had been forgiven.
>
>                    (*CP*, 38)

Moore's revision of this passage is very slight (she changes "there would always be" to the more fictionalized "there was always to be") in light of her more weighty decision to maintain Bishop's correlation between Christ and the cocks. What began both versions of the poem as an emblem of the most horrific selfishness is by the end metamorphosed into Judeo-Christian culture's most resonant sign of self-sacrifice and forgiveness. Though the birds who introduce both poems are decidedly un-Christlike, they endure mounting opposition, as Christ did among the "speakers" of his time, in language that increasingly insists on the connection between them. In a scene that echoes the Crucifixion, the roosters were, in Bishop's words, "elected to shoot at on a post" (*CP*, 36), whereupon the speaker of both versions then angrily exclaims, "what right have you to give / commands and tell us how to live. . . ?" When Christ was summoned before the high priest Caiaphas he, too, was asked to justify his claim to authority: "'I adjure you by the living God, tell us if you are the Christ, the Son of God.'" When Jesus affirmed that this was so, the priest "tore at his robes, and said, 'He has uttered blasphemy. Why do we still need witnesses?'"[25] Both demands are rhetorical, providing vehicles for the speakers' exasperation more than an opportunity for enlightened exchange. Along these lines, the birds in each poem are bedecked with "crowns of red" while heroically "defying / even the sensation of dying" (37). Finally, Moore honors the roosters' emblematic journey from sacrifice to resurrection as their life-less "metallic feathers" are eternally perched atop the papal weather-vane.

The two poems literally "pivot" upon this parallel, as Peter's tears of remorse signal its completion: "There is inescapable hope," writes Bishop, "the pivot: // yes, and there Peter's tears / run down our chan-ticleer's / sides and gem his spurs. . . . Poor Peter, heart-sick, // still cannot guess / those cock-a-doodles yet might bless, / his dreadful roosters come to mean forgiveness" (CP, 38). Typically, Moore is less lenient on "the Prince / of the Apostles," cutting the sympathetic pic-ture of him from her poem. Nevertheless, she too contests the bound-aries between speaker, reader, roosters, and Peter, as forgiveness is only arrived at through a blurring of subject positions and the collapse of opposing views. Each speaker's distanced disdain gives way to a contemplation of forgiveness, a progression that is engendered by a growing awareness of one's own capacity for that which one also con-demns. Accordingly, the speakers in each poem participate in Peter's plight, while our investment as readers is measured by the degree to which we can do so as well. At the same time, because Moore *is* less for-giving of Peter, we must infer that she is also less forgiving of the speaker, whose complicity still survives her revision. As Kalstone remarks, Bishop's version "allows her to explore *and escape* the full and final burden of her poem";[26] Moore, on the other hand, allows herself less relief.

It is this potential for escape that I believe troubled Moore most about "Roosters," sparking her deep-rooted fear of "disassociated" art and its "warped" "sense of proportion." While a reading of Moore's omissions and revisions reveals a consistent discomfort with Bishop's "interiorizing," this discomfort acquires a thoughtful depth of purpose in light of what Moore didn't touch: by keeping Bishop's focus on human imperfection through a speaker who is at once less involved and less absolved, Moore fortifies the critique of warlike aggression that, according to Bishop, lay at the heart of her poem. Ignoring this twofold dimension of Moore's response to "Roosters" encourages an incomplete comprehension of a poet whose complexities far outstrip her limits.

Such selectivity brings us face-to-face with the problem of feminist interpretation with which this chapter started: by reading Moore's response to "Roosters" strictly in terms of its moralizing, a moralizing that is, furthermore, disconnected from the issue of self-consciousness to which it is wed, Moore's deep commitment to justice can only be understood as antiquated propriety. Given Bishop's critique of masculinist presumption, a critique that Moore's version in fact accentuates, it is especially ironic that this poem has come to signal Moore's unfeminist impenetrability. At the heart of this reading is a tendency among feminist readers to privilege autobiography as a conduit to political consciousness, which is why Bishop's more uncertain, interiorized version of "Roosters" garners feminist acclaim at the expense of Moore's. But such "interiorizing" signals a repressed, more authentic self only if selfhood can be unearthed, retrieved from the forces that mute its pleas for unobstructed being. While Bishop may have sometimes longed to redeem her suffering in these terms, her longing was, as we shall see, always balanced by a view that undermined such illusions of autonomy.

# 3 Elizabeth Bishop's Ambivalent "I"

lthough Elizabeth Bishop was at least as wary of women-iden-
tified feminisms as was Marianne Moore, she was less assertive
on the page, seduced by situations and objects of inquiry that
resisted resolve or revelation. At the same time, Bishop was more likely
to populate her poems with obviously personal details, especially in
the later half of her career. To those in search of autonomous self-defin-
ition, these characteristics of Bishop's writing appear contiguous
though incongruous, evidence of the poet's evolution from self-deflec-
tion to self-empowerment.[1] While I am indebted to such readings for
bringing Bishop's personal life into focus, I reject the conclusion that
Bishop's feminism was at odds with her ambivalent voice. For Bishop,
writing as a feminist had less to do with self-expression than it did with
probing the complex and often discomforting nature of self and its
attendant claims to agency, which means that the personal details in
Bishop's later poems are enabled by—not anathema to—the slippery
and often surreal voice with which they are told. Hence, the "sidelong"
perspective that permeates an overtly personal poem like "In the Wait-
ing Room" is best read as akin to "Elizabeth's" shyness; far from arrest-
ing her intrepidness, the seven-year-old's self-consciousness *propels* her
"right straight through" the *National Geographic* and "those awful hang-
ing breasts" into the "blue-black" maw of her becoming (*CP*, 159). More
strategic than mere insecurity, Bishop's ambivalence signals the contin-
gent, not coherent, nature of self.

Allowing that Bishop's ambivalence may be ally to her feminism is
to shift our focus from the quest for identity to the less tenable
processes of differentiation. As "In the Waiting Room" reveals, the
parameters that delimit one's individual being are defined by one's
images of the abject—in "Elizabeth's" case, those "black, naked
women" and their "awful hanging breasts." I will return to this poem
and its depictions of otherness in more detail at the end of this chapter,
but for now I want to stress the crucial link in Bishop's poetry between

her dramatizations of self and her explorations of difference. From the Gentleman of Shalott's disjointed being to Bishop's racially and economically marked characters, we witness an unbroken commitment to subversions of the autonomous self and its attending markers of difference that continues through "Santarém" and "Pink Dog" in 1979. Moreover, the proximity of poems such as "The Gentleman of Shalott" and "The Map" with poems like "Cootchie" and "Songs for a Colored Singer" in *North & South* should not be overlooked as coincidence; the transformation of black faces into a "conspiring root" in part 4 of "Songs for a Colored Singer" (*CP*, 50–51) carries over the tropes of division, unconscious processes, perspective, and reconstruction that pepper poems like "The Weed," "The Man-Moth," "Sleeping Standing Up," and "The Gentleman of Shalott." This does not mean that Bishop's interrogations of difference are innocent of her own prejudices as a white, middle-class woman of (for the most part) midcentury America; I agree with Adrienne Rich when she describes Bishop's racial portraits as a "risky undertaking."[2] Nevertheless, I believe that Bishop's passionate willingness to expose the tension between her attempts to identify with those marked as radically different from herself *and* her own investment in maintaining those very distinctions is what creates the opportunity for us to reexamine our own claims to agency while reading her poems.

Recognizing the interdependence in Bishop's work between the unstable "I" and her portraits of exotic and disenfranchised others enables us to place these poems within the logic of her oeuvre as a whole and not, as they are often read, as "something other than . . . Elizabeth Bishop['s] poem[s]."[3] Throughout her poetry Bishop reminds us that we can only rupture the cycle of you versus me, or self versus other, if we can understand our sense of identity as dependent on this opposition in the first place. Maintaining the illusion of wholeness depends upon one's refusal to identify with anything alien from one's own sensational ego, and a concurrent clinging to those images that reflect one's ego back. For this reason, destabilizing the coherent self is indispensable to the feminist goal of dismantling staid conceptions of difference. In *The Threshold of the Visible World*, Kaja Silverman articulates a theory of desire that illuminates this aspect of Bishop's poetic: rather than lament identification as an inevitable means by which we are coerced into the status quo, Silverman maintains that under certain conditions we "might be carried away from both ideality and the self, and situated in an identifactory relation to despised bodies."[4] Because identification is always in part an unconscious process, this sort of "ethical" looking can happen only in retrospect, and then only provisionally, since it is through the act of looking *again* that we might learn to restructure our ways of seeing, and thus our interactions, with others and ourselves. In doing so, we must constantly admit of our desires for identifying with the ideal just as we remain committed to the deconstruction of those desires. The anticipated result of this "productive look" is an understanding that it is through our own psychic projections (and not because of the other's "essential" character), that one body or image may appear ideal and an other abject. In the process, argues Silverman, we may finally "'leap out of 'difference' and into bodily otherness,'" to a state of awareness in which loving oneself does not mean either seamlessly meshing with the ideal or repudiating all that is other" (37).

Bishop's poetry is marked by this struggle, a kind of resistance that is often interpreted as insecurity, or indecision. Characters such as the man-moth, the Gentleman of Shalott, and certainly seven-year-old "Elizabeth" long for the ecstasy of coherent selfhood, the promise of plenitude that identification with the normative ideal confers, just as they expose the impossible and ultimately coercive nature of such representations.[5] Along these lines, I maintain that Bishop's early, more abstract explorations of difference and her gradual turn to autobiography are compatible, not in conflict—indeed, that Bishop's later focus on her self is in perfect keeping with her lifelong poetic reticence. The focus on personal history in the later poems is *defined* by Bishop's focus on the other, a signature concern of the poet's that brings her late-life verse face-to-face with her earliest pieces. Thus, what may appear in Bishop's work to be a gradually liberated expression of her self is more suitably described as an increasingly sophisticated understanding of her lack—of the lack at the heart of all subjectivity—and the ways in which her own observations are embroiled in the dual project of revealing this lack and covering it up.

There is no "split." Dreams, works of art (some) glimpses of the always-more-successful surrealism of everyday life, unexpected moments of empathy (is it?), catch a peripheral vision of whatever it is one can never really see full-face but that seems enormously important. . . . What one seems to want in art, in experiencing it, is

the same thing that is necessary for its creation, a self-forgetful, per-
fectly useless concentration.[6]

The latter portion of this quotation from Bishop's letter to Anne Steven-
son has been circulated many times throughout Bishop criticism, but it
is rarely contextualized within the rest of this excerpt. Important here is
Bishop's insistence that there is no "split" between the waking process
of conscious artistic production and the sleeping life of unconscious
dreams, an assertion born out by Bishop's habit of recording her
dreams and attempting to use their contents as material for her poems.
Like the Yeats who believed that "art / Is but a vision of reality,"[7]
Bishop articulates her conviction through the vocabulary of seeing:
"glimpses," "peripheral vision," "what one can never really see full-
face." This diction summons perhaps the most notorious aspect of
Bishop's early work—its heady fusion of dreamlike imagery and a con-
stant preoccupation with perspective. In the first stanza of "The Map,"
the first poem in *North & South*, we are introduced immediately to these
defining aspects of her poems.[8]

> Land lies in water; it is shadowed green.
> Shadows, or are they shallows, at its edges
> showing the line of long sea-weeded ledges
> where weeds hang to the simple blue from green.
> Or does the land lean down and pull the sea from under,
> drawing it unperturbed around itself?
> Along the fine tan sandy shelf
> is the land tugging at the sea from under?
>
> (CP, 3)

By the second line of the poem the speaker's perspective is subjective,
questionable. Are they shadows or are they shallows? A reflection of
the land, or its actual presence? The distinction between the "real" and
"representation" is quickly offered just as it is rendered untenable to
the speaker's eye; though the question is posed, it is never answered,
and indeed, the rest of the poem is a meditation on the process of rep-
resentation itself. At the same time, the meandering imagery of the
poem moves, much like the ocean, in and out of "long sea-weeded
ledges," "a clean cage for invisible fish," and "women feeling for the
smoothness of yard-goods." In short, the poem unfolds like a dream-

scape, syntactically more akin to the scattered patchwork of uncon-
scious imagery than to the narrative logic of waking conversation.

In an effort to explain the relationship between visual imagery and
the "productive look," Silverman provides a summary of Freud's
explanation of how unconscious stimuli become conscious thoughts:

> In *The Interpretation of Dreams*, Freud . . . [suggests that] visual stim-
> uli enter the psyche from the "side" of the unconscious, and are
> processed in complex ways before arriving at a state of conscious
> perception. As these stimuli traverse the imaginary "space" of the
> psyche, they pass through two mnemic reserves, one unconscious
> and one preconscious. At the level of the preconscious a process of
> classification occurs, whereby the stimulus in question is "recog-
> nized" through its paradigmatic grouping with other, similar stim-
> uli. . . . Freud problematizes the notion of objective vision through
> the delay which he insists obtains between the introduction of a
> stimulus into the psyche and its conscious perception.[9]

"The Map," like any number of Bishop's early poems, dramatizes pre-
cisely this relationship between the seeing eye and the path of con-
scious identification. The repetition of "s" sounds that introduce the
speaker's observations creates a shifting sensory field within which the
images of sea and land slide imperceptibly in and out of their respec-
tive shadows. We are ushered immediately into an economy wherein
visual accuracy is highly valued, while the distance between visual per-
ception and conscious understanding of what one has seen is widened.
As the poem proceeds—as we "traverse the imaginary 'space' of the
psyche"—the initial image of land and sea forms a chain of associations
with several ostensibly disparate pieces of "visual stimuli" (the
Eskimo, the cage for invisible fish, and so on), eventually giving way to
metaphors in which Norway becomes a "hare" that "runs south in agi-
tation," and continents become "profiles" that investigate the sea. The
success of such metaphors depends, of course, upon the "recognition"
to which Freud refers, a process wherein a particular visual stimulus is
"paradigmatically" grouped with other visual stimuli, and thus given
conscious meaning—that is, upon the string of metonymic associations
that make up the middle of the poem.

As "The Map" and nearly every other poem in *North & South* insists,
"There is no 'split'"; unconscious and conscious procedures are contin-

gent upon one another, and a consciousness that remains alert to this fact is more likely to understand its own processes of identification, however subjective and peripheral that understanding is bound to be. As a result, one is more likely to enter into "unexpected moments of empathy" and, in turn, begin the "enormously important" act of making and experiencing art that will facilitate this literally "self-forgetful" state of being.

For Bishop, such a state depends upon remembering the tenuous nature of one's sense of self. According to Lacan, the subject first apprehends herself as a "me" upon recognizing herself in a localized mirror image. At this moment, the subject garners an illusory sense of coherence, or identity, as the visual image literally frames and contains her.[10] As Silverman notes, this formulation suggests the oft-overlooked implication of Lacanian psychoanalysis that the subject's *corporeal* limits provide the basis, indeed, the "limit or boundary," inside of which identification, and thus the formation of one's ego, can occur.[11] And since, within normative processes, one's ego formation or self is developed in tandem with one's sense of other, the entire notion of "difference" is derived from one's vision of bodily being.

These insights are of particular relevance when discussing Bishop's poetry because they illuminate the consistent interweaving of visual, sensual acuity and explorations of selfhood within which her later, seemingly more straightforward use of the lyric "I" is couched. Especially in the early poems of *North & South*, we are led again and again to mirror images, distorted and exaggerated corporeal parameters, askance perspectives, dreamworlds, and fragile identities. The title character of "The Gentleman of Shalott," a poem written at the start of Bishop's career in 1936, embodies precisely this nexus between being and seeing:

> Which eye's his eye?
> Which limb lies next the mirror?
> For neither is clearer
> nor a different color than the other,
> nor meets a stranger
> in this arrangement
> of leg and leg and
> so on. To his mind
> it's the indication

of a mirrored reflection
somewhere along the line
of what we call the spine.
                    (*CP*, 9–10)

In this first stanza we are introduced to the issue at the heart of the
poem: the interplay between seeing and being. The gentleman's "I"
(importantly never named as such) is punningly contingent upon the
"eye" through which the poem's imagery is framed. Unlike Tennyson's
Lady of Shalott, who "in her web she still delights / To weave the mir-
ror's magic sights,"[12] Bishop's gentleman cannot distinguish between
"reality" and the mirrored reflection. "Which eye's his eye?" asks the
speaker, a question that, typically, is posed only to expose the impossi-
bility of an answer. The gentleman does not assume that one's mirrored
reflection frames his body once-removed; on the contrary, as in "The
Map," reflection (or representation) and "real" are fused to generate his
sense of being.

At the same time, the gentleman maintains that he is *part* mirrored
reflection, "Half," to be precise, so that his perception of self assimilates
that which is, according to Lacan, normally always exterior: the visual
imago that by its very distance from the viewing subject will always
generate in him or her a sense of lack, and thus desire. In other words,
the gentleman embodies the driving paradox at the center of Lacan's
mirror stage: "On the one hand, the mirror stage represents a *mécon-
naissance* [misrecognition], because the subject identifies with what he
or she is not [the mirror image]. On the other hand, what he or she sees
when looking into the mirror is literally his or her own image." Conse-
quently, the ego is simultaneously based upon the "otherness" and
"sameness" of the mirror image, which explains in part why one's own
sense of self is always to some extent dependent on one's sense of
other.[13] The gentleman *is* the mirror, *and* the reflection, *and* that which
exists before the mirror altogether. But just as the poem names these
distinct elements of the gentleman's being, it renders each element, for
all intents and purposes, neither "clearer / nor a different color / than
the other." The distance between representation-of-self and self is col-
lapsed in this poem, so that "he's in doubt / as to which side's in or out
/ of the mirror" (*CP*, 9). The gentleman knows that "There's little mar-
gin for error, / but there's no proof, either" (9), as Bishop's poems in
general suggest. Existing *as* the "threshold of the visible world" rather

than on either side of it, hovering within the exchange between one's eye and "I," Bishop's gentleman exposes the dialectic of seeing and being at the heart of all human experience of "self." He insists that subjectivity is an unfinished process, or in his words, "that sense of constant re-adjustment."

The stakes of the gentleman's plight are made clearer when we turn to Bishop's unpublished drafts. In her notebook from 1934 to 1936 there is a much-worked-over stanza that was never included in the final version of the poem:

he'd like to hold dear
the part *not* in the mirror
but one eye cannot discern

where he should put his love.[14]

This passage emphasizes the gentleman's quest for total, secure selfhood with a poignancy that's smoothed to humor in the final published draft. Extending our understanding of the poem through an analysis of this forsaken stanza, we may better detect the conflicted heart of Bishop's gentleman: he longs to be one with the "real" that exists both before and beyond the disruptive "re-adjustments" that representation, or his reflection demands, but at the same time, try as he might, he simply cannot "discern // where he should put his love." In other words, he cannot locate a part of his identity that exists outside the domain of symbolic representation. And as the language of this stanza makes clear, it is the gentleman's love, his ability to desire, that is literally paralyzed because of it. Not only is the gentleman unable to love himself, but as the published version asserts, he cannot meet "a stranger" either. The gentleman is bound within his narcissistic world, not having moved *through* the mirror stage to the scopic domain where one's vision of oneself is achieved at a distance. Consequently, he is both closer to *and* farther from his "self" than normative subjects are, which accounts for the paradoxical perspectives rendered by this poem—that we are at once embroiled, almost suffocated, within the gentleman's self-reflexive world, while at the same time, we have little sense of his "self," his bodily parameters.

This confusing portrait is enriched by the fact that the gentleman never speaks for himself. Instead, an anonymous speaker presents us with the gentleman's intimate world; he is, quite literally, without a voice of his own, though the poem is structured according to the shifting corporeal dimensions of the gentleman's body. Though we become intensely familiar with the gentleman's fraught sense of self and his clumsy and endearing passion for self-reflection, we never actually meet him one-to-one. As readers, we occupy the place all "stranger[s]" do in relation to the gentleman—the place beyond the mirror, the register of symbolic life where, as Tennyson's Lady of Shalott discovered, moving through the mirror stage means the death of unmediated selfhood and the birth of insurmountable lack.

Like any number of Bishop's early poems, "The Gentleman of Shalott" reminds us that one's perspective is mapped by one's physical location, which, in turn, is apprehended only through one's bodily sensations. But as the gentleman reveals, there are *two* not necessarily aligned experiences of the body going on here: on one level we have the gentleman's reflection in the mirror, that once-removed half of his being that, though indistinct from the "real" half, is ostensibly quite different. But on another yet simultaneous level, we have the gentleman's hazy sense of his "actual" body, that which is described to us as "this arrangement / of leg on leg and / arm and so on," what the gentleman can only conceptualize as "the indication / of a mirrored reflection / somewhere along the line / of what we call the spine." Caught in the precarious balance between his sensual ego and his visual image, the gentleman at first searches for *his* eye, *his* limbs, longing for a feeling of wholeness. Living at the literal juncture of his sensual self ("this arrangement / of leg on leg and / so on") and his visual imago ("the indication / of a mirrored reflection"), the gentleman's search for his "real" half is overwhelmed by his deepening inability to distinguish the real from the reflected. Eventually, the gentleman accepts this: "he's resigned / to such economical design" (*CP*, 9), and in doing so, admits of the impossibility of finding an a priori self beyond or before the mirror. At the same time, however, the gentleman feels the split in his being. Though he cannot distinguish between these different aspects of his subjectivity, he nonetheless cannot escape the awareness that they exist as such. In this way, the gentleman, like so many of Bishop's characters, longs for normativity while exposing the impossibility of satisfying his desire.

In the short poem "To Be Written on the Mirror in Whitewash," written in 1937, just one year later than "Gentleman" (published in *The*

*Complete Poems* under the heading "Uncollected Poems"), Bishop constructs what might be read as the mirror image of the gentleman's mirror image, an inverted version of this selfish, selfless being who further illustrates the futility of looking inside to discover one's self:

> I live only here, between your eyes and you,
> But I live in your world. What do I do?
> —Collect no interest—otherwise what I can;
> Above all, I am not that staring man.
>
> (*CP*, 205)

Whereas the gentleman's physical presence determined the parameters of his poem at the expense of his speaking "I," this poem is anchored assertively through the mysterious speaker's first-person narrative at the expense of his bodily ego. It is as if the speaker of "Whitewash" embodied the gentleman's missing voice, a voice articulated from the threshold that the gentleman could only know through his hazy bodily contours. Yet the confidence of this speaker's "I" is belied by the absence of a corporeal presence. As Bonnie Costello observes in her reading of this poem, the "'here' the writer designates has no spatial register. . . . The 'I' seems to exist only as an effect of the writing itself and is thus inherently unstable."[15] And though the speaker seems to know quite well where he lives ("between your eyes and you"), it is *we*, this time, who cannot distinguish between our reflections and our selves as we are invited to locate the speaker's riddled being; or at the very least, the unanswerable question around which the poem is written suggests the futility of thinking that we can. In processing this poem we are faced with the split that exists at the core of our ostensibly coherent egos: the threshold "between your eyes and you," a split that generates the illusion of an "I" that, as the abstractions of this poem suggest, reflects no "real" or essential body that exists "*not* in" the mirror's symbolic reflections.

By exposing the split conditions through which both the "Whitewash" speaker and the gentleman exist, Bishop foreshadows Silverman, insisting that the sensational ego "is *always* initially disjunctive with the visual image, and that a unified bodily ego comes into existence only as the result of a laborious stitching together of disparate parts."[16] Clearly, neither poem offers the experience of coherence that results from this "laborious stitching." Instead, we are privy to the backstage mechanisms that are naturalized and made invisible by the smooth meshing of these "disparate parts." It is perhaps for this reason that Bishop excised the unpublished stanza from the final draft of "Gentleman," since to include it would have been to tip the scales of the poem toward the possibility of plenitude, assuring us that though the gentleman can't find it, the "part *not* in the mirror" may indeed exist. Bishop's refusal to resolve the "disparate parts" of subjectivity into an illusory and comforting whole explains the uneasy feeling that lingers around most of her early pieces. From the weed's "divided heart" to the man-moth's distorted "shadows," the illusion of causality between a biologically determined body and a cohesive self is "inverted and distorted. . . . I mean / distorted and revealed" (*CP*, 17). But, as was always the case for Bishop, this is not cause for despair. Like her gentleman, who in the end "loves / that sense of constant re-adjustment" (*CP*, 10), Bishop's poems proffer an "uncertainty" we find "exhilarating": "Half," we must concede, will always be more than "enough" (*CP*, 10).

Parallel to the tension between life in the symbolic register and a longing for the real in "The Gentleman of Shalott" is Bishop's general refusal to delineate clean lines between the abject and the ideal in her poems about race and class relations; this is in part what makes these poems a "risky undertaking." In "Cootchie," for instance, we are introduced to the title character, "Miss Lula's servant," whose "life was spent / in caring for Miss Lula, who is deaf, / eating her dinner off the kitchen sink / while Lula ate hers off the kitchen table" (*CP*, 46). Clearly, this description begs our sympathies for Cootchie, whose suicide provides the impetus for the poem: "black into white she went / below the surface of the coral-reef." The opening stanza layers opposition upon opposition: servant versus master, life versus death, freedom versus servitude, black versus white. The "sable" faces at Cootchie's funeral stand in stark contrast to the "egg-white" skies that, as the canopy above the funeral, align the heavenly and sublime with whiteness and Miss Lula while death and blackness seem to signal the domain of Cootchie and her mourners. The binary of black versus white weighs heavily upon the first stanza of this poem, framing it and concluding it with images wherein whiteness occupies the register of immortality and nature, while blackness, along with Cootchie herself, continually slides "into [the] white."

Yet, as Margaret Dickie notes, "the poem is titled 'Cootchie' not

'Miss Lula,'"[17] and the exaggerated emphasis on dark versus light within the first half of the poem suggests a mockery behind the speaker's words; it is the absent maid whose presence is immortalized through this poem, and as we move from the first to the second and last stanza, the moonlight disbands the stark contrasts of black versus white that came before it:

> Tonight the moonlight will alleviate
> the melting of the pink wax roses
> > planted in tin cans filled with sand
> placed in a line to mark Miss Lula's losses;
> > but who will shout and make her understand?
> Searching the land and sea for someone else,
> the lighthouse will discover Cootchie's grave
> and dismiss all as trivial; the sea, desperate,
> > will proffer wave after wave.
>
> > > > > (*CP*, 46)

Foreshadowing the "conflux of two great rivers" and their impact on "literary interpretations" in "Santarém" (*CP*, 185), the moon here "alleviates" more than the melting of the flowers. In the silvery light of night the lighthouse's beam crosshatches the moon's, and in place of sharp binaries we are left with a shifting, shadowy landscape in which such contrasts are literally unsustainable. At the same time, the speaker's purpose becomes more nebulous. No longer charting loyalties and injustices along a deepening division of black versus white, the poem concludes with philosophical ambivalence: does the lighthouse "dismiss all as trivial" because, within the shadow of endless tides and infinite lives, Cootchie's death and Miss Lula's "deafness" are mere undulations in the greater scheme of things? Or is the lighthouse's dismissal an echo of Miss Lula's uncomprehending ear, yet another gesture of the world's injustice that will always triumph over the sea's silent urgings? The answer is, of course, a matter of perspective, and one possibility does not exclude the other. Having carefully teased our habits of seeing with familiar oppositions, Bishop abruptly asks that we look again, this time at our own patterns of identification and the need to make sense of things in the absence of established resolve.

In the later "Faustina, or Rock Roses" (*CP*, 72–74), Bishop picks up where "Cootchie" leaves off. Having posed the laden opposition of black versus white in the earlier poem, Bishop relentlessly deconstructs the traditional alignment of whiteness and ideality in "Faustina." Like "Cootchie," this poem is named after a black female servant who tends an aging white woman. But unlike the earlier poem, "Faustina" is structured upon an exaggerated, disquieting field of white-on-white into which blackness—Faustina's "sinister kind" face—emerges disproportionately in the last third of the poem. Furthermore, the whiteness that at least postured as a sign of immortality and natural superiority in "Cootchie" is rendered frail and illusory in "Faustina" from the start. In the first two-thirds of the poem we are introduced to the "white woman [who] whispers / to herself," propped up in her "chipped enamel" bed, surrounded by "white disordered sheets / like wilted roses" (*CP*, 72). The table near her "bears a can of talcum / and five pasteboard boxes / of little pills" in addition to a "white bowl of farina" (73). The woman's "fine white hair" blends associatively into her "gown with the undershirt / showing at the neck" (72) and "the pallid palm leaf fan / she holds but cannot wield" (73). Meanwhile, a "visitor sits and watches / the dew glint on the screen" while an

> eighty-watt bulb
> 　　　betrays us all,
>
> discovering the concern
> within our stupefaction;
> lighting as well on heads
> of tacks in the wallpaper,
> on a paper wall-pocket,
> violet-embossed, glistening
> 　　　with mica flakes.
> 　　　　　(72)

The brightness of the eighty-watt bulb leaves nothing untouched by its glare, and it does not discriminate: tack-heads are no less structurally important in this description than is "our stupefaction." Twelve short stanzas link image after image of whiteness into a cohesive scene, like a series of props, while the repetition of their small identical structures functions much like acts in a play, drawing attention to the manipulation of discrete parts into an illusory whole. It is as if we are being led behind the scenes, to the barefaced world without makeup or soft lighting where imperfections stand out and rolling hills are revealed as two-dimensional cardboard paintings. Consequently, tired efforts (the older woman's, Faustina's, the speaker's, the visitor's) to maintain the triumphant status of the white lady's world are exposed, becoming sources of embarrassment through their failures to do so:

> Clutter of trophies,
> chamber of bleached flags!
> —Rags or ragged garments
> hung on the chairs and hooks
> each contributing its
> shade of white, confusing
> > as undazzling.
>
> The visitor is embarrassed
> not by pain nor age
> nor even nakedness,
> though perhaps by its reverse.
> > (*CP*, 73)

Hardly a trope of natural superiority in this poem, whiteness is the mark of vulnerability, failed illusions, and tenuous, decayed control. The "shade[s] of white" that might, through a different perspective, represent a "clutter of trophies" have been reduced to a disheartening "chamber of bleached flags." What was presumably once the white woman's winning mastery (of herself, her surroundings, and Faustina) is exposed as no more or less than a "laborious stitching together of disparate parts"—the haphazard combination of scattered images through which the woman is sketched in this poem. Because the images of whiteness that construct this woman are, like the various garments hung up around her on "chairs and hooks," both distinct from one another and always slightly unaligned (e.g., the juxtaposition of "white disordered sheets / like wilted roses" and the "Clutter of trophies / chamber of bleached flags!" [*CP*, 73]), we are urged to see the space between the trope of whiteness and the subject who embodies it. The nameless woman is made visible to us almost entirely by way of her surroundings, a descriptive strategy that underlines both her particularity and her constructedness: the scene inside the woman's disordered house is littered with her personal touches—her pills, her farina, her hair, her "pallid palm-leaf fan"—so that the exaggerated whiteness that she clearly represents stands at an awkward distance from the frail individual she is "betray[ed]" to be. At the same time, this distance is measured by "our stupefaction," by the embarrassment we feel right along with the visitor, and most likely Bishop herself, in the face of such disillusionment. Thus, making sense of our feelings as readers means confronting our own "confusing" discomfort with the old woman's pathetic attempts—or more precisely her *failures*—to represent the stereotypical ideal that whiteness traditionally signifies.[18]

The reduction of the trope of whiteness to its disparate, "undazzling" shades is what ushers confusion into this poem, as we are refused the image of an ostensibly unmediated ideal around which to organize our identifications. Furthermore, we must remember that the puzzling discomfort that this poem establishes within the first eight stanzas is the context into which Faustina is introduced,

> complaining of, explaining,
> the terms of her employment.
> She bends above the other.
> Her sinister kind face
> presents a cruel black
> coincident conundrum.
> Oh, is it
>
> freedom at last, a lifelong
> dream of time and silence,
> dream of protection and rest?
> Or is it the very worst,
> the unimaginable nightmare
> that never before dared last
> more than a second?
> (*CP*, 73–74)

Read against the backdrop of carefully crafted disorder established in the first two-thirds of the poem, Faustina's looming dark face will inevitably be a "coincident conundrum," as it no longer signifies the abject side to her mistress's white ideal. As Silverman explains, to "invest the other with the ability to return our look is seemingly to accept the other as an other, or . . . to concede that he or she is also a subject."[19] Moreover, because "every idealizing attribution . . . at present implies its opposite, and since the imposition of all these forms of difference depends upon the imaginary alignment of certain subjects with what is negative rather than ideal" (19), to dismantle the ideal of whiteness also means to deconstruct the abjection of blackness. Thus, Faustina drinks cogñac and openly discusses the terms of her employment while her mistress eats farina and whispers to herself. To deconstruct this hierarchy without establishing a clear replacement of any sort—indeed, to blend the perspectives of Faustina and her mistress into a climactic series of questions that could emanate from either woman—is, as the opening stanza asserts, to yield a "crazy house" replete with a "crooked / towel-covered table" and floorboards that "sag / this way and that" (*CP*, 72). As in Bishop's poems about fantastical others, the slightly surreal or "crooked" perspective through which the poem unfolds is a manifestation of her refusal to accommodate normative, oppositional processes of ideality and identification.

Like "Cootchie," "Faustina" ends with deliberate ambiguity:

> The acuteness of the question
> forks instantly and starts
> a snake-tongue flickering;
> blurs further, blunts, softens,
> separates, falls, our problems
> becoming helplessly
>        proliferative.
>
> There is no way of telling.
> The eyes say only either.
> At last the visitor rises,
> awkwardly proffers her bunch
> of rust-perforated roses
> and wonders oh, whence come
>        all the petals.
>
>                (*CP*, 74)

The question sparked by Faustina's entrance could be either woman's, or even the simultaneous musings of each. More important than deciphering the origins of the eyes that "say only either," however, is the tension generated by the question itself, a tension that deepens exponentially as its "acuteness" is increasingly felt. The mutual dependence the two women share with one another cannot be extricated from the limits such dependencies impart, and in turn, the mechanisms of exchange between Faustina and her mistress become inextricable from our own efforts to understand them, so that the opposition of self and other "blurs further, blunts, softens, / separates, [and] falls." Under Bishop's eighty-watt eye "difference" thus becomes "our" problem, and a "helplessly / proliferative" one at that. It is the visitor, after all, whose mounting discomfort draws an end to the poem, as she "awkwardly proffers her bunch / of rust-perforated roses"—an organic yet manicured mingling of white and brown—and clumsily leaves the scene (CP, 74).

It is likely that this lack of resolution, or clear moral assertion, is partly responsible for the sketchy approval among the readers of Bishop's poems concerning race and class. And it is just as likely that Bishop's own racism, however unwitting it may have been, explains in part the moments of marked ambivalence that structure these poems. What is so provocative about these pieces, though, is Bishop's willingness to interrogate her own discomfort in the face of otherness, a willingness necessitated by her restless desire to transcend the mundane exchanges of self versus other, or one-way perspective. While Bishop's passion for honest observation does not yield firm political conclusions within her poetry, it does demonstrate what David Kalstone described as "a language, open-eyed, that is unembarrassed by anomaly."[20] Such endurance is necessary for confronting one's own limits of perspective, one's provisional look, and for accepting the predicate of lack upon which one's relations to others is based. To borrow from Silverman, this "would seem the juncture to reiterate, once again, that productive looking necessarily requires a constant conscious reworking of the terms under which we unconsciously look at the objects that people our visual landscape."[21] Indispensable to this process is, as Bishop's poems suggest, the "opening up of the unconscious to otherness."[22] Though visibly uncomfortable for a variety of reasons—the impending death of the white woman; the disruptive rearrangement of power relations between mistress and servant, white woman and woman of color; the recognition of her own implicatedness in the "helplessly proliferative" "problems" of difference—the visitor in "Faustina" perseveres through twelve stanzas, rising "At last" to go. But her awkward departure is, typically, foiled by the offering of rock-roses she makes, a tenacious flower that grows in rocky soil and is, as Costello points out, "viable and mutable, defying the barren whiteness of the scene."[23]

The "problems" of difference that start "a snake-tongue flickering" at the end of "Faustina" show up repeatedly in Bishop's work, with an increasingly explicit proximity to Bishop's own life as the years go on. In the first three *Brazil* poems of *Questions of Travel*, for instance, Bishop interrogates the relationship between self and other and its attending impact on notions of difference through the lens of travel in South America, where she herself lived for nearly fifteen years with her lover, Lota de Macedo Soares, to whom the collection is dedicated.[24] Examples like this motivate many readers to refer to Bishop's later work as more personal, while some feminist critics cite this development as a symptom of her coded devotion to autobiography. But as I have suggested, Bishop's focus on the self cannot be understood in isolation from her relentless refusals of the coherent ego and her concurrent deconstructions of difference.

While dismantling the trope of whiteness in "Faustina, or Rock Roses" de-essentialized the normative ideal, Bishop's poems about travel explicitly interrogate the viewing subject's role in "leaping out of 'difference' into bodily otherness." Tellingly, "Questions of Travel" went through many versions under the heading "Problems of Travelers" before Bishop finally settled on the published choice.[25] This early title suggests that the voyeuristic eye of the visitor in "Faustina" becomes the focus of inquiry in this later poem, as when the speaker asks,

> Should we have stayed at home and thought of here?
> Where should we be today?
> Is it right to be watching strangers in a play
> in this strangest of theatres?
> What childishness is it that while there's a breath of life
> in our bodies, we are determined to rush
> to see the sun the other way around?
>
> (CP, 93)

The rest of the poem offers a provisional answer to this series of questions:

> But surely it would have been a pity
> not to have seen the trees along this road,

really exaggerated in their beauty,
not to have seen them gesturing
like noble pantomimists, robed in pink.
. . . . . . . . . . . . . . .
Yes, a pity not to have pondered, blurr'dly and inconclusively,
on what connection can exist for centuries
between the crudest wooden footwear
and, careful and finicky,
the whittled fantasies of wooden cages.

(*CP*, 93–94)

Obviously the speaker thrives, even depends upon "watching strangers in a play / in this strangest of theatres," as the gorgeous series of descriptions that make up this poem attest. But at the same time, the speaker is aware of the limitations of her own vision; she can only "ponder" "blurr'dly and inconclusively" upon the observations she collects. Though the "inexplicable old stonework" the speaker admires is "inexplicable and impenetrable, / at any view," it is, to the eye of this observer, "instantly seen and always, always delightful" (*CP*, 93). The speaker of "Questions of Travel" is cognizant of the liminal position she occupies between native and tourist, self and stranger, and ultimately, as the liaison between us, the readers, and the subjects of her observations. Consequently, while she idealizes the customs and objects in her view ("always, always delightful") the speaker recognizes that such idealization is always mediated by her own eye/"I" ("the choice is never wide and never free" [*CP*, 94]). Moreover, though the speaker calls the land and its inhabitants "strange" in the second stanza, this sentiment is complicated in the opening lines of the poem by the familiarity with which the speaker describes the "crowded streams," the "waterfalls," and the "many clouds" like "mile-long, shiny, tearstains" that, "in a quick age or so as ages go here," "probably will" turn to waterfalls as well (*CP*, 93). Just as Bishop does not maintain neat lines of demarcation between the symbolic and the "real" and the abject and the ideal, she frustrates the fine line between romanticizing and identifying with the other in this poem.[26] Subsequently, "Questions of Travel" (along with "Arrival at Santos" and "Brazil, January 1, 1502") enacts what Costello describes as the "double impulse of nostalgia and novelty":

Bishop's travelers are driven by contradictory impulses. They want change, renewal, originality, but also mastery . . . over the world they approach, in terms of the world they left behind. Bishop sees this double impulse of nostalgia and novelty as inescapable; she also sees both aims as illusory.[27]

Bishop's romanticizing of this "strangest of theatres" is checked by the continual questioning of her motives: the trees' "exaggerated beauty," the breathless determination to see "the sun the other way around," the "always, always delightful," are subject to scrutiny within the interrogative, self-questioning tenor of the poem as a whole. Just as we are enticed by the exotic otherness of these images, we are asked to "ponder," however "blurr'dly and inconclusively," if such idealizations are, after all, "right." The mastery of this poem is the way in which it maintains a productive tension between these two gestures. While romanticizing the other, the speaker consistently makes us aware of the part she plays in constructing the other's ideality or "strangeness." While the land and its inhabitants are described as "strangers," they are also positioned as actors "in a play / in this strangest of theatres," a play for which the poem itself functions as script. It is for this reason that Costello argues that Bishop's "dual impulse" is necessary, just as its aims are "illusory."

Consciously reviewing our habits of idealization while admitting the necessity of the act is what allows us to idealize "at a distance," to identify with others without either repudiating that otherness or thoroughly assimilating it within our own sense of self. The "problems" of "difference" within Bishop's poetry are always "helplessly proliferative," affirming neither the abject nor the ideal, but rather the degree to which one's sense of self depends upon the play between the two. Consequently, her poems are inflected with a "reticence," or the "undazzling" confusion of intermediary shades in place of stark, familiar contrasts. In a letter from Brazil to her friend and doctor Anny Bauman, Bishop wrote that it "seems to be mid-winter, and yet it is time to plant things—but my Anglo-Saxon blood is gradually relinquishing its seasonal cycle and I'm quite content to live in complete confusion, about seasons, fruits, languages, geography, everything" (*OA*, 243). The beauty of Bishop's art resides, in part, in her ability to translate this "confusion" into questions that challenge us all to relinquish our "seasonal cycles." The brilliance of Bishop's poems lies in her knowledge that this "choice is never wide and never free." Thus, we may under-stand the image of home that frames "Questions of Travel" as not only ironic, but utterly precise in its proximity to "this strangest of theatres": though "difference," for Bishop, is always at the heart of her questions of travel, home is where such queries lead us, "wherever that may be" (*CP*, 94).

The contingency between travel and home, or other and self, that runs through "Questions of Travel" becomes a crucial backdrop to the overtly personal poems of *Geography III*.[28] This last published collection of Bishop's lifetime includes some of her most well known pieces, such as "In the Waiting Room," "Crusoe in England," "The Moose," and "One Art," poems generally heralded as final proof of Bishop's autobi-ographical, hence feminist, bent. Yet it is within this assembly of poems, and particularly in the most self-referential poem of them all, "In the Waiting Room," that Bishop offers her keenest challenge to the notion of a coherent selfhood that the term *autobiography* often under-scores or assumes.

As we have seen, Bishop's poems focus on the psychic processes of ego formation from the start. Beginning with *North & South* and contin-uing through the publication of *Questions of Travel*, Bishop gracefully and relentlessly pushes the bounds of being, exploring the deepest implications of looking, loving, and living among others. In doing so, Bishop calls our attention to what it means to be positioned within the inescapable exchange between our "selves" and others. This means, as the growth of Bishop's oeuvre suggests, that understanding "whatever it is . . . that seems enormously important" leads us to a deepening sense of our relationships, since, as Bishop's gentleman made clear, charting one's self means grasping one's lack and one's attending need for communion with the world. Bishop's later poems become more autobiographical because it is ultimately through reformulating the way we see *ourselves* that we may restructure our ways of seeing *others*. Thus, the emphatic "I" of "In the Waiting Room" is named Elizabeth because this "I" is so conscious of her lack and the details of her own relations to the other. Or to put it somewhat differently, the individual-ity that characterizes the speaker of this poem is a manifestation of the profound degree to which Bishop has unraveled the autonomous "I," not an affirmation of its triumphant endurance.

Like Bishop at the end of her life, Silverman concludes *Threshold of the Visible World* by shifting her emphasis slightly away from the parameters of the other to the locus of self. Pursuing her explication of the productive look, she now writes:

> Instead of assimilating what is desirable about the other to the self, and exteriorizing what is despised in the self as the other, the subject whose look I am here describing struggles to see the otherness of the desired self, and the familiarity of the despised other. He or she attempts, that is . . . to recognize him- or herself precisely within those others to whom he or she would otherwise respond with revulsion and avoidance.[29]

Silverman's formulation provides the perfect preamble to the seven-year-old Elizabeth who, though horrified by the images of "black, naked women with necks / wound round and round with wire" in the *National Geographic,* reads it "right straight through" because, she says, she is "too shy to stop" (*CP,* 159). While sitting in the dentist's waiting room among adult strangers, waiting for her "foolish, timid" Aunt Consuelo, the young Elizabeth is then seized by the understanding that she is "an *I,*" "an *Elizabeth,*" "one of *them.*" Why, she asks herself, "should you be one, too? / I scarcely dared to look / to see what it was I was."

> I knew that nothing stranger
> had ever happened, that nothing
> stranger could ever happen.
> Why should I be my aunt,
> or me, or anyone?
> What similarities—
> boots, hands, the family voice
> I felt in my throat, or even
> the *National Geographic*
> and those awful hanging breasts—
> held us together
> or made us all just one?
> (CP, 160–61)

Elizabeth's understanding of being an "I" is wholly dependent in this poem upon her articulation of what she despises in the images of those around her: the foolish timidity of her aunt, and the black, naked, "awful hanging breasts" of the women in the *National Geographic*. Not only is Elizabeth's "I" expressed, typically, through its association with what she is not, but what makes those others *other* is revealed in this poem more clearly than in any piece that Bishop ever wrote.

Looking at the original drafts of this poem, it becomes apparent just how central the "struggle to see the otherness of the desired self, and the familiarity of the despised other" was for Bishop while writing "In the Waiting Room." More worked over than any other portion of the poem, the description of the black women's breasts went through six versions before Bishop settled on the final one. What was initially "Their breasts filled me with awe" becomes "Their breasts filled me with awe and terrified me," and then "their black breasts horrified me" ("frightened" is written in the margin). Working through variations of these phrases Bishop eventually decided on the somewhat less explicit "Their breasts horrified me" of the published version.[30] What these drafts reveal is the degree to which the image of these black breasts both attracted *and* repulsed Bishop, and the interlacing of blackness and femaleness at the core of this tension. This image clearly fascinated Bishop; like the young Elizabeth, she can't stop looking at, or rewriting, them, and according to the sequence of drafts, what the poet is initially cognizant of is the awe she feels in their presence. *Awe* is an especially revealing word in this context, meaning a "fearful or profound respect or wonder inspired by the greatness, superiority, grandeur, etc. of a person or thing."[31] It suggests from the outset that allure and aversion are bound inextricably, a suggestion that is certainly borne out by the poem as a whole. These drafts also underline the link that exists for Bishop between race and gender and, given the focus on "I" in this poem, the central role this link occupies in the articulation of identity for the poet. With this understanding, it becomes all the more clear why earlier poems like "Cootchie" and "Faustina" are not only at the heart of Bishop's poetic project, but why they are key in comprehending the feminist pulse of her poetry at large.

The small Elizabeth indeed struggles with the apprehension of her self, and it is this struggle that charts the flow of the poem. While "suddenly" realizing the "similarities" that link her to Aunt Consuelo and "those awful hanging breasts," Elizabeth simultaneously sees such kinship as "'unlikely'"; it is just when she comprehends the overlap between her "self" and others that she grasps the lack that, paradoxically, fosters her subjectivity, an insight literalized by the "sensation of falling / off the round, turning world / into cold, blue-black space" that permeates the poem (*CP,* 160). Realizing that the utterance of her "I" is enabled by her relationship to what she deems most horrific, Elizabeth describes the oneness of being as, indeed, "unlikely." This understanding is what allows her to "recognize . . . herself precisely within those others to whom . . . she would otherwise respond with revulsion and avoidance." Both attracted and repulsed by the black women's breasts and the foolishness of her aunt, Elizabeth's "I" is simultaneously crystallized and destabilized through her interactions with them, and in turn, their images become joined inextricably; it is after the moments when Elizabeth most keenly articulates her proximity to those she's repelled by that her "self" is most anchored ("I said to myself: three days / and you'll be seven years old" [160]) *and* most uprooted ("I was saying it to stop / the sensation of falling off / the . . . world" [160]). Maintaining this tension throughout the poem, Elizabeth resists the appeasement of self-sameness in favor of "constant readjustments," never once losing sight of what it is "Outside" (161) that keeps her safe, in the waiting room, while the wintry night and war-torn world spin ceaselessly around her.

The horror that Elizabeth feels when gazing at the black women's breasts does not preempt her desire to keep looking—indeed, it seems to fuel her desire to do so. Consequently, what began for Bishop as "awe" becomes, for Elizabeth, a never-ending journey along the slippery path from ideality to abjection and back again. Constructing this journey around the act of Elizabeth's literal *looking* (at the magazine, and then at those around her) not only reminds us of the central place perspective always occupies in Bishop's work, but of the dynamic relationship between seeing and being that lies at the heart of Bishop's poetic, as well as Moore's and Swenson's. Like her ancestor the gentleman, Elizabeth steers her course through revelation by way of her eyes. While Aunt Consuelo is "inside / what seemed like a long time," the young girl picks up the *National Geographic* and "carefully / studie[s] the photographs" (159). It is this act that leads her to the images of black breasts, and then, to her next look, "at the cover: / the yellow margins, the date" (159), in an effort, as Lee Edelman explains, "to contextualize the text so as to prevent her suffocation, her strangulation within it."[32] Throughout the poem Elizabeth maneuvers her look to stop herself

from "falling off / the round, turning world" or sliding into the seduc-
tions of easy oppositions. It is her "sidelong glance," for instance, that
enables her to see "what it was I was" without looking "any higher"—
allowing her, that is, to be both one of "them" and something quite sep-
arate from the "trousers and skirts and boots / and different pairs of
hands / lying under the lamps" (160). We are led by Elizabeth's eye,
held aloft in the face of "blue-black space," and brought microscopi-
cally close to "awful black breasts," insides of volcanoes, and "rivulets
of fire." The camera-like lens of "In the Waiting Room," with its abrupt
turns and twists, its sudden zooms and cuts, constantly reminds us of
the particular look—Elizabeth's look—through which we are viewing
her world.

Just as Bishop's speakers routinely tread the threshold that marks
you-versus-me, frustrating the possibility of subsuming one in the
other in the dialectic of self-sameness, Elizabeth's look remains slightly
ajar from the greater gaze constructed by those around her in the poem.
Her sidelong glance emanates at an angle against the horizontal plane
of "shadowy gray knees, / trousers and skirts and boots," so that just
as it reveals the "similarities" between her self and the others, her look
insures the distance between them as well. It is no coincidence that this
kind of crooked vision brings us back to Bishop's earliest pieces, in
which perspectives are skewed and subjects seem utterly fantastic.

And so we have Elizabeth's "I," the most self-assertive proclamation in
all of Bishop's poetry, an "I" that does not engender a sense of jubila-
tion, but rather, one whose very utterance begins the disorienting cycle
of its own displacement. Such a gesture, however, cannot happen as a
matter of choice; as Silverman is careful to reiterate, we cannot simply
decide to idealize differently, and then do so. Rather, we can only learn
to look again, revising how we see in retrospect, with the hope that
such efforts will transform the way we see in the future. Thus,
"[M]emory implies more than anything else the possibility of effecting
change at the level of representation,"[33] and it is for this reason that the
majority of poems from *Geography III* are ones in which Bishop looks
back to her past. As she herself observed in an essay of 1934,

We live in great whispering galleries, constantly vibrating and
humming, or we walk through salons lined with mirrors where the

reflections between the narrow walls are limitless, and each present moment reaches immediately and directly the past moments, changing them both.[34]

Written her senior year at Vassar, this bit of imagery bears an uncanny likeness to the world of poems she had yet to produce. Acutely aware of "whatever it is one can never really see full face but that seems enormously important," Bishop never gave up her efforts to articulate the whispers that urged her observational eye. From the gentleman's mirrored world to Elizabeth's sidelong glance, her ambivalence is so productive precisely because of its ability to shape what will come through what has come before.

## 4   Elizabeth Bishop and May Swenson

Writing about Bishop's treatment of sexuality, Lorrie Goldensohn has observed that for Elizabeth Bishop, "to be personal meant to be misread, to be trapped within the conventional feminine."[1] I would reword this slightly: to be personal risks being misread as reinforcing the conventional feminine, a category that Bishop's poetry challenges consistently. I augment Goldensohn's important point in order to emphasize both the strategic element of Bishop's restraint and the degree to which this aspect is often elided when discussing Bishop's sexual poetics. Indeed, a methodological gap seems to be growing in Bishop criticism between her interrogations of self and her depictions of sexual desire; while critics such as Langdon Hammer and Bonnie Costello assert Bishop's challenges to essentialist notions of identity, there remains a pervasive tendency, especially among feminist critics, to read her sexual reserve according to the very standards of self-expression that underwrite those same essentialist ideals—standards that privilege the explicit over the indirect, as if the truth were something we could attain by proclaiming its presence.

May Swenson, an intimate correspondent of Bishop's and one of her most astute readers to date, struggled to reconcile exactly those aspects of Bishop's poetic that underpin this critical gap.[2] With this struggle in mind, it is perhaps no surprise that the correspondence between Swenson and Bishop echoes so precisely the exchanges between Bishop and Moore. Just as Bishop was both fascinated and frustrated by Moore's morality, so Swenson was intrigued and exasperated by Bishop's sexual reserve. Likewise, while Bishop's struggles to make sense of her mentor trace the defining paradox of Moore's poetic, Swenson's efforts to understand Bishop chart a similar tension. In their correspondence Swenson was often frustrated with her friend's "prudish ears"—ears that bear a notable likeness to Moore's (*MWW*, 252). Nevertheless, Swenson was inspired deeply by Bishop's ability to produce poems that are "exacting, flawless, and plain," poems that allow "no self indulgence."³ Negotiating these ostensibly opposing aspects of Bishop's poems meant arriving at an understanding of the powers of self-restraint. While it is increasingly common to emphasize Bishop's honesty at the expense of her reserve, Swenson was determined to articulate the ways in which the two go hand in hand. In the process, however, Swenson needed to confront the conflict in her own poetry between a "craving to get through . . . to thing as they *are*" and her awareness that the world is always "becoming."⁴

Like Bishop and Moore, Swenson believed that explicitness often works against the process of revelation that poetry should engender:

> [T]he poetic experience is one of constant curiosity, skepticism, and testing—astonishment, disillusionment, renewed discovery, re-illumination. It amounts to a virtual compulsion to probe with the senses into the complex actuality of all things, outside and inside the self and to determine relationships between them.⁵

To emphasize the self that is seeing instead of the thing being seen is, Swenson implies, to curtail the discoveries that a poem might otherwise spark. At the same time, Swenson was distinct from Moore and Bishop in her passion for effusive, erotic detail. Reconciling these aspects of her own poetry enabled Swenson to make sense of the tension at the heart of her friend's. We encounter such awareness in "Her Early Work," the last of the poems Swenson wrote about Bishop (*IOW*, 58). Begun in March 1983, almost five years after Bishop's death, this short poem pivots upon a grasp of Bishop's sexual reserve. The title begins the poem, which then continues:

> Talked to cats and dogs
> to trees, and to strangers.
> To one loved, talked through
> layers of masks.
> To this day we can't know
> who was addressed,
> or ever undressed.
> Because of the wraparounds,
> overlaps and gauzes,
> kept between words and skin,
> we notice nakedness.

Wild and heathen scents
of shame or sin
hovered since childhood,
when the delicious was always
forbidden. "A Word With You"
had to be whispered,
spoken at the zoo,
not to be overheard
be eavesdropping ape or cockatoo.

                                    (58)

While it would be a mistake to overlook the costs of closeted desire to which this poem calls our attention, we limit our readings no less by discounting the subtle logic of these lines: masks, overlaps, and gauzes do not only hide, they have the power to reveal, to emphasize, to help us "notice nakedness." I will return to this poem toward the end of the chapter, but for now I want to stress that Swenson's reading grants Bishop's "whispered" words a conscious agency, and hence respect, that they are sometimes denied. Swenson's instructive grace lies in her commitment to spinning clarity from contradiction, to nurturing complexity where oppositions more readily triumph; though Bishop clearly struggled against the confines of heterosexist culture, her careful explorations of sexual desire can't be chocked up to coded cries of repression. On the contrary, Swenson's readings reveal that Bishop's silences were often strategic, in the service of unearthing assumptions instead of giving answers.

Little has been made of the correspondence between Bishop and Swenson, and I suspect that this is due in part to the portrait of Bishop that emerges from these letters. In response to the curious, attentive Swenson, Bishop appears most often in these pages as the Bishop of self-restraint, an advocate of personal distance, a remarkably Moore-like mentor in diction and self-expression.[6] Moreover, while Bishop's genuine love and respect for Swenson are obvious, she is also at times condescending, competitive, elitist, and, as she herself put it, "nasty" when giving advice to her junior of only two years.[7] When the bulk of Bishop-Swenson correspondence became available to scholars in 1990, the wave of criticism devoted to emphasizing Bishop's autobiographical bent was just starting to pick up speed. Readers looking for clues to

Bishop's intimate life details will find few in these letters. But what we do find is no less rewarding: a nearly thirty-year discussion between two of America's best poets about why they write the kinds of poems that they do.

Swenson and Bishop were drawn to one another by way of their writing. They met at Yaddo, and letters from the first ten years of their correspondence (when their exchange was heaviest) are weighted with close readings and critiques of each other's poems, most of which elicited lengthy responses. Throughout their relationship Bishop assumed, and was granted, the role of established superior. Particularly with regard to her early work, Swenson sought her friend's advice regularly and received it unsparingly: "There's a favor I want to ask of you—a big one, I hope you can do it—to read the manuscript of my book and help me strike out the no-good poems. I find myself vacillating so about my own opinions of them that I haven't been able to decide in certain cases what to leave in—and then, too, it's too big a collection I suspect even though I've weeded and weeded."[8] In response to this letter in 1963 Bishop mailed Swenson a dense, five-page critique of *To Mix with Time: New and Selected Poems,* Swenson's third book (for which Bishop would also write a dust-jacket blurb). Bishop's letter, its tiny margins overflowing with microscopic notes, advises Swenson on everything from punctuation to content, addressing the text page by page and almost line by line.

While Swenson was not shy in sharing her opinions of Bishop's work, Bishop was far less solicitous of those opinions than Swenson was of hers. This situation makes sense: at the time of their meeting, Bishop was a fairly well known and certainly a well-respected poet, with literary liaisons securing her firmly in the folds of American contemporary poetry. *North & South,* for which Bishop received the Houghton Mifflin Literary Fellowship Award, had been published four years earlier. She had been awarded a Guggenheim, and the year before she met Swenson at Yaddo Bishop served as poetry consultant at the Library of Congress. In contrast, Swenson's career was just beginning in 1950. Though she had published several poems in various places (the most notable being James Laughlin's *New Directions in Prose and Poetry*), it would be another four years before Swenson's first book of poems, *Another Animal,* appeared in print. But despite these differences and other more substantive ones, each recognized in the other a related way of approaching poetry that set them apart from the current of self-expressive verse that was beginning to swell poetry circles at midcentury.

In 1963, after Bishop had endorsed Swenson's two most recent books with dust-jacket comments, Swenson broached the issue of Bishop's influence as candidly as she ever would:

> I guess it's because you endorsed my book that reviewers have decided I'm following in your tracks—a foolish conclusion to jump to . . . the fact is I *have* been influenced by you a lot—not as to method, but as to attitude. I'd like to be more so. But when I write I find I can't do just as I intend to—it goes its own way. I would like to find the casual and absolutely natural tone that you have in your poems—they are never over-colored or forced the least little bit—they are very honest, and never call attention to their effects. Their brilliance is inside, and not on the surface. And they are subtle, not obvious. I think my greatest fault is being obvious—and I never know it until the poem's been printed—quite long after that, and its too late. (*MWW*, 242–43)

This passage provides a telling backdrop to the oft-quoted response Swenson gave to Karla Hammond in an interview in 1979:

> Have I been influenced by [Elizabeth Bishop]? Not necessarily, although neither of us writes confessional poetry. Elizabeth Bishop has always stayed with the objective, the large view, the impersonal which contains the personal if you look deeply. I have this tendency, but not because of any influence of hers. I think we share some of the basic perceptive equipment.[9]

What interests me here is not the degree to which Bishop directly did or did not influence Swenson's poetry (nor Swenson's discomfort with the idea), but the "absolutely natural" way in which Swenson slides from Bishop's "casual" honesty to her beneath-the-surface subtlety, from the "objective, large view" to the "personal" that's always lurking between the lines. To Swenson, honesty and subtlety are not antonyms; these aspects of Bishop's poetry nurture one another, and the "attitude" Swenson shares with Bishop is made manifest in her intuitive grasp of this relationship and her insatiable efforts to achieve an articulate understanding of its logic—efforts, like those between Bishop and Moore, that stoke the fire in this friendship for years to come.

From the start Swenson's admiration of Bishop was both fueled and furrowed by this characteristic of Bishop's poetry, what she once referred to as Bishop's "cagey" poetics.[10] Especially in the early years of their friendship, Swenson's comments on Bishop's poems turn again and again to this aspect of Bishop's work:

> THE SHAMPOO I like *very* much . . . but would have a deuce of a time saying why . . . that is, it feels like something has been left out—but this makes it better, in a way . . . a mysteriousness, although the expression is perfectly straightforward. . . . I remember a poem of yours about his "green gay eyes" that seemed even more mysterious in the same kind of way. I felt the emotion or the impression being expressed, but couldn't seize an outline of what was behind it. Guess maybe I try to read symbolism or special significance into this, when it [is] simply a comparison between someone's hair streaked with gray and the lichen on a cliff. No, that's not all—it's a kind of tribute to someone. . . .Well, it certainly has *occupied* me, hasn't it? It's ridiculous to try to say in reportorial fashion what a poem "means"—but I so frequently never find out whether other people receive the same basic associations I think I've put into something—they will never tell you in so many words what they think it is saying. (*MWW*, 200–201)

Though Bishop liked Swenson's interpretation, her response is just as cagey as the poem it attends to:

> I am awfully pleased with what you say about the little *Shampoo* & you understood exactly what I meant and even a little bit more. . . . The Shampoo is very simple: Lota has straight long black hair,—I hadn't seen her for six years or so when I came here and when we looked at each other she was horrified to see I had gone very gray, and I that she had two silver streaks on each side, quite wide. Once I got used to it I liked it—she looks exactly like a chickadee. . . . Shiny tin basins, all sizes, are very much a feature of Brazilian life. . . . And I am surrounded with rocks and lichens—they have the

sinister coloration of rings around the moon, exactly, sometimes—
and seem to be undertaking to spread to infinity, like the moon's,
as well.[11]

Bishop's rather transparent attempt to brush aside the "special signifi-
cance" of the "little" poem is belied by her affirmation of Swenson's cri-
tique (CP, 84). Though Bishop does, "in so many words," explain the
imagery of the poem for her friend, she does not make explicit the link
between the depictions of life with Lota and what Swenson called the
"mysteriousness"—the erotic desire, that "little bit more"—that hovers
among her words.

In summoning a likeness between "The Shampoo" and "While
Someone Telephones" (the third in a series of poems called "Four
Poems" from which Swenson recalled the image of "his green gay
eyes") Swenson hints to Bishop the "little bit more" she understood
about her friend's "cagey" motives.[12] Like "The Shampoo" and "Varick
Street" (another poem Swenson comments on along these lines), "Four
Poems" is a typical Bishop love poem; anxious love and tender desire
are woven into a sequence of stark yet slippery images: "The tumult in
the heart / keeps asking questions," while "Beneath that loved and cel-
ebrated breast, . . . I cannot fathom even a ripple. / (See the thin flying
of nine black hairs / four around one five the other nipple)" (CP,
76–79). Swenson's handling of Bishop's caginess here is characteristic;
while Swenson pushes relentlessly the limits of Bishop's poems, she
salutes them with a caginess of her own. Without naming that "little bit
more" that she intuits, Swenson makes it obvious in a letter she sent to
Bishop in 1955, two years after her interrogation of "The Shampoo":

> I don't understand the Four Poems, that is, I get their *mood*, but I
> can only imagine what they're talking about—my imagination goes
> pretty wild and comes back with strange answers, none of which fit
> exactly. It's like smelling a strong odor, or hearing a keen sound
> and not being able to discover what it comes from. Didn't "While
> Someone Telephones" used to have a different title? . . . Reading
> these four poems now I have to furnish them with my own experi-
> ences because you've left yours out (their labels)—you had to, I
> suppose, to get them said at all. . . . So I'm left outside here, sniffing
> and listening, and no use pounding on the door. (MWW, 208)

Bishop's response to this letter is almost apologetic: "The *Four Poems* are pretty mysterious, I'm afraid. I hoped they'd have enough emotional value in themselves so that I wouldn't have to be more specific— a little like a few lyrics from *Maud,* say, with the narrative parts left out. Any meanings you want to attach are all right, I'm sure—the wilder the better."[13]

It is tempting to catalog the palpable caginess of this correspondence as the symptom of sexual masking. Swenson and Bishop were both lesbians who would not lodge themselves within a growing climate of woman-identified poetry, and maintaining this distance perhaps made them wary of identifying with each other in these terms. To acknowledge openly the relationship between one's "cagey" poetics and one's desire may well have meant sacrificing the distance that, ironically, allowed them to maintain their friendship over the years. Moreover, an unfinished poem addressed to Bishop that Swenson wrote sometime between 1961 and 1962 suggests that their friendship had the potential, at least from Swenson's perspective, for sexual intimacy. The most explicit lines of this sort appear near the end of the untitled poem:

> I was nuts
> about you. And I couldn't say
> a word. And you never said the
> word that would have loosened
> all my doggy love.[14]

Whether or not Swenson's feelings were reciprocated (I have found nothing in Bishop's archive that suggests they were), Bishop was clearly unwilling to unleash the "doggy love" that she perhaps detected in her friend. At the same time, though, Swenson's attraction to Bishop turned upon this very resistance. Although she seemed to long at times for a more forthright and open communion with Bishop, Swenson was drawn insatiably to the process of *implication* to which their relationship was wed. Thus, Swenson's unfinished love poem concludes with these lines:

> Little Elizabeth who still keeps me
> wild at the end of your chain—
> . . . because because

I have never known you years
and years—and love the
unknown you.

Read in isolation, this confession seems to be a response to unre-
quited love, a hunger for the hard-to-get. But if we consider it alongside
the published poems that Swenson wrote about Bishop and the letters
from which these poems were gleaned, this admission reveals a mind
far more complex. While Bishop found Swenson's understanding of the
lesbian desire in her poems reassuring, Swenson was both exasperated
and intrigued by her friend's unwillingness to make that desire more
explicit. But Swenson's response to this aspect of Bishop's work had as
much to do with her own developing poetic as it did with her friend's.
As we've seen, Swenson will eventually confide to Bishop that her
"greatest fault is being obvious," a fault made more manifest when
compared to Bishop's "very honest" verse that never calls "attention to
its effects." No doubt it was in part Bishop's early criticism that helped
shape Swenson's sense of her "greatest fault"; while Swenson was busy
prodding Bishop about her cagey depictions of desire, Bishop was per-
sistently calling Swenson to task for her use of explicit anatomical
words. In response to Swenson's second book, *A Cage of Spines,* Bishop
sent Swenson a four-page letter packed with criticism, laced with
praise.[15] At the heart of Bishop's concern about the book was its use of
"ugly words" that "stick out too much and distort the poem":

> My next point . . . will make you think I am a hopeless reactionary
> and prude as well, probably. I don't like words like "loins,"
> "groins," "crotch," "flanks," "thighs," etc. . . . . Also the poems I like
> best, those I think almost everyone would agree *are* your best,
> almost never use them. . . . I am NOT saying this from any Puritani-
> cal feeling, I swear. They are in general ugly words that startle the
> reader in a directly physical way, perhaps more than you realize.
> We have come a long way in the last 100 years in freedom of speech
> and writing—but we are still not comfortable with those words,
> *usually.* . . . I imagine that now you'll say that that's exactly why you
> use them, to startle and make the poem "strong," give it "impact,"
> etc. . . . . [But those words] are, or some of them sometimes are,
> euphemisms, and that's what makes them extra-indecent.[16]

Bishop's critique of Swenson's "ugly words" unmistakably echoes Moore's discomfort with the "sordidities" in Bishop's own "Roosters." We may recall that almost twenty years earlier, when Bishop's career was only somewhat less advanced than Swenson's at the time of this letter, Moore spent an entire night rewriting her younger friend's poem. As I recount in chapter 2, Moore defended her actions to the startled Bishop in the following manner: the "trouble is, people are not depersonalized enough to accept the picture rather than the thought. . . . [F]ew of us, it seems to me, are fundamentally rude enough to enrich our work in such ways without cost" (*SL,* 403–4). Nearly twenty years after the infamous "Roosters" episode, Bishop now stands where Moore once stood, advocating subtlety over starkness in an effort to explain that the most poignant expression is often enabled by restraint, a belief she articulates most succinctly in her next letter:

> It's a problem of placement, choice of word, abruptness or accuracy of the image—and does it help or detract? If it sticks out of the poem so that all the reader is going to remember is: "That Miss Swenson is always talking about phalluses"—or is it phalli—you have spoiled your effect, obviously, and given the Freudian-minded contemporary reader just a slight thrill of detection rather than an esthetic experience. (*OA,* 360–61)

Unlike her mentor, however, Bishop was distinctly uncomfortable with this role, as her repeated qualifications ("I am NOT saying this from any Puritanical feeling, I swear") make clear. Indeed, in a rather suggestive moment, Bishop invokes the "Roosters" exchange in an effort to deflect the prudishness that Swenson's interrogations sometimes imply. Returning for the final time to Swenson's comments about "The Shampoo," Bishop confides to Swenson:

> No one but you and one other friend have mentioned *The Shampoo* . . . I sent it to a few friends and never heard a word and began to think there was something indecent about it I'd overlooked. Marianne among others. . . . I'm afraid she never can face the tender passion. Sometime I must show you her complete re-write of *Roosters*—with all rhymes, privies, wives, beds, etc. left out . . . It is amazing, and sad, too.[17]

Once again, the oppositional thinking that underwrites Bishop's sim-
plified portrait of Moore is belied by the sensibility she adopts in her
less guarded moments. Many critics have remarked on Bishop's dual-
istic character, both in her person and her poems. What I find most rel-
evant about this manifestation of Bishop's dualism is not so much her
unconscious ambivalence toward Moore, but the way in which Swen-
son's interrogations bring this ambivalence to a head. Throughout their
correspondence, and especially in the first ten years, it is striking how
often Bishop's manner resembles Moore's in the early years of *their* cor-
respondence. Instances like the one above abound in these letters,
adding weight to other, more subtle moments that might otherwise go
unnoticed. For example, in a handwritten letter containing her dust-
jacket comments for *To Mix with Time*, Bishop writes, "I hope you can
read this. Use what you want—& turn it around any way you want.
The only things I want to keep especially are the 'ungrudging' business
(I'm proud of that) and 'one's pleasure is in hers,' etc."[18] Swenson was
thrilled with what Bishop wrote, and of course took it to press in its
original state. The phrases Bishop felt a special fondness for read as fol-
lows: "A great part of one's pleasure in her work is in *her* pleasure; she
has directness, affection, and a rare and reassuring ungrudgingness."[19]
If these words seem strangely familiar, it is because we encountered
their ancestral shapes in Moore's first review of Bishop, "Archaically
New," in which the older poet praised the younger for her "ungrudged
self-expenditure" that is as "automatic, apparently, as part of the
nature."[20] That Bishop summoned these phrases with particular pride
suggests not only that Bishop's pleasure in Swenson's poetry derived
from the ways it reflected *her* own, but that Swenson's poetry conjured
that conflicted place in Bishop's mind where her poetic crossed with
Moore's—that slippery line where self-assertion parts from self-con-
sciousness, where the "very honest" recoils from the "obvious."

For Bishop, this line became especially knotted around the issue of
sexuality, which is in part why Swenson's sensuous poetry struck such
a conflicted chord. In reply to Bishop's Moore-like critique of her "ugly
words," Swenson defends that aspect of her poetic with which Bishop
had taken issue:

> The physical is the beautiful to me—it's awfully strong in me—and
> then I don't see, logically, why buttock is an uglier word than, say,

> thumb. Or that groin is an ugly word, or image either. It depends
> on the poem's intentions, of course. The effect of all words, I grant
> you, comes from their associations. I guess I like physical associa-
> tions. Worse, there is almost a compulsion to employ them. . . . I
> think my taken-for-granted belief is that, as human animals, we
> have *nothing but* our sensual equipment, through which all expres-
> sions and impressions flow: thought and philosophy, reason and
> the spiritual all included. (*MWW*, 227).

This conception of the "physical" has more in common with Moore's
explorations of materiality and embodiment than it does with Bishop's
labyrinthine poems about lesbian desire; as I suggested in chapter 1,
Moore's "asexual" reputation has occluded an understanding of the
ways in which her poetry is fascinated with the contingency between
language and corporeality, with "our sensual equipment, through
which all impressions and expressions flow." And as I propose in the
following chapter, Swenson's effusive fleshiness is often read at the
expense of her celebratory skepticism of bodily innocence or truth. But
it is exactly this sort of cost that Bishop warns against when she takes to
task those "ugly words," a price that she herself inflates unwittingly
when she labels Moore's similar caution a lack of "the tender passion."

   As we have seen, Swenson was inspired by Bishop's ability to render
startlingly honest observations without, as Moore once put it, being
"insultingly unevasive," a balance that Swenson strove after with no
less impressive success. Nevertheless, Swenson's desire for Bishop to
explicate the "mysteriousness" in her love poems in particular betrays
a lingering belief that sensuality—the "physical"—signals authenticity,
a realm of experience unmediated by language or cultural context. At
the same time, though, Swenson's skepticism of the "obvious"—her
understanding that "the effect of all words . . . comes from their associ-
ations" even as all expressions flow through "our sensual equip-
ment"—checks and challenges this impulse.

   Swenson's early letters to Bishop are charged with her relentless
efforts to work her subliminal sense of this conflict into conscious com-
prehension, and her poetry of this time bears the stamp of this struggle.
In addition to her discomfort with Swenson's "ugly words," Bishop
took issue with Swenson's early experiments with punctuation, specif-
ically her poems that abandoned it altogether. Swenson defends her
motives in the following manner:

The non-punctuation, I'm afraid I'm committed to. . . . You say no punctuation limits one's range, but I've found that frequently an effect can be gotten from the absence of punctuation itself, that adds to the particular quality of a poem. And it causes one to work for exactness and compactness, the whole burden being on the *words* and how they are combined. The reader is induced to concentrate a little harder, too—must drop his "for granted" attitude, can't skim over the surface so easily. Doesn't it lure him deeper into it—force him to follow more subtle clues to understanding? (*MWW*, 200)

Bishop's disapproval is gentle but clear: "If the qualities you expressed can be better expressed by using no punctuation (that's a better way to put it than "without") that's all right—but I don't think you want to label yourself with a style that you may soon want to abandon."[21] Bishop's objection is a symptom of her keen understanding of the relationship between language and meaning, what James Longenbach describes as her comfort "with the idea that poems cannot break through their lin-guistic fabric, just as the self cannot be separated from the social codes from which it's made."[22] Swenson's attempts to elicit from Bishop a more explicit expression of sexual desire are linked to her experiments with form by a mutual logic: both efforts imply the possibility of breaking through form or formality to an essential authenticity, an a priori coher-ence that Bishop's poems routinely call into question.

But once again, Swenson's essentializing is checked. The "particular quality" that Swenson hopes to achieve in her poems by forsaking punctuation is not transparency, but just the opposite; she wants to force the reader "to follow more subtle clues to understanding." Char-acteristically, Swenson's enthusiastic interrogation of her own logical tangles leads her to a sense, however rough, of this disjunction:

Of course there are other ways to snare the reader—I mean, one does want to capture him and make him like it. I remember, though, how opposite my earlier defense was—something about poetry must be so clear it doesn't need guides. Maybe this inconsis-tency in argument proves not using punct. is only a conceit. You've made me think about it at any rate. (September 14, 1953)

Just as Swenson eventually abandons her experiments with punctu-ation, she also achieves a deeper understanding of Bishop's sexual restraint. Both processes, however, take almost a lifetime to unfold. Guiding this growth throughout is Swenson's generous courage, her thirst for pushing the limits of her own creative perspective. For Swenson, making sense of the relationship between Bishop's sexual reserve and her hallmark honesty meant refining the balance in her own poetry between a "compulsion" toward the physical and her disdain of the obvious.

In 1963, at the height of their correspondence, Bishop wrote Swenson a letter typical for its fusion of personal life-details and observations of everyday life in Brazil. While Bishop often described her fifteen years in Brazil as the happiest of her life, her contentment was at the start of its decline at the time of this letter. Bishop's lover, Lota, was immersed in her high-profile job directing the construction of a public park in Rio, an intensely demanding commitment that Bishop would eventually blame in part for Lota's suicide four years later. While the two women had enjoyed a relatively secluded life together in Samambia (the home that Lota designed among lush mountain foliage above Rio), Lota, who hated being alone, was now spending most of her time without Bishop in their city apartment. The stress Lota encountered at work resulted in a deteriorating state of health from which she was never to recuperate.

After some routine remarks about the mail system, Bishop's letter begins with a reference to Lota's latest hospitalization for "intestinal occlusion":

> Lota is recovering and went back to work two weeks ago—much too soon. But there was a big show at the Museum of Modern Art here—models, airplane photographs, etc., of all her "job"—It opened last week and was a huge success—almost 5,000 people. . . . Lota had to cut a ribbon, receive sheaves of roses, etc—and we watched the whole thing over again on TV Monday night.[23]

Two paragraphs later Bishop's tone shifts from anxious pride to unchecked exuberance as she describes her latest delight, a new collection of birds:

> Oh—I have three new birds—Betty T had about 20 and gave them all away except one lonely little yellow and green creature she handed to me—it turns out to be a female wild canary and I think

I'll have to get it a husband. Then I couldn't resist a pair of Bica Lacquas—(Lacquer beaks—or maybe sealing-wax beaks—the word's the same)—I wish I could send you a pair and I wonder if they import them. They're the most adorable bird I know—about 3" long, including the tail—extremely delicate; bright red bills and narrow bright red masks. The male has a sort of mandarin-drooping mustache—one black line—otherwise they're just alike. They're tiny, but plump—and the feathers are incredibly beautiful, shading from brown and gray on top to pale beige, white, and a rose red spot on the belly—but all this in almost invisible ripples of color alternating with white—wave-ripples, just like sand ripples on a sand flat after the tide has gone out—all so fine I have to put on my reading glasses to appreciate it properly. They're almost as affectionate as love-birds, and they have a nest—smaller than a fist—with a doorway in the side, that they both get in to sleep. The egg is about as big as a baked bean—rarely hatches in captivity—but I'm hoping—From the front they look like a pair of half-ripe strawberries—you'd like them! But now I have two unwed female wild canaries—must find them husbands in order to have a little song around here—We're all silent together at present. (August 27, 1963)

Inspired perhaps by the proximity of domestic unrest and the lavish descriptions of affectionate birds, Swenson began a poem composed largely of Bishop's own words from this letter. "Dear Elizabeth," Swenson's best-known poem about Bishop, is a mischievous, riddled exploration of lesbian love and desire, what Richard Howard describes as "an intricate meditation on sexuality and exoticism . . . a kind of causerie between the two lesbian poets about their situation as lesbians, as poets."[24] It is also the product of twenty-two drafts and fifteen letters that, when read together, reveal a determined evolution in Swenson's understanding of Bishop's "cagey" poetics, a private forging of the path that links her early unrest to the distanced acceptance she possessed in late life.

Swenson began working on the poem immediately after receiving Bishop's letter. Her first draft is dated September 17, 1963. A week later she wrote of her efforts to Bishop, enclosing a draft with her letter: "Elizabeth, I've written a poem about those *Bica Lacquas* that you described in a recent letter—I've used *your words*, almost exactly, because the way you expressed their appearance and habits, etc., is so charming. . . . It's written like a letter. . . . Have the wild canaries got husbands yet?[25] The copy of the poem that Swenson enclosed was, however, several drafts away from the first; in the week preceding this letter, Swenson completed eight different drafts of "Dear Elizabeth," and an examination of these early versions reveals why Swenson never showed them to Bishop. By draft number 8, Swenson had untangled what appears to have been the most knotty part of the poem for her to write, the passage that received the most attention in drafts. In the final, published version it appears as follows:

> They must
> be very delicate, not easy to keep. Still,
> on the back porch on Perry St., here, I'd
> build them a little Brazil. I'd save every
> shred and splinter of New York sunshine
> and work through the winter to weave them
> a bed. A double, exactly their size,
>
> with a roof like the Ark. I'd make sure to
> leave an entrance in the side. I'd set it
> in among the morning-glories where the
> gold-headed flies, small as needles' eyes,
> are plentiful. Although "their egg is apt
> to be barely as big as a baked bean . . ."
> It rarely hatches in captivity, you mean—
>
> but we could hope!
>
> (*N*, 133–34)

These two stanzas mark the exact middle of this eight-stanza poem. They also contain the point at which Bishop's words give way most notably to Swenson's—the moment when Swenson's careful, gradual pastiche assumes a mission, a determined eagerness that seems to say, "Yes! Don't you *see?*": "*I'd* save *every* / *shred and splinter* of New York sunshine / and work *through the winter* to weave them / a bed." The speaker's insistence clearly builds on the excitement in Bishop's descriptions, but her enthusiasm turns to urgency as the stakes of this poem are made clear: while the tiny egg lies unhatched in Bishop's

Brazil, it just might come to life on Swenson's back porch, where the flies "small as needles' eyes" share a world more their size.

Bishop ends her letter by drawing a parallel between her own domestic strain and the birds' inaudible song: "We're all silent together," she confesses. Swenson seized upon this parallel, sighting a moment pregnant with possibility for the working through of her thoughts about Bishop. "Dear Elizabeth" is Swenson's most sustained published effort to process the frustration she felt toward Bishop's sexual reserve. What begins as a straightforward response—"Yes, I'd like a pair of *Bicos de Lacre*" (*N*, 133)—becomes a gentle critique of her friend's songless love. Stifled by "captivity," the "affectionate" birds can't hatch their eggs; there is a cost, implies Swenson, to Bishop's cagey ways. In contrast, the porch on Perry Street is teaming with life— the "gold-headed flies" are plentiful, buzzing amid blossoms whose hungry vines find food in this urban haven.

The importance of this image for Swenson is emphasized by the prominence it assumes in the very first draft. While the Perry Street porch doesn't appear until halfway through the published version of the poem, it is immediately introduced in the original. After ten or so lines describing the *bicos de lacre*—the same lines that launch all twenty-two drafts—we arrive at the following passage:

> "Extremely delicate," you say.
> Never mind. On the back porch
> on Perry St. here, I will
> build them a little Brazil.
> I will save every shred of
> sunshine, from June to September,
> and sew them a bed.[26]

This is the first of several scribbled-over, scratched-out versions in which Swenson struggles to contain the pulse of her poem. Though the image of Swenson's "little Brazil" remains much the same throughout the poem's development, the tone with which it is delivered goes through many transformations. Indeed, the tone of this passage may be said to bear the burden of the poem's purpose, since Swenson's revisions are focused largely upon its modulations.

As it appears in this first draft, the juxtaposition between Swenson's liberating porch and Bishop's barren Brazil is as abrupt as it ever gets. By placing quotation marks around Bishop's description of the birds' delicacy ("'Extremely delicate,' you say") Swenson distances herself from this image of refined fragility, and perhaps from a diction that echoes an earlier displeasure with "ugly words." With one clipped flourish Swenson then dismisses this emphasis as insignificant: "Never mind," she asserts, and quickly moves on to the business at hand—the porch on Perry Street, where delicacy is neither here nor there. In the next draft Swenson moves this passage to the place it will occupy henceforth in the poem. At the same time, she removes the quotation marks from Bishop's description of delicacy, only to put them back next time around; abrupt impatience begins to soften as Swenson cautiously blurs Bishop's words and her own.

Swenson explores this image of delicacy and her discomfort with it in the next several drafts. Eventually, Bishop's "extremely" is blunted to "very," and by draft number 5 Swenson's curtness allows some empathy: "I understand they're delicate, not easy to keep. But never mind." At the same time, as if to make up for an escaped edge of exasperation, Swenson repositions herself as wanting to please. "I'll do my best to manage their care," she writes in the margins; "You can depend on it." For seven days straight Swenson worked on this poem, engrossed largely by this section and her attempts to curb the "obvious." In draft number 7 Swenson pauses over this passage, setting it apart in a shape distinct from the rest of the poem. With number 8 she blends it back into the structure at large:

> "Their nest," you say, "is smaller
>
> than a fist, with a doorway in the side just wide
> enough for both to get in to, to sleep. They're very
> delicate . . ." I understand. Not easy to keep.
>
> Well, never mind. On the back porch, on Perry
> St. here, I will build them a little Brazil.
> I will save every shred of New York
>
> sunshine, from June to September, and work
> through the winter to weave them a bed—
> a double, exactly their size—inside a house with

the right kind of door, in among the morning-
glories, where the gold-headed flies,
minute as needles' eyes, are plentiful.

". . . Although their egg is apt to be barely
as big as a baked bean . . ." It rarely hatches
in captivity, you mean. Still, we could hope . . .

While this version of the poem still bears an impatience ("Well,
never mind") not present in the final draft, Swenson was satisfied
enough to show it to Bishop; it is less oppositional, more invitational,
and as a result the driving issue of this poem is made both clearer and
more complex. No longer is the thrust of this central passage deter-
mined by the distance between Bishop's Brazil and Swenson's back
porch. In her determined efforts to make sense of her own frustration,
Swenson has, however reluctantly, developed a degree of sympathy for
Bishop's ways—"I understand," she assures. The focus of the poem has
shifted from Swenson's exasperated sense of her difference from
Bishop to the murkier, more interesting place where commonality
breeds opposition: crafting a fertile nest for these birds is a delicate mat-
ter—no matter where, they're "Not easy to keep." Building a little
Brazil on the Perry Street porch is more complicated than it first seemed
to be; any bed won't do—it must be "exactly their size—inside a house
with / the right kind of door." Presumably this door differs from the
locked sort that left Swenson "outside," "sniffing and listening" several
years earlier as she read "The Shampoo." Nevertheless, in writing
"Dear Elizabeth" Swenson has come to understand that her visions of
liberation must contend with a "captivity" that links her life to Bishop's
as well as the birds': the heterosexual imperative that the *bicos de lacre*
both symbolize and shake up with their unhatched eggs; that pervasive
presence that, like the sun in this poem, both bathes Swenson's porch
and spawns the birds' bed.

As Swenson's sympathy grows, so does her emphasis on the birds as
a *couple,* hence the contingency above between the birds' sleeping
arrangements and Swenson's back porch, a contingency that will be
maintained for all subsequent drafts. At the same time, Swenson makes
the heterosexual presumption that usually underpins such imagery
more explicit in the poem. Shortly after Swenson first sent the poem to
Bishop, the following lines appear in her drafts: "I'd weave them a bed

... *shaped like an Ark*" (emphasis added). In the final version of the poem these lines look like this: "I'd save every / shred and splinter of New York sunshine / and work through the winter to weave them / a bed. A double, exactly their size, // with a roof like the Ark" (*N*, 133). While most of Swenson's readers may visualize any number of sun-woven beds, our imaginations converge immediately upon this familiar image of primordial, naturalized love: we can easily recall pages in picture books of happy animals filling the ark, two by two, "one of each." But Swenson's placement of this image also stresses the degree to which this narrative fails the "affectionate" couple, for inside the ark-covered nest lies the tiny, infertile egg. As we will see in the next chapter, this double gesture, with its simultaneous summoning and subversion of heterosexual tropes, becomes central to Swenson's evolving poetic, a poetic that gains shape in part through Swenson's struggles to make sense of Bishop's sexual reserve.

Bishop was pleased by the draft of "Dear Elizabeth" that Swenson sent her: "I think the poem might work out rather well," she wrote in return (*OA*, 418–19). In her next letter to Swenson, Bishop transcribed a passage about the *bicos de lacre* from a "big, colored-photograph, children's Bird Book." The male bird describes himself:

> My great grand-parents were born in Africa. They came to Brazil long ago. They adapted themselves so well to the new land that they seemed like natives. Frankly, I consider myself as Brazilian as you are . . . My voice is very nice, but weak, and I have no song. Even so, people like me, and find me pretty and "simpatico" . . . I do not mind being caged (?) as long as I am well-treated and have plenty of seed. I can live with other small birds and make friends with them. I get along beautifully with my wife. Occasionally we fight, but it's nothing, and we soon make up. My nest is small and round and I help to hatch the eggs.[27]

Bishop follows this passage with a subtle critique of its contents, further complicating the opposition upon which "Dear Elizabeth" turns.

> A young botanist & natural historian who's working with Lota has lent me some books, including the one I've quoted from. One is called "The Bird-Lover," and besides all the birds, it gives complete and rather awful instructions how to catch them, build traps and

cages, etc. . . . I know some dull men who know all about birds and keep 40 or 50 in their apartments—take them for airings the way the Chinese do, etc. I don't really approve—but at least they *see* them and that's something. . . . I'm about to buy another pair of Bicos de Lacre tomorrow—seeing they're so sociable.

Bishop's coda to the picture-book portrait of the *bicos de lacre* focuses on captivity, that laden image that distinguishes Bishop's Brazil from Swenson's back porch in the poem. In criticizing the "dull men" who hoard birds in their cages and the authors who show them how, Bishop subtly cautions Swenson against a reductive reading of her reserve. Moreover, Bishop caps her critique of the "dull men" by acknowledging her complicity with their greedy ways; she is, she tells Swenson, "about to buy another pair of Bicos de Lacre."

In her reply, Swenson does not respond directly to Bishop's commentary, and she addresses the picture-book passage in only a cursory way. But what she does say is rather revealing:

About the *Bicos Lacres*. . . . I *will* go up to the Bronx Zoo (where they have a splendid bird pavilion with everything in the world in it) and meet the little wonders personally. I was up there . . . about six weeks ago. Zambesi and Ranee, the lioness and tigress that I once wrote a poem about, are *gone*. I saw in another cage an old lioness that *looked* like Zambesi—but all alone.[28]

Written in 1955, "Zambesi and Ranee" (*N*, 152–54) is an unusually caustic condemnation of homophobic zoo-goers, those who would "prefer these captives punished, who / appear to wear the brand some captivated humans do" (*N*, 154). In sparking a return to this poem, Bishop's letter urged Swenson to revisit the pervasive intolerance and injustice that can darken even a trip to the zoo. As a result, Swenson was forced once more to rethink her stance in "Dear Elizabeth." Indeed, in the same draft in which the ark first appears, the brusque "Never mind" is quietly dropped, to be replaced by the softened "Still, on the back porch of Perry St. here . . ." Concurrently, Swenson's assertion that she "will build" shifts to the more deferential "I could," eventually becoming "I'd build them a little Brazil."

In her determination to find a balance between her frustration and fascination with Bishop, Swenson needed to make peace between her celebratory thirst for goodness—"but we could hope!"—and her uncomfortable understanding that Perry Street is no less captive than Bishop's Brazil, that the dominant ideology, like the linguistic structure of poems, cannot be so simply rejected. Guiding this process is a growing awareness of how it is that her kinship with Bishop's restraint ("I understand") might instruct her own strategies of resistance. After all, as Bishop herself observed in the postscript to her picture-book letter, "Apparently all of the Bicos de Lacre here are descended from some that escaped."

Above all else, "Dear Elizabeth" is a poem about language, an exploration of that mysterious slippage between our mind's eye and our tongues, a probing of the sometimes rich, sometimes wearing path from impassioned intention to the vagaries of interpretation. It is a poem woven from the threads of overlapping letters, a poem whose intricate evolution reveals the contiguity between language and being, writing and meaning. As Swenson worked through the tangles that inspired "Dear Elizabeth," she developed a deeper awareness of the issues that fed her attraction to Bishop. What began as intrigued exasperation with Bishop's sexual reserve shifts to a more subtle emphasis on the contingencies that determine all kinds of expression. Swenson never stopped flirting with the desire to break free—of convention, tradition, of language itself: "The past," she once wrote, "is so settled, trampled over. It's no fun unless you stand on the end of the diving board, alone, naked, not thinking of 'how' or 'why' or the best technique, but just the sensation—let impulse do it, instead of heavy knowledge" (*MWW*, 238). But Swenson's thirst for pushing the limits led her, paradoxically, to an ever-widening understanding of their productive capacity. In its redeployment of Bishop's descriptions, "Dear Elizabeth" dramatizes the relationship between "captivity" and creativity: in her efforts to unravel her uncomfortable attraction to Bishop's reserve, Swenson is literally bound by the very language she struggles against. And while the final lines assert Swenson's distinction from Bishop, they conclude a poem that also flaunts the terms of their debt. As Swenson struggled to decipher her conflicting feelings toward her friend, she came to realize that behind her fascination with Bishop's restraint lurked the power of language, its ability to both reveal and conceal, to hold captive and create.

The next poem that Swenson wrote about Bishop builds upon this realization. "In the Bodies of Words" (*N* 135–36) takes place on the occasion of Bishop's death in 1979. It is both a mourning and a celebration of the friendship these poets shared. It is also a poignant meditation on the nature of language itself:

> Until today in Delaware, Elizabeth, I didn't know
> you died in Boston a week ago. How can it be
> you went from the world without my knowing?
> Your body turned to ash before I knew. Why was there
> no tremor of the ground or air? No lightning flick
> between our nerves? How can I believe? How grieve?
>
> (*N*, 135)

The unnerving displacement Swenson feels upon hearing of Bishop's death mirrors the conflicted currents that chart their thirty-year correspondence. Like the song of the *bicos de lacre*, whose "note is" not "something one hears, / but must watch the cat's ears to detect," the bond between Swenson and Bishop was both intuitive and elusive. Swenson and Bishop shared an implicit, unspoken understanding that was, despite its inaudible song, made manifest in their mutual love of linguistic measures. At the same time, as we have seen, the unnamed pulse of their exchange sparked both frustration (there's "no use pounding on the door") and connection ("I understand. Not easy to keep"). In her efforts to break through Bishop's self-restraint, Swenson was led again and again to the dynamics of their exchange, to the "cagey" nature of communication: "How can it be / you went from the world without my knowing? . . . For a moment I jump back to when all was well and ordinary. / Today I could phone Boston, say Hello. . . . Oh, no! / Time's tape runs forward only. There is no replay" (*N*, 135).

"In the Bodies of Words" is saturated with this sense of missed messages, failed expressions, perverted attempts at understanding.

> I meet a red retriever, young, eager, galloping
> out of the surf. At first I do not notice his impairment.
> His right hind leg is missing. Omens. . . .
> I thought I saw a rabbit in the yard this morning.
> It was a squirrel, it's tail torn off. Distortions.
>
> (*N*, 135)

Those small but exquisite moments that bear life's beauty are deployed in this poem as reminders of the pain without which joy would have no meaning. Images that appear full of promise and communion yield disappointment and isolation: "Light hurts. . . . Ocean is gray again today, old and creased aluminum / without sheen. Nothing to see on that expanse" (135). The sandy beach is scraped "hard as a floor by wind," and a "life is little as a dropped feather. Or split shell / tossed ashore, lost under sand" (135).

But this sad and silent expanse is pierced by emotional contact when the speaker spots "a troupe of pipers— / your pipers, Elizabeth!—their racing legs like spokes / of tiny wire wheels" (*N*, 136). For a brief but ecstatic moment Swenson feels a connection with Bishop once more. Through the image of these birds Swenson is reminded of Bishop's sandpiper, who looks "for something, something, something. / Poor bird, he is obsessed! / The millions of grains are black, white, tan, and gray, / mixed with quartz grains, rose and amethyst" (*CP*, 131). Hope emerges in this instant, born of the realization that while language sometimes fails us, it also exceeds our limits. "In the Bodies of Words" mourns the loss of a friend, but perhaps more to the point, it signals the abrupt arrest of an exchange that for Swenson was left unfinished. In her efforts to grapple with her loss, Swenson is returned to the poetry that attracted her from the start, and it is at this moment that she receives from Bishop the unambiguous answer she'd always sought: "But vision lives! / Vision, potent, regenerative, lives in bodies of words. / Your vision lives, Elizabeth, your words / from lip to lip perpetuated" (*N*, 135). It is through language that we grow our selves, with words that we learn to see; reserve becomes regeneration when language turns from masking to that which "multiplies . . . in the bodies of words" (*N*, 136).

In its title alone, Swenson's commemorative poem immediately announces the contingency between the corporeal and the linguistic; words in this poem are *embodied* : "vision lives . . . in the bodies of words." By celebrating the productive (as opposed to prohibitive) quality of Bishop's language in overtly physical terms (terms that are emphasized through the refrain of the poem), Swenson bridges her love of "the physical" and her early mistrust of Bishop's cagey ways. In doing so, Swenson revels in her articulation—"But vision lives!"—of that elusive, intuitive "attitude" she indeed shared with her friend.

It is no surprise, then, that in her last poem to Bishop Swenson returns overtly to the issue that divided them most. "Her Early Work" (*IOW*, 58) is a concise, explicit reckoning with the knotty problem of sexual restraint. While Swenson admits of her lingering desire to get beyond Bishop's "masks" ("To this day we can't know / who was addressed, / or ever undressed" [58]), she also suggests that such a desire in some sense misses the point: "Because of the wraparounds, / overlaps and gauzes, / kept between words and skin, / we notice nakedness" (58). Or in other words, Bishop's reticence spawns revelation. All of the unpublished drafts of "Her Early Work" underscore the importance of these lines for Swenson herself: "*But because,*" they insist, as if answering an unrest that the poem initially poses (emphasis added).[29] And indeed, this poem provides Swenson's last homage to those instructive frustrations that Bishop inspired.

"Her Early Work" is a response in part to Bishop's early poem "A Word with You," in which the speaker uncharacteristically confides

how hard it is, you understand
this nervous strain in which we live—
Why just one luscious adjective
infuriates the whole damned band.
                    (*CP*, 218)[30]

Swenson must have smiled knowingly upon reading this passage, recalling how Bishop had taken her to task for those "ugly words" years ago. But in her late-life response to Bishop's poem Swenson articulated an awareness still nascent in her earlier reply to Bishop's critique. While "Her Early Work" clearly speaks to a persistent longing for a more authentic, more personal truth, it just as emphatically answers that longing with a discovery more profound: linguistic "masks" don't simply compete with the "physical" truth; they accentuate, they regenerate, indeed they impart "nakedness." Moreover, this poem offers its concession within the terms of a conversation, and thus provides a quiet conclusion to the correspondence from which it grew. Though "A Word with You" "had to be whispered, / spoken at the zoo," Bishop's poetry engulfs the "obvious" in its embrace of a more subtle truth. As Swenson once put it upon introducing her friend, "Good poets—there are few, they have always been few—are couriers of consciousness and yes, of conscience, too."[31]

## 5   May Swenson's Performative Poetics

**M**arianne Moore enjoys talking. I am awkward at it and would rather listen."[1] Thus wrote May Swenson in 1964, and as usual, her observation unsettles easy assumptions. For if anyone's poetry is effusive, it's Swenson's, while Moore's mazelike verse always feels more contained. But Swenson thrived on the unlikely observation, or more precisely, on collapsing the distance between *like* and *unlikely*. We have seen how this characteristic of Swenson's shaped her keen understanding of Bishop's work, and the same can be said of her reading of Moore. Indeed, Swenson felt she possessed an almost intuitive grasp of Moore's poetry, as she once confessed in a letter to Bishop: "I have the feeling I *know* how to read [Moore]. It bores me to read critical articles, but I am going to look up critiques of her work and check whether anyone has found the key-points to her method in the way that it seems I can sense them" (*MWW*, 243). Central to Swenson's "sense" of Moore's method is an admiration of Moore's self-restraint: "There is neither self-pity nor self-aggrandizement in her poems. Where a capital *I* begins an observation, it is never to say, using the excuse of being a poet: 'See how *I* have loved, or suffered. . . . See what *I* have discovered.'"[2] At the same time, Swenson celebrated Moore's "extensive, hypnotic peacock-display of language," her "strong, limber, complex, organic trellis of technique," calling forth a commanding poet who is anything but reticent or timid. Moore's "individual conviction . . . is monarchical," wrote Swenson, and we've "all been given courage by her beautiful daring, her abundance, her naturalness that is cunning. . . . She is a rascal and a revolutionary of form, of aesthetics. She is an uncompromising idealist as to content, to truth."[3] Swenson burrows into the landscape of Moore's complicated poetry, clarifying its contours while maintaining its opulence—a none-too-easy maneuver that is itself an expression of Moore-like flexibility and grace. It is not surprising, then, that when asked about influences, Swenson spoke most often of Moore.[4] Above all else, Swenson was attracted to Moore's unmatched ability to criticize and even moralize without promoting herself as authority. And so we return to the question of Swenson's with which this book began: "Who of us is able to be such an acute instrument for the objectification of sensual perceptions and states of mind as she, without emphasizing *self* as subject?"[5]

Like Moore, Swenson insists on the interdependence of extremes, revealing connections where oppositions normally endure. It is for this reason above all others that Swenson found in Moore a "grand and indelible example" for "we *women poets*," whose "deviation into creative rather than procreative tracks is grudgingly sanctioned these days, but on a carefully segregated basis."[6] Near the end of "A Matter of Diction," Swenson goes on to pose the question that she never asked the older poet in person: "Is there a distinction as fixed as pigmentation between the intellect and the imagination of male and female poets? Does each depend on some different Hormonal Muse?" Swenson's query is, of course, sarcastic, because Moore's "poetry itself annihilates the debate" (48).

This is a fitting place for the dexterous Swenson to end her tribute to Moore, for just as she salutes Moore's feminist instincts, she checks the sort of feminist praise she herself would eventually garner. Swenson's lush and fleshy language celebrates the sensual, exploring the erotic in human and nonhuman existence alike; we may recall her confession to Bishop that the "physical is the beautiful to me. . . . I like physical associations. Worse, there is almost a compulsion to employ them" (*MWW*, 227). This characteristic of Swenson's verse has attracted spare but steady critical approval from woman-identified feminists for the past thirty years. Though Swenson's distaste for confessional poetry and wariness of women-only anthologies kept her on the banks of the feminist mainstream while she lived, her relationship with feminism in general was much less strained than either Moore's or Bishop's. Throughout the 1970s Swenson's poems appeared in a handful of same-sex collections (several of which were edited by friends), and the feminist poet-critic Alicia Ostriker began her enthusiastic promulgation of Swenson's work at about this time.[7]

But there has been a cost to Swenson's currency in the feminist canon, a tendency to read her sensuality at the expense of her wariness of authenticity, sexual or otherwise. As Swenson explained to Louise Bogan in 1963, "I think your statement that 'Women function differently, in art as in life' is open to a lot of argument. I like to think that a good work of art is not subject to the limitations of either gender, but can combine the strengths of both sexes."[8] Moreover, Swenson believed that "poetry is made with words of a language . . . in order to make the mind re-member (by dismemberment) . . . the buried grain of language on which depends the transfer and expansion of conscious-ness—of sense. . . . To *sense* then becomes to *make sense*."[9] In other words, Swenson's focus on "the physical" is a means of getting under our most basic assumptions, beyond "the flat ground of appearances," probing notions like a prediscursive or material real that sensual expe-rience is often assumed to signify.[10] While Swenson loved the "physi-cal," that love is underwritten by a fascination with the productive powers of language. As a result, her explorations of the corporeal are navigated by a skepticism of the irreducible "truth" that the body—especially the female body—is often said to represent. In this way Swenson's poetry complements Moore's: while the latter's crisply cere-bral and supposedly asexual verse in fact reveals the discursive prac-tices that make up sex to begin with, Swenson immerses herself in the sensual and in the process deconstructs the standard of female sexual-ity by which both authors are so often seen as opposites. In each instance sexual frankness ironically becomes a standard by which the literary analysis of women is limited, not liberated. And indeed, while the "beautifully . . . Sapphic" nature of Swenson's poetry has been much admired,[11] her persistent use of traditionally gendered and het-erosexual imagery has gone largely without critical comment.[12]

Swenson is known among critics for her portraits of lesbian love and desire. Also a feminist ("I began to be a feminist at age three-and-a-half"),[13] Swenson wrote heavily anthologized poems like "Bleeding" and "Women" that offer obvious critical commentaries on gender inequality and heterosexist desire. At the same time, however, an over-whelming number of Swenson's love poems employ blatantly hetero-sexual or stereotypically gendered tropes, a strategy that is central to the relationship between sensuality and subjectivity that shapes Swen-son's poetic. In the previous chapter we witnessed the tension in Swen-son's writing between her desire to break through limits and her awareness of the interdependence between those boundaries and her very sense of being. At the heart of this tension lies Swenson's penchant for "the physical," that dimension of experience which seems at once most essential and most mutable. Swenson's compulsion toward the sensual led to a particularly keen balancing act within her work, to what makes her poetry so remarkable: an unparalleled celebration of bodily being that contests the authenticity of material existence. In the following pages I suggest that Swenson's appropriation of heterosexual, normative imagery marks her most successful strategy for maintaining this balance. Through a performative redeployment of gendered tropes, Swenson rewrites the terms of desire and broadens our scope of subjectivity. In the end, we may see how the promise of Swenson's effulgence is realized through the power of restraint, so that sexual frankness no longer measures feminist concern, and desires contest the limits of self-expression.

As Sue Russell has noted, although Swenson "did not go out of her way to disclose her lesbianism, neither did she go out of her way to hide it."[14] Swenson gladly granted permission in 1957 to Joan Larkin and Elly Bulkin to include her poem "To Confirm a Thing" in their lesbian anthology *Amazon Poetry* (1975), but she refused the same editors an inclusion of her work six years later in a more comprehensive collection titled *Lesbian Poetry: An Anthology* (1981).[15] Her reasoning is of particular relevance here because it reveals a steadfast wariness of the nature of representation. In a letter to Larkin explaining her refusal, Swenson wrote, "I have not sent you any poems for inclusion in the proposed anthology—nor would I do so—any more than I would submit any writing to a book titled, for instance, 'The Heterosexual Women's Poetry Anthology'" (July 30, 1980).[16] In a later letter she wrote that the term *lesbian* "strikes me as a label placed on a collection simply in order to arouse attention, and I believe it invites misunderstanding. . . . People attracted to such a title would not, I think, be looking principally for first-rate poetry." Furthermore, Swenson would have preferred the title *Amazon Poetry II* because it is "suggestive," but not "crude" (August 19, 1980).

Richard Howard captures the way this resistance toward labeling figures into Swenson's work: within her poetry there is an "impulse to identify" alongside a "reluctance to call a spade a spade; it is an impulse implicit in the very paradox supported by the word *identification*, which we use both to select an object in all its singularity, and to dissolve that 'identical' object into its likeness with another."[17] Thus, in "In the Yard" Swenson writes:

Fat-tailed she-dog
grinning's thrasher-
red. Oriole there

by the feeder's cheddar
under black bold head.

And later, as the poem ends:

You're back,
barefoot, brought
some fruit. Split me
an apple. We'll
get red, white
halves each, our
juice on the
Indian spread.
                    (N, 94)

Distinguished by a singular color (red, cheddar, black, white), each
entity (dog, oriole, apple, companion) is isolated and held apart,
defined through visual contrast with that which comes before and
after. Yet this isolation is introduced only to be confounded by an
increasing overlap of specificity, a contiguous, not evolutionary
process of identification in which the "I" delimited by narrative dis-
tance is only given shape in the poem within the "we" of mingled col-
ors and mixed-up halves.

It is precisely Swenson's invocation of identity at the liminal site
*between* bodies, between self and other, in the slippage between repre-
sentation and reality, that marks her portrait of selfhood as contingent,
a view clearly suggested when she writes that

no one
can be sure
by himself
of his own being
and the world's seeing
.  .  .  .  .  .  .  .  .
is suspect.
                    (LP, 41)

Howard goes on to state that "the refusal, or the reluctance, to *name* in
order to more truly *identify* is what we notice first about May Swenson's
poetry."[18] But although Swenson's refusal to name is indeed an identi-

fying mark of her work, this refusal seems to be more of a *challenge* to the constraining, representational power of the name itself than a "reluctance" to be trapped "within the numbing power of proper names."[19] This is a subtle distinction, but an important one, because to resist the "numbing power" of the name in an effort to more "truly identify" is to imply the existence of a prediscursive identity that *can* be numbed by the intrusive constraint of the name. While Swenson's poetry repeatedly flirts with such a perspective, it rejects it regularly as well, as in "The Key to Everything," a very early poem (1949) in which the power of naming is clearly called into question:

> If I knew what your
> name was I'd
> prove it's your
> own name spelled backwards or
> twisted in some way the one you
> keep mumbling but you
> won't tell me your
> name or
> don't you know it
> yourself that's it
> of course you've
> forgotten or
> never quite knew it or
> weren't willing to believe it.
>
> (*LP,* 50–51)

In an attempt to garner the love of the addressee, to fix her attentions, the speaker imploringly seeks a specific name, "your / own name spelled backwards." Different from merely "your name," it is the "key to everything" through which the speaker hopes to establish control. But the explanatory power of this somehow more revealing name is rendered insufficient, indeed illusory; first of all forgotten, its existence is then questioned to begin with. In a burst of disillusioned revelation, the narrator exclaims,

> Then there *is* something I
> can do I
> can find your name for you

that's the key to everything once you'd
repeat it clearly you'd
come awake you'd
get up and walk knowing where you're
going where you
came from.

(51)

However, in the next and final stanza the euphoria is gone, replaced by
the sober realization that

no once you'd
get there you'd
remember and love me
of course I'd
be gone by then I'd
be far away.

(51)

The "name spelled backwards" is no different, after all, from the pub-
lic, unriddled one. The beloved is no more, but no less, than her repre-
sentation. Swenson is not rejecting the name *because* of its power,
endowing it thereby with the authority it assumes; rather, she confronts
the very integrity of this power itself.

Swenson's focus on the power of naming, on the act of representa-
tion, implies that the act of representation is just that—an action, a pro-
ductive power by which subjectivity is not passively reflected, but
actively produced. In a journal entry dated May 20, 1965, Swenson
ruminates on exactly this relationship between language and human
consciousness:

My theory: That the universe began to exist at the point when
human language was born. That it began simultaneously with its
*expression* through thought & word—through recognition & nam-
ing & defining & relating. "In the beginning was the word"—
Human recognition and expression concomitantly created the past,
the history of existence, with the present, and it projects the future.
Reality as a mental concept . . . There can be no material before the
designation "material"—no energy before the name energy—and

all properties and phenomena come into *being* only at the instant that *human* consciousness lifts them from the void into mind; light.[20]

The implications of Swenson's theory on notions of selfhood and perception are explored in a poem she began about a year before the above entry and published for the first time in *Half Sun Half Sleep* (1967). One of the longer poems in Swenson's oeuvre, "Spectrum Analysis" begins as follows:

When I say
>*I*
>>I swim
in a yellow
>>room.
When I think
>>*my mind*
>>my mind
pulls to me a
>>sun
that magnetizes to itself a
>>million
>>million
butterflies dandelions and
coins eggyolks strands
of ambergris the eyes
of cats and owls and
beakers ampoules beads
of topaz and of honey and of
>>urine.

>>>(*HS*, 93)

It is when the speaker names herself—utters "I"—that she ushers her *self* "into *being*," a being that is, interestingly, defined by its bodily weight, its ability to swim. Language here is what lights the senses, sparks the ability to *be* even physically. Probing the parameters of this revelation ("Reality as a mental concept"), the speaker contemplates her mind and pulls to her a sun bursting with energy, suffusing the "yellow room" of her self-knowing with, indeed, a dazzling light.

Moreover, this light also "magnetizes" a "million million" subjects that we may recognize from Swenson's poems—butterflies, dandelions, egg yolks, eyes of cats and owls, and so on, so that this poem itself comes into being by exploring its own genesis. In parallel fashion, the speaker's isolated *I* is at once distinct from the "I" that names it as such and no more than its magnified reflection: it arrests our attention, asks pause, alone and exaggerated in a line all its own. But its soft vowel sound melts into the *I*s that surround it, so that it does indeed "swim" along the walls of self-awareness, both marking and blurring the bounds of its existence. This curiously double gesture reflects the notion that "the universe began . . . *simultaneously* with its *expression* through thought & word." It is this simultaneity that frustrates our need for ontology. Self and representation of self are stretched apart like a rubber band, and when we let go, they snap back to the serpentine, circular, unfixable experience that "being" always is.

In this way Swenson explores the generative, not merely prohibitive, functioning of the name, calling to mind Foucault's important critique of the repressive hypothesis. Foucault asserts that we ought to reconceive the law and its representations as productive, as creating the illusion of repressed desire as a way of naturalizing its own existence. By essentializing particular identities through the insistence of their repression, the law emerges as a natural inevitability, determined by the very identities it in fact works to produce.[21] In this light, subjectivities are produced through the terms by which they are simultaneously constrained. To name is in part to *create*, not merely to reflect, express, or authorize what is already there. To think of naming as a form of power is to recognize this productive aspect of description, to understand that observations are never innocent.

Swenson was acutely aware of this paradoxical nature of naming, and her distinctive poetic is an expression of the degree to which she reveled in the challenges it posed. Like Moore and Bishop, Swenson wrote poetry that is characterized by an intense thirst for exact, expansive observations *and* a simultaneous unwillingness to spell them out. If we take into account the productive, performative power of language, as I believe these poets ask us to, then such a strategy is not at all contradictory, and the restraint of each may be understood as an effort to participate more rigorously in the provisional process of revelation. As such, Moore's conviction that "complexity is not a crime" and Bishop's surreal, distorted vision are akin to Swenson's lifelong love of

riddles,[22] for as Richard Wilbur observed, a riddle is "at first a conceal-
ment, the withholding of a name; but as and when we solve its dark
metaphor, the riddle is a revelation."[23]

At the heart of Swenson's poetry is a devotion to self-exploration
that gives way to the realization of one's inevitable incompleteness.
"Spectrum Analysis" turns upon this revelation:

> I whirl—not
> grassward but
> brassward . . .
> . . . my
> *I* dissected
> naked
> frayed to anonymous
> *its*—reversed and
> tossed out
> lost.
>
> (*HS*, 93)

This revelation, of course, motivated Moore and Bishop as well, and calls
to mind the wily pangolin and the thoughtful "Elizabeth," among oth-
ers. But Swenson surpassed both Moore and Bishop in the outright
ecstasy she brought to this perspective: though the speaker in "Spectrum
Analysis" confesses, "I know not what / point *my* / *point* / points to,"
she nevertheless declares that "it is a / point intent upon / itself" and is
empowered by the decentered but delicious contours of her being.

> When I taste
> *I*
> I taste something akin
> to suprafruit or neutronic
> flower
> a solar heart engorged with light's rich
> juice
> infrared.
>
> (*HS*, 93)

Exuberant, effusive, indulgent, this concluding stanza reveals indeed
the "solar heart engorged" that pumps such powerful life into Swen-

son's poems: to confront the mainstays of subjectivity with a skeptical, unwavering rigor is not to forsake the pleasures of loving who we are.

Swenson's reluctance to "call a spade a spade" is integral to an analysis of her sexual imagery. Her poetry asserts that the relationship between the name and the named, representation and real, is always unfixed and fluid, an interactive process that necessitates a responsible, careful awareness of one's own ability to represent and potentially revise. Judith Butler's work on sexuality and desire illuminates the relationship between Swenson's treatment of selfhood and her sexual imagery. Butler insists that it is exactly the naturalized link between representation and reality, figured most clearly in the opposition between identification and desire, that normalizes what she calls the "heterosexual matrix." The "heterosexual logic," observes Butler, "that requires that identification and desire be mutually exclusive is one of the most reductive of heterosexism's psychological instruments: if one identifies *as* a given gender, one must desire a different gender."[24] The logic that seeks to construe heterosexuality as normal and homosexuality as aberrant is dependent upon a view of representation (such as poetic imagery) as a mere reflection of the material, essential nature of things, a nature that is both located in and legitimized by those very representations. From this view, it becomes clear "why refusing to draw lines of causal implication between [gender and sexuality] is as important as keeping open an investigation of their complex interimplication," for such a refusal opens up the possibility of reading Swenson's manipulation of oppositional, often heterosexual imagery as strategic, rather than hopelessly confused or coded. If, as Butler explains,

> to identify as a woman is not necessarily to desire a man, and if to desire a woman does not necessarily signal the constituting presence of a masculine identification, whatever that is, then the heterosexual matrix proves to be an *imaginary* logic that insistently issues forth its own unmanageability. (239)

It is with this understanding that I read Swenson's sexual imagery as subversive in its appropriation, and reconfiguration, of normative tropes. Swenson's imagery often seems to reiterate familiar heterosexual codes, while the dramatic script of the poem subtly subverts or

revises the power dynamics that such imagery might otherwise natu-
ralize. Take, for instance, "A Couple":

> A bee rolls in the yellow rose.
> Does she invite his hairy rub?
> He scrubs himself in her creamy folds.
> A bullet soft imposes her spiral
> and, spinning, burrows
> to her dewy shadows.
> The gold grooves almost match
> the yellow bowl.
> Does his touch please or scratch?
>
> (N, 150)

The feminized flower and the masculinized bee establish the conven-
tional, binary roles of passive receptacle versus active desire: the bee
"rolls," "scrubs," and "imposes," while the rose is determined by her
"creamy folds," her "dewy shadows," characteristics only illuminated
by the hungry action of the probing insect. The interrogatives accentu-
ate the voicelessness of the feminized rose, while further entrenching
the poem's continuum of desire along an oppositional, active/passive
axis. However, the poem takes a turn as it ends:

> When he's done his honey-thieving
> at her matrix, whirs free leaving,
> she closes, still tall, chill, unrumpled on her stem.
>
> (N, 150)

Although the questions are left unanswered, the ending asserts their
structural insufficiency. Pleasure here is not found through a strict
opposition, and therefore can't be contained within the diametrical
map of active desire versus passive resistance, or acquiescence versus
imposition. The flower's role is ostensibly passive and her pleasure
remains ambiguous, yet her final act of closing intimates her ability to
have done so all along, endowing the flower's prior passivity with a
consciousness that complicates the victimized passivity that the poem
seems to construct outwardly. Tellingly, in the first several drafts of the
poem, Swenson paired the rose's "unrumpled" stance with the bee's
"fumbling touch," a juxtaposition that further highlights the flower's
relative power.[25]

The narrative progression of "A Couple" is later echoed in "The Wil-
lets":

Her back to him pretended—
was it welcome, or only dazed
admission of their fate?
Lifting, he streamed a warning
from his beak, and lit

upon her, trod upon her
back, both careful feet.
The wings held off his weight.
His tail pressed down, slipped off. She
animated. And both went back to fishing.

(N, 117)

Although he treads upon her back, his feet are careful, and it is the
strength of *her* wings that checks and orchestrates the weight of his
desire. His tail presses down and she animates, yet, reminiscent of the
unrumpled rose, consummation is ultimately consumed by indiffer-
ence, as they both go back to fishing.

"Poet to Tiger" is an especially interesting poem, exploding with tra-
ditionally gendered imagery and the psychological processes of hetero-
sexist manipulation:

You went downstairs
saw a hair in the sink
and squeezed my toothpaste by the neck.
You roared. My ribs are sore.
This morning even my pencil's got your toothmarks.
Big Cat Eye cocked on me you see bird bones.

(LP, 32)

Although there are no gendered pronouns in the poem, roles are fig-
ured playfully along familiar masculine and feminine lines: He roars,
she "snuggles in the rug" of his belly; he "bounds," she's getting "thin-
ner"; he orders her gruffly, she pleads longingly. At the end of the
poem an obvious assertion of feminized power seeks to dislodge the
mainstays of the tiger's masculinized oppression, but it is arguable
whether or not a mere inversion—"I'm going to / do the cooking /
now

instead / of you. / And sneak some salt in / when you're not look-ing"—does so effectively. More interesting, however, are the simulta-neous and conflicting plays on standard gender roles within the poem in and against which this inversion takes place. On the one hand, the masculine tiger, bestial and gruff, stands in direct contrast to the femi-nine, willowy poet, reworking what is perhaps the most pervasive of all binary tropes: nature as woman, spirit as man, in which woman is coded as sensual, bodily, and material, while man emerges as cerebral, untethered by materiality, indeed, divine. Within the confines of this poem the narrator-poet's physical presence seems to diminish in direct proportion to the tiger's increased vitality, a vitality that is in turn more raw and sensate with each stanza. Untamed and animalistic, the tiger assumes the overwhelming "natural" presence traditionally reserved for Woman, while the feminine poet inhabits the analytical, mindful role of Man. On the other hand, this very reading can be used to show that Swenson's imagery *relies* upon, rather than rejects, a different but no less insidious set of gender stereotypes, those of the bestial, sensual man versus the chaste, refined lady. It is important to note that it is pre-cisely this latter stereotype that has been used historically to legitimate the abusive behavior of men toward women, behavior that is at least echoed in the actions of the tiger in this poem.

What is Swenson intending here? Is she revising or reifying these gender codes? What purpose do they serve in this context, and what is Swenson saying about sexual desire? Sue Russell notes that this poem was one of two that, in the year before she died, Swenson allowed into an anthology titled *Gay and Lesbian Poetry in Our Time* (1988), also edited by Joan Larkin.[26] Although Swenson's late-life decision to accept this heading that she rejected in earlier years is curious, it is of less rel-evance here than the fact that she obviously felt this an appropriate poem to exist under the title *lesbian*. And indeed, toward the end of the poem we discover that the tiger is, after all, a female. In the first stanza of the last section of "Poet to Tiger" we encounter the solitary clue that gives away her sex: settling into a bath, the tiger "wet[s] that blond / three-cornered pelt" while lying back, her "chest afloat" (*LP*, 34). Nearly buried within the poem's profusion of binary tropes, these two telltale lines take on a layered, and typical, Swensonian luster; as they reveal the lovers in the poem to be women, these lines can't help but reemphasize the weighty presence of normative, often antigay codes through which this revelation takes place. For this reason, I am surprised by Russell's claim that "Poet to Tiger" is "one among many poems which communicate the nuances of domestic life in women's long-term partnering with more clarity than perhaps any other poet has done before or since."[27] What I find odd is not Russell's reading of this poem as describing a lesbian relationship in the absence of a more "typically lesbian" imagery, if there is such a thing, but rather, that her praise of this poem as particularly sensitive to the depiction of lesbian life elides the heterosexist script through which this depiction is dramatized.

This juxtaposition of lesbian love and heterosexist imagery recalls an earlier poem of Swenson's called "Zambesi and Ranee." Written in 1955, this poem foreshadows "Poet to Tiger" (1970) in many ways and may be read as its precursor. Inspired by an installment at the Bronx Zoo of two female cats, a tiger and a lion, who "were reared together by hand from early infancy" and "strongly resent[ed] separation," Swenson ends this more explicit poem with a bitter rebuke to the homophobic onlooker (or reader):

> *Refused to nurse them,* simpering mothers read,
> and tighten the hold on Darling's hand: "Look
>         at the pussy cats!" they coax, they croon,
>         but blushing outrage appalls their cheeks—
> and this menage calls down no curse,
> not only is excused, but celebrated.
>             They'd prefer these captives punished, who
>         appear to wear the brand some captivated humans do.
>                                                 (*N*, 152)

One of the "captivated" who shares the "brand" of lesbianism with the cats, the author of this poem is certainly upfront—more so than usual—about her intentions here. Moreover, this critical turn at the end the poem highlights the stereotypically gendered way in which Swenson catalogs the cats at the start: "the tiger looks the younger and more male" (152), while the "lion, square-bodied, heavy-pelted, less grand / her maneless, round-eared head held low," slinks around the cage "watchful and slow" (153). Swenson's appropriation here of standard male and female tropes destabilizes the heterosexual presumption they often naturalize. Though the visitors can successfully fit the cats into their conditioned ways of perceiving, they cannot align the animals with the heterosexuality that they believe such roles should signal. As a result, the visitors' ways of seeing and understanding are exposed as insufficient, hence the "blushing outrage" and visceral fear that makes Mother "tighten the hold" on "Darling's hand."

Like "Zambesi and Ranee," "Poet to Tiger" is a poem devoted at least in part to the depiction of two lesbian lovers—indeed, Swenson wrote it for her partner of nearly twenty years, Rozanne Knudson[28]—and when read alongside the earlier poem, we may conclude all the more confidently that Swenson's imagery in "Poet to Tiger" should be read as strategic. The directness with which heterosexist assumptions are condemned in "Zambesi and Ranee" prepares us to better appreciate the more subtle, and I believe more profound, degree to which the less explicit poem does the same. "Poet to Tiger" sets up the most obvious props used to signal heterosexual relations, but does so in such a way that ultimately pits one trope against the other. Rather than working in successive layers to strengthen the marriage of masculine and feminine representations, the simultaneous employment of the nature/culture and bestial male/pure female tropes turn in on each other, preventing a sense of progression or resolution between the two partners in the poem while illuminating the precarious logic that lies at the heart of heterosexist assumptions of sexuality and gender. Interestingly, this typical double gesture is mirrored in the composition of the poem. Unpublished drafts reveal that Swenson started with the image of her lover squeezing the toothpaste by the neck; with each new version (there are twenty-two in all) the poem becomes both more intimate—"we're riding pillion" appears about halfway through—and more traditionally gendered.[29] When we contextualize these intrinsic conflicts of the poem within the contours of a lesbian relationship, the sense of purposeful irresolve that this poem implies is heightened. And although the lovers in the poem are both women, it is important to note that the poem offers no place *beyond* the reaches of its gendered imagery in which a resolution of their troubled relations can take place. Just as much a product of heterosexist culture as anyone else, the female lovers in this poem do not represent a purer, more idyllic life beyond the bounds of binary logic. Indeed, part of what makes this poem more forceful than "Zambesi and Ranee" is the fact that the speaker is clearly complicit in the very dynamic she criticizes. At the same time, the pat, dialectical evolution that is traditionally figured through such oppositional tropes gives way instead to a lingering sense of unease in which the naturalized chart of gender codes proves useless in mapping the trials of love. By crafting an obvious opposition along gendered lines that Swenson then blurs by the absence of gendered pronouns and reworks through the manipulation of the very imagery upon which these oppositions rest, "Poet to Tiger" indeed suggests the "imaginary logic" of the "heterosexual matrix," exposing its construction and thus the very possibility of its revision.

It is crucial that Swenson appropriates, rather than rejects, the mechanisms through which gender and sexuality are naturalized. While her poetry insists on the constructedness of gender and subjectivity, it likewise suggests the impossibility of a pure or prediscursive identity that exists outside of, or apart from, the terms it seeks to subvert. The lovers in "Poet to Tiger" play out the terms of heterosexist naming in ways that parody its claim to truth, but there does not exist a truer, more "lesbian" space in which they can escape the troubled dynamics of their relationship. This strategy is especially striking given Swenson's "compulsion" for "the physical" and her lifelong fascination with limits. In reworking the terms by which sexuality is both named and naturalized, Swenson honors both her fascination with sensuality and her "theory" that "there can be no material before the designation 'material.'"

Swenson's manipulation of sexual imagery implies that there is no such thing as an identity not ideologically saturated, that any attempt to explicate or dislodge the mainstays of the dominant cultural codes will always be entangled in the very terms they work to subvert. Given her view of sexuality and selfhood as produced by the terms they seek to resist, Swenson's poetry suggests that perhaps the most effective strategy of change is one that flaunts blatantly the lawful apparatus it works against. Butler puts it this way: "The resignification of norms is thus a function of their *inefficacy*, and so the question of subversion, *of working the weakness in the norm*, becomes a matter of inhabiting the practices of its rearticulation."[30] This "working the weakness in the norm" is at the heart of Butler's theory of "performativity," a method of resistance that helps elucidate Swenson's erotic verse:

Performativity describes this relation of being implicated in that which one opposes, this turning of power against itself to produce alternative modalities of power, to establish a kind of political contestation that is not a "pure" opposition, a "transcendence" of con-

temporary relations of power, but a difficult labor of forging a
future from resources inevitably impure.[31]

Performative writing, then, depends upon language as a source of
agency, a belief that language and personal power are interdependent,
that one does not wholly determine or preexist the other: "We do things
with language, produce effects with language, and we do things to lan-
guage, but language is also the thing that we do. Language is a name
for our doing: both 'what' we do . . . and that which we effect, the act
and its consequences."[32]

Butler's articulation returns us immediately to the "simultaneity" of
speaking and being that Swenson wrote of in her journal at midcareer,
and to the sometimes paradoxical ways in which Swenson accounted
for linguistic agency. Throughout her life Swenson treated poetic lan-
guage as *alive,* as an organic entity. She referred repeatedly to her
poems as tangible objects, as bodies of energy with lives of their own:
"I think of a poem as a mobile, almost a construct, something you can
look around, that moves, that is concrete. . . . Poetry has to give more
than one aspect, more than one dimension";[33] "I want my poems to be
like three-dimensional objects instead of just words on a page. I want
them to have immediacy, as if you could walk around them, see them
from several aspects, notice many facets."[34] Not only did Swenson
visualize her poems as physical entities, as possessing the ability to
move through time and space, but she also saw poetry as a potentially
transformative source:

> Poetry is used to make maps of that globe, which to the "naked
> eye" appears disk-like and one-dimensional. . . . It then enlarges
> and reveals its surprising topography, becomes a world. And *pass-
> ing around* it, our senses undergo dilation; there is transformation of
> perception by means of this realization of the *round.*[35]

Poetry has the power to *change* us. It asserts itself as a bulk around
which we move, through which we may more clearly sense and under-
stand, by which we uncover the relations that bind us to that which we
may otherwise overlook or even disdain. Swenson's descriptions edge
toward an essentialist view of language, signaling a tendency we've
seen before in her work. But I believe that Swenson's characterizations

articulate a much more subtle and sophisticated understanding, one that always summons and surpasses her desire for an authentic dimension: it is the *productive force* of language—exactly that aspect which underwrites its arbitrary nature—that Swenson sees as alive, organic, literally life-changing. Swenson's descriptions endow language with a fleshy pulse, a throbbing immediacy, but to read this as essentialist is to fall prey to the belief that sensuality is somehow less mediated than language, a view that Swenson's poetry routinely contests.

In the context of writing, to be performative is to approach language as a kind of dramatic process, indeed, a performance that by definition succeeds because of its proximity to some kind of "reality" *and* a simultaneous marking of its made-up nature. It is this double gesture that Swenson aims for in her embodiment of language. Performative theory builds on the belief that *all* language is potentially performative, that it creates realities just as it covers up the process of creation. Swenson's work builds from such a perspective, which may explain in part her brief but intense foray into playwriting. In 1967 (shortly after the aforementioned journal entry was written and "Spectrum Analysis" was published), Swenson completed a one-act play called *The Floor* with support from the Ford Foundation.[36] The play echoes Beckett in its wry parody of human constraints and was given eighteen performances.[37] Two years before the play was finished, Swenson also published what could be read as a companion poem, "To Make a Play," in which she explores explicitly the performative relationship between writing and subjectivity.[38] The second half of the poem begins as follows:

> To make a play
> is to make people,
> to make people do
> what you say . . .
>
> You can make
> people, or you
> can unmake. You
>
> can do or you
> can undo. People
> you make up make up

and make people;

people come to
see—to see
themselves real.
            (*HS*, 106)

The short, repetitive lines dramatize the process of building up and breaking down that the "making" of people, not to mention poems, entails. Likewise, the playfulness of the poem emphasizes the speaker's *performance* as such, as a parodic caricature of itself. Through most of the poem the ability to "make people" belongs almost entirely to the speaker, the person wielding the words, who mocks her astonishing agency just as she revels in it. The poem's momentum comes from the speaker's need to work through this strangely frightening empowerment. And indeed, about half of Swenson's early drafts include the revealing refrain, "It's *as if* you made them . . . *As if* you unmade them" (emphasis added), wherein the *as if*s suggest a degree of discomfort that was processed out of the poem upon its completion.[39] But as the poem ends, this agency proliferates, so that once again, "To make a play / is to make / people," but now to make people who make

themselves; to
make people
make themselves
new. So real.
            (*HS*, 106)

In making a poem about making a play the speaker makes people make themselves *new;* Swenson is literalizing the performative process of living through language, so that we must read the "real" with which the poem ends as both serious and sarcastic.

It is exactly this double edge upon which the performative acts, since the constant, two-way slippage between language and identity is where "new" ways of being are forged. The performative practice must draw from the old in order to "make" something new; in this way it can always only provisionally succeed. Its success depends on an ability to both "echo prior actions" and "break with prior context" so that ordinary language "takes on non-ordinary meaning in order . . . to contest what has become sedimented in and as the ordinary."[40] However, we must be wary of the power of reiteration to subvert *merely* by means of a constant articulation, and thus exposure, of the mechanisms that naturalize behavior. Returning to Swenson's sexual imagery, it is important to recall Butler's caution: "[T]here is no guarantee that exposing the naturalized status of heterosexuality will lead to its subversion. Heterosexuality can augment its hegemony *through* its denaturalization, as when we see denaturalizing parodies that reidealize heterosexual norms *without* calling them into question."[41] This kind of reification through reiteration is exemplified by the unfortunate choice of the front-cover photo by John Brooks on *The Love Poems of May Swenson.* The black-and-white photograph of man and woman in bed, in a traditional about-to-be missionary position, is misleading—not because it suggests a heterosexuality within the poetry that *should* be read as lesbian, but because, in its soft-lit, antiquated glow, it renaturalizes the gendered constructions that Swenson's work calls into question. Obviously a marketing device, as all book covers are, the heterosexual presumption of this design works, however unwittingly, to suture the cracks in the normative terms that the poetry inside creates.

Once beyond the cover, however, we find that it is precisely the performative, self-conscious aspect of Swenson's poetry that enables the re-creation of "alternative modalities of power," an expanded continuum of pleasures and erotic identifications. Within these poems the limits of self/other, active/passive are exposed, reworked, and ruptured. If, as Swenson's poetry asserts, sexualities are always products of the norms by which they are likewise constrained, then sexuality can never be disentangled from power, and power can never be disengaged from sexual pleasure. Thus, Swenson works through, and not around, the terms she attempts to challenge, reshaping them in the process. The means by which sexualities are produced and policed are themselves reconstructed, allowing an expanded realm of desires and pleasures to unfold within her words. Consider, in particular, "Four-Word Lines":

Your eyes are just
like bees, and I
feel like a flower.
Their brown power makes
a breeze go over

my skin. When your
lashes ride down and
rise like brown bees'
legs, your pronged gaze
makes my eyes gauze.
I wish we were
in some shade and
no swarm of other
eyes to know that
I'm a flower breathing
bare, laid open to
your bees' warm stare.
I'd let you wade
in me and seize
with your eager brown
bees' power a sweet
glistening at my core.

(*LP*, 1)

Once again we have a feminized narrator constructed in seeming oppo-
sition to the masculinized look of her companion: the feminine flower
is almost hypnotically "laid open" to the "pronged," piercing "gaze" of
the lover; she is "breathing bare" while he rides, wades, and seizes. Sig-
nificantly, the activity of the bee's eyes is figured within the field of his
*gaze*, a trope that calls to mind the school of psychoanalytic feminist
film studies within which many theories of female subjectivity and
identification have arisen in the last thirty years. Inside this theoretical
forum the cinematic apparatus is often analyzed as essentially sexist by
way of feeding a masculine voyeuristic pleasure. By universalizing the
gaze as masculine and the pleasure of looking as only male, female
spectatorship is rendered extremely problematic, indeed incoherent.[42]

In "Four-Word Lines," however, the binaristic framework of mascu-
line voyeur versus feminine fetish is restructured as the gaze is literally
*given shape* by the narrator's feminized voice. "She" defines the opposi-
tional roles in the first lines of the poem: "Your eyes are just / like bees,
and I / feel like a flower." It is *her* narrative power, her agency as
author, that literally articulates "his" look, that enables it and directs it.
Motivating the progress of consummation within the poem are the nar-
rator's sensuous needs. At once an effect of her own assertiveness and

of his "pronged gaze," her proneness is not an indication of desubjecti-
fication; rather, it marks an active desire, a desire that in turn enables
*his* activity. Objectification becomes simultaneously passive *and* active,
an intensely erotic expression of desire in which power and pleasure
are inseparable. The masculinized eyes are literally subject to the pres-
ence of the flower's proneness for their pleasure, a pleasure that in turn
underscores the *power* of the speaker's passivity. Thus, the assertive
and invitational "I'd let you" of line 18 does not contradict the preced-
ing "I'm a flower breathing / bare, laid open to / your bees' warm
stare." As when Swenson describes female genitals as "carnivora of
Touch" (*LP*, 20), the active/passive, subject/fetish formula of desire is
here twisted out of shape. Lingering at once on either side of the binary
divide, Swenson weaves a web of desire that, like her riddles and
"iconographs," confounds expected answers and positions.

In "One Morning in New Hampshire" sensuality transgresses the
bounds of corporeal sexuality, endowing the natural world with a
questing eroticism that in turn refigures the speaker's own possibilities
of pleasure:

> In the sun's heart we are ripe
> as fruits ourselves, enjoyed
> by lips of wind our burnished slopes.
> All round us dark, rapt
> bumble-eyes of susans are deployed
> as if to suck our honey-hides. Ants nip,
> tasting us all over
> with tickling pincers. We are a landscape
> to daddy-long-legs, whose ovoid
> hub on stilts climbs us like a lover,
> trying our dazzle, our warm sap.
>
> (*N*, 99)

The distinction between the narrator and the narrator's companion is
subsumed within the distinction between the landscape of their bodies
and the explorations of the wild and its creatures. The dialectical rela-
tionship of self/other is reworked into a contiguous "we" whose
desires are not opposed or even symmetrical but, rather, one and the
same. There is an intense pleasure here in the act of *being enjoyed;* the
probing of the ants and spiders does not occur at the expense of the

lovers' desires; rather, they are energized, infused with "dazzle" and "sap" by the ostensible passivity of their pleasure. Erotic satisfaction is no longer confined or orchestrated by the anatomical axis of give/take, self/other, male/female, but polyvalent and simultaneous, continually opening up and branching out.

As naturalized boundaries of pleasure are transgressed, so identity is refigured. Once again we are led to Swenson's focus on the inextricable relationship between sexuality and subjectivity, as in the poem "Untitled."[43]

I will be earth you be the flower

You have found my root you are the rain

I will be boat and you the rower

You rock you toss me you are the sea

How be steady earth and that's now a flood

The root's the oar's afloat where's blown our bud

We will be desert pure salt the seed

Burn radiant sex born scorpion need

[*New and Selected* 139]

The lack of punctuation accentuates the contingency of being, where to *be*—"I will be" / "you be" / "How be"—is redrafted in the shifting nexus of desire. "I" becomes "you" becomes "I" becomes "we," as the poem constructs subjectivity as transitive, always specific but never isolated. The hand-drawn lines throughout the poem underscore further this sense of interweaving: crossing directly between "you" and "me," Swenson's careful scribbles separate self and other while uniting them as well. The lines both meet and diverge from this liminal place among subjectivities, suggesting the importance of the point of contact *between* them, a place further emphasized by the exaggerated spaces between words. By drawing our attention to these boundaries this poem, like many others, insists on the creative, active occupation of limits that are otherwise naturalized as fixed, inert, or invisible. It is perhaps in this vein that we can contextualize Swenson's notorious manipulation of poetic form. By introducing untraditional formats Swenson forces the reader to consider the function that form itself occupies in the production of meaning. As "Untitled" suggests, identity is always a negotiation, always dependent yet ever-specific; to be produced is not to be predetermined.

It is this attention to specificity that marks the material potential of Swenson's work, the actual, fleshy feasibility of the identities within her words. Her poetry challenges the universality of heterosexuality while it stays grounded within the details of sensual experience. Swenson asserts the *reality* of constructed selfhood, affirming that to expose the instability of identity is not at all to argue that identity is therefore less meaningful, powerful, destructive, or pleasurable. On the contrary, the intensely expansive effect of her poetry suggests that to view identity as nonessential is to render it all the more relevant as a site for personal responsibility than can perhaps otherwise be imagined. To consider the constructedness of gender and selfhood is to be ever more conscious of the fine and shifting nuances of lived experience, not to be nonexistent or hopelessly ungrounded. In "A History of Love," Swenson writes:

At last acquainted smoothed by contiguity
sharpened each by opposite tempers we divined
about our nacreous effigies outlined
the soft and mortal other
Under the body's plush a density
awkward ambiguous as bone
Real as our own.

(LP, 36)

It is through the drama of their relationship that the lovers outline their selves, selves not fixed or holistic, but rather "nacreous," as sculpted as "effigies." Although inessential, these selves are nonetheless vulnerable, "soft and mortal." Defined by and through the other—the "Other than self" of the poem's first verse—identity *becomes* "a density," and although selfhood is a result of "their amalgam mingled," it is nevertheless as "Real as our own."

Swenson's insistence on reappropriation is what gives her poetry such a celebratory effect. There is something intensely uplifting about her work, an unsettling courageousness that magnifies the beauty in life while it recreates the lenses through which we've come to view it:

> the youngest nerve and keenest stem
> in secret shade, reach up to meet
> radiance, swell to make radiance;
> as all pouting blossoms do,
> I turn, as earth to its sky, to you.
>
> *(LP,* 72)

Her work insists on the possibility—the necessity—of change *within* the parameters of lived, actual existence, suggesting likewise the futility of efforts that seek new subjectivities outside the confines of the dominant fiction. As she said repeatedly, "I take the literal first before anything else."[44] Swenson makes this clear in "You Are":

> once I thought
> to seek the limits
> of all being
> I believed
> in my own eyes' seeing
> then
> to find pattern purpose aim
> thus forget death
> or forgive it
> . . . . . . . . . .
> now I know
> beginning and end
> are one
> and slay each other
> but their offspring is what *is*
> not was or will be.
>
> *(LP,* 42)

Both dreamer and realist, Swenson saw the world with wonder no less wide-eyed for its assertive lack of innocence. Revealing phallocentrism as rigid but removable, Swenson's plethora of sexual identifications is no longer reducible to something like "false consciousness," in which women are seen as the unsuspecting thus unresisting victims of an impenetrable patriarchy. Quite the contrary: through a provoca-tive—and playful—appropriation of phallic privilege by subject posi-tions construed as its victims, heterosexual representation is exposed as both irresistible and insufficient. The cost of this confrontation is, of course, the admittance of impurities between the sheets. Thus, love will inevitably be "baptized in the cool font of evil" (*LP*, 58), a place in which we are constantly "Open to joy to punishment in equal part" (*LP*, 39).

Perhaps no poem of Swenson's illustrates this more clearly than "Strawberrying," whose speaker asserts at the start, "My hands are murder-red" (*IOW*, 8). A richly decadent poem, "Strawberrying" shows Swenson at her most unsettling, and at her best:

Hunkered in mud between the rows, sun burning
the back of our necks, we grope for, and rip loose
soft nippled heads. If they bleed—too soft—
let them stay. Let them rot in the heat.

(8–9)

Picking strawberries "near the shore," their "Fingers find by feel / the ready fruit in clusters" (8). "Here and there" they discover the "squishy wounds" of "Flesh [that was] perfect / yesterday," "sweet hearts" that were "young and firm before decay" (8).

From the first line to the last, when the speaker, "Red-handed," leaves the field, she is clearly a "marauder" like the blackbird in the opening stanza who, shrieking his "ko-ka-ree," has "left his peck in some juicy cheeks." Aligned in part with the masculinized bird, the speaker of "Strawberrying" indulges excessively and forcibly in the feminized, sexualized crop of fruit. Groping, probing hands "rumple" under "rough-veined" leaves to find fruit so soft it might bleed at one's touch. And though such vulnerability is, in the end, left alone, it is not out of the speaker's sympathy or kindness: no longer "young and firm," these untouchables will only "rot in the heat." Their fate is that of the "clump of heart-shapes / once red, now spider-spit gray, intact but empty, / still attached to their dead stems" (9) that determine the sated speaker's decision to "rise and stretch," and to leave—but not before eating "one more big ripe lopped / head" (9). Sexual desire, imagined as the ravaging of ready fruit, is aggressive and sensuous, an echo of Whitman's "red marauder" whose "Blind loving wrestling touch, sheath'd hooded [and] sharp-tooth'd" overwhelms his impassioned speaker: "Unclench your floodgates, you are too much for me."[45]

Like Whitman, Swenson treads the fine line between danger and desire; the speaker of "Strawberrying" knows she's guilty, but for what, or by whom, we are never to know for sure. Is guilt intrinsically wed to erotic satisfaction within the terms of Swenson's poetic? Perhaps, but only insofar as innocence begs corruption. For, as we are told, a "crop this thick begs for plunder. Ripeness / wants to be ravished, as udders of cows when hard, / the blue-veined bags distended, ache to be stripped" (*IOW*, 8). Like the prone flower or the willowy poet, sexual ripeness should not be left "to rot in the heat"—it *wants* to be consumed. So while the speaker shares the blackbird's intrusive position, she also shares that of the children in the poem who, despite their mother's warnings against overindulgence, are "Mesmerized / by the largesse," and "squat and pull / and pick handfuls of rich scarlets, half / for the baskets, half for avid mouths," until "whole faces are stained" (8). Ostensibly exemplars of innocence, the berry-picking children are marked indelibly with the juices of sexual gorging. Simultaneously ripeness and ravishers, the children provide the site in the poem through which innocence and corruption blend. In turn, the speaker's desire and ensuing pleasure cannot be disentangled entirely from the children's, the blackbird's, or the strawberries', though each clearly occupies a different position within the poem. Thus, forging new sites for subjectivity and sexuality will always be a "dangerous game of change" (*LP*, 36). It is the effusive promise of Swenson's poetry, however, that profound rewards can only come from such risks.

Typically, "Strawberrying" does not offer us revelations or guidelines. Instead, it reminds us of what we already know, but are often unwilling to admit. Like the three poets who make up this project, this poem disrupts conventional categories, and perhaps this is why it was not included in *The Love Poems of May Swenson*. But love the poem certainly celebrates, in all its rawness, pain, urgency, and joy—a love, as Swenson once put it, "based on a craving to get through the curtains of things as they *appear*, to things as they *are*, and then into the larger, wilder space of things as they *are becoming*."[46] Indeed, *the wild space of becoming . . .* untenable yet immediate, disorienting yet intimate; it is the province of the poets who have brought this book into being. To explore insatiably the nature of self is to be consumed by connections both infinitesimal and immense: the undulations of "ink— / bespattered jelly-fish"; images of otherness that make "us all just one"; the palpable "ache" of sexual appetite. As the arc of my narrative has meant to suggest, self-restraint enables an understanding of identity as inextricable from the mutable and sometimes oppressive contexts in which we live. Hence, what began here as a probing of strategic reserve concludes in the grip of desire. The feminist goal of self-empowerment, then, is less a quest for liberation than a call to relationship at its most elemental; as Moore, Bishop, and Swenson insist, our capacity to fully *be* is dependent, paradoxically, upon confronting the contingencies that make us real. In the wake of autonomy, self-realization demands no less.

# Notes

INTRODUCTION

1. Marianne Moore, in a speech delivered at Barnard College in 1955, quoted in Charles Molesworth, *Marianne Moore: A Literary Life* (New York: Atheneum, 1990), 365.

2. See, for instance, the following letters by Moore, both of which are reproduced in *SL*, 178 and 45–46, respectively: letter to Winifred Bryher, August 31, 1921, and letter to family, April 5, 1908. See also Moore's letter home dated February 14, 1909, MMC (photocopy, Bryn Mawr, Excerpts).

3. Alicia Ostriker, *Stealing the Language: Emergence of Women's Poetry in America* (Boston: Beacon Press, 1986), 11. Feminist critics who have advocated an alternative female tradition in poetry include, in addition to Ostriker, Paula Bennett, *My Life a Loaded Gun: Female Creativity and Feminist Poetics* (Boston: Beacon Press, 1986); Joanne Feit Diehl, *Women Poets and the American Sublime* (Bloomington: Indiana University Press 1990) and *Elizabeth Bishop and Marianne Moore: The Psychodynamics of Female Creativity* (Princeton, N.J.: Princeton University Press, 1993); Sandra Gilbert and Susan Gubar, *No Man's Land: The Place of the Woman Writer in the Twentieth Century*, 3 vols. (New Haven: Yale University Press, 1988–94); Margaret Homans, *Bearing the Word: Language and Experience in Nineteenth Century Women's Writing* (Chicago: University of Chicago Press, 1968) and *Women Writers and Poetic Identity: Dorothy Wordsworth, Emily Bronte, and Emily Dickinson* (Princeton, N.J.: Princeton University Press, 1980); Suzanne Juhasz, *Naked and Fiery Forms: Modern American Poetry by Women* (New York: Harper and Row, 1976); and Cheryl Walker, *The Nightingale's Burden: Women Poets and American Culture before 1900* (Bloomington: Indiana University Press, 1982) and *Masks Outrageous and Austere: Culture, Psyche, and Persona in Modern American Women Poets* (Bloomington: Indiana University Press, 1991).

4. Bennett, *My Life a Loaded Gun*, 5.

5. Ostriker, *Stealing the Language*, 11.

6. Bennett, *My Life a Loaded Gun*, 11.

7. See Bonnie Costello, *Marianne Moore: Imaginary Possessions* (Cambridge: Harvard University Press, 1981); and Cristanne Miller, *Marianne Moore: Questions of Authority* (Cambridge: Harvard University Press, 1995). Other critics who have focused (with varying conclusions) on the strategic or antiessentialist elements of Moore's or Bishop's poetic reserve include Louis Cuculla, "Trompe L'Oeil: Elizabeth Bishop's Radical 'I,'" *Texas Studies in Literature and Language* 30, no. 2 (1988): 246–71; C. K. Doreski, *Elizabeth Bishop: The Restraints of Language* (Oxford: Oxford University Press, 1993); Celeste Goodridge, *Hints*

*and Disguises: Marianne Moore and Her Contemporaries* (Iowa City: University of Iowa Press, 1986); Langdon Hammer, "The New Elizabeth Bishop," *Yale Review* 82, no. 1 (1994): 135–49; James Longenbach, *Modern Poetry after Modernism* (Oxford: Oxford University Press, 1997), chaps. 1 and 2; Taffy Martin, *Marianne Moore: Subversive Modernist* (Austin: University of Texas Press, 1986); Jeredith Merrin, *An Enabling Humility: Marianne Moore, Elizabeth Bishop, and the Uses of Tradition* (New Brunswick, N.J.: Rutgers University Press, 1990); and Robert Dale Parker, *The Unbeliever: The Poetry of Elizabeth Bishop* (Urbana: University of Illinois Press, 1988).

8. Cristanne Miller's wonderful book on Moore has been indispensable to my project, affirming and further illuminating what I see to be the direct relationship between Moore's restraint and her feminist poetic. Nevertheless, our projects do differ in significant ways. For instance, while my analysis of Moore is part of a larger exploration of the ways in which feminist reading practices have shaped our understanding of the poetics of self, Miller's study focuses on the often oppositional agency that underpins Moore's poetry by situating it within specific historical, cultural, and familial influences. Of course, these approaches are overlapping and complimentary, mirroring our mutual conviction that feminist poetry often employs a destabilized sense of self. In the end, the distance between our projects is largely a matter of emphasis. As Miller puts it, "[W]hile I recognize that authority inheres both in a writer's felt and enacted entitlement to speak and in the changing receptions of that writer's work through successive generations, I focus on the former" (vii); in comparison, my book may be said to focus on the latter.

9. Lynn Keller and Cristanne Miller, eds., *Feminist Measures: Soundings in Poetry and Theory* (Ann Arbor: University of Michigan Press, 1994).

10. Longenbach, *Modern Poetry after Modernism*, 6.

11. "Stillborn" is Lombardi's term, *Elizabeth Bishop: The Geography of Gender*, 6, "Sapphic" Grace Schulman's, in "Life's Miracle: The Poetry of May Swenson," *American Poetry Review*, September–October 1994, 10.

12. Silverman's term "dominant fiction" appears in *Male Subjectivity at the Margins* (New York: Routledge, 1992). I draw most heavily, however, from her more recent book, *The Threshold of the Visible World* (New York: Routledge, 1996). Judith Butler's books have been indispensable to this study: *Gender Trouble: Feminism and the Subversion of Identity* (New York: Routledge, 1990), *Bodies That Matter: On the Discursive Limits of Sex* (New York: Routledge, 1993), and *Excitable Speech: A Politics of the Performative* (New York: Routledge, 1997).

13. Donna Haraway, *Simians, Cyborgs, and Women: The Reinvention of Nature* (New York: Routledge, 1991).

14. See Martin, *Marianne Moore*. For instance, in her *Naked and Fiery Forms*, Suzanne Juhasz claims, "When [Moore] writes about 'the particular strength' that chastity confers, she writes from direct experience" (4). More recently, in *Women Poets and the American Sublime*, Joanne Feit Diehl argues that Moore's poetry "reinforces a disengagement of affect from voice. Moore's poetry displays the absence of eros and its attending desires" (46), while Jan Clausen

describes Moore's poems as having the "appearance of neutered chastity." See Jan Clausen, "Lowell, Teasdale, Wylie, Millay, and Bogan," in *The Columbia History of American Poets,* ed. Jay Parini and Brett C. Millier (New York: Columbia University Press, 1993), 204.

15. Louise Bogan, *Achievement in American Poetry, 1900–1950* (Chicago: Henry Regnery, 1951), 102.

16. "'The Work!' A Conversation with Elizabeth Bishop," interview by George Starbuck, in *Elizabeth Bishop and Her Art,* ed. Lloyd Schwartz and Sybil Estes (Ann Arbor: University of Michigan Press, 1983), 327.

17. For example, in the only full-scale biography of Moore, published in 1990, Charles Molesworth writes that Moore's work is "an intimate modernism, almost precious, but redeemed from mere precocity by great skill and moral balance" (*Marianne Moore,* 95). To his credit Molesworth does give insight into Moore's persona that directly challenges this "myth," particularly with regard to her early suffrage activities. See also Costello, *Marianne Moore;* Merrin, *An Enabling Humility;* Goodridge, *Hints and Disguises;* Miller, *Marianne Moore;* and Martin, *Marianne Moore.*

18. Miller, *Marianne Moore,* 22.

19. Adrienne Rich, *Blood, Bread, and Poetry: Selected Prose, 1979–1985* (New York: Norton, 1986), 125.

20. Critics who claim Bishop's feminism by way of an autobiographical emphasis include Lorrie Goldensohn, *Elizabeth Bishop: The Biography of a Poetry* (New York: Columbia University Press, 1992); Marilyn May Lombardi, "Another Way of Seeing," in *Elizabeth Bishop: The Geography of Gender,* ed. Lombardi (Charlottesville: University of Virginia Press, 1993); and Merrin, *An Enabling Humility.* Many critics assert an autobiographical evolution in Bishop's poetry without explicitly linking this evolution to a feminist consciousness. See David Kalstone, *Becoming a Poet: Elizabeth Bishop with Marianne Moore and Robert Lowell,* ed. Robert Hemenway (New York: Farrar, Straus and Giroux, 1989); Brett C. Millier, *Elizabeth Bishop: Life and the Memory of It* (Berkeley: University of California Press, 1993); and Thomas Travisano, *Elizabeth Bishop: Her Artistic Development* (Charlottesville: University Press of Virginia, 1988).

21. My phrasing here reflects my debt to Langdon Hammer's brief but incisive rebuke of recent feminist readings that position Bishop as a primarily autobiographical poet ("The New Elizabeth Bishop").

22. The exceptions are few but notable: John Hollander, *The Work of Poetry* (New York: Columbia University Press, 1997), 288–98; Richard Howard, "May Swenson: 'Turned Back to the Wild by Love,'" in *Alone with America: Essays on the Art of Poetry in the United States Since 1950* (New York: Atheneum, 1969), 517; Alicia Ostriker, "The Nerves of a Midwife: Contemporary American Women's Poetry," *Parnassus* 6 (fall–winter 1977): 69–87, and "May Swenson and the Shapes of Speculation," *American Poetry Review,* March–April 1978, 35–38, reprinted in Ostriker's *Writing Like a Woman* (Ann Arbor: University of Michigan Press, 1982), 86–101; Sue Russell, "A Mysterious and Lavish Power: How

Things Continue to Take Place in the Work of May Swenson," *Kenyon Review* 16, no. 3 (1994): 128–39; Schulman, "Life's Miracle"; and Ann Stanford, "May Swenson: The Art of Perceiving," *Southern Review* 5 (winter 1969): 58–75.

### CHAPTER 1

1. Betsy Erkkila, *The Wicked Sisters: Women Poets, Literary History, and Discord* (Oxford: Oxford University Press, 1992), 104.

2. May Swenson, "A Matter of Diction," in *A Festschrift for Marianne Moore's Seventy Seventh Birthday by Various Hands,* ed. Tambimuttu (New York: Tambimuttu and Mass, 1964), 45.

3. Letter from Mrs. Mary Warner Moore to Marianne Moore, January 7, 1908, MMC, VI.14.02. Throughout this chapter all bracketed citations of Moore's archival materials will refer to the Rosenbach's collection.

4. Letter from Mary Warner Moore to John Warner Moore, October 1, 1915, MMC, VI.21.11.

5. Andrew Kappel argues that Moore's poetic is almost completely determined by her religious devotion, noting that according to Calvinist thought, to be self-centered is a grave sin. He claims that because of this, Moore "does not share with her contemporaries any veiled self-expressive—in the long-run autobiographical—ambitions" ("Notes on the Presbyterian Poetry of Marianne Moore," in *Marianne Moore: Woman and Poet,* ed. Patricia Willis [Orono, Maine: National Poetry Foundation, 1990], 43). Several other critics, such as Charles Molesworth, Cristanne Miller, and Taffy Martin, have contested Kappel's extremism. I would venture that Moore does indeed harbor self-expressive ambitions, but perhaps not self-referential ones.

6. Letter home from Moore, January 21, 1906 (photocopy, Family Correspondence, Bryn Mawr, 1906). Throughout this chapter I will maintain the practice of leaving Moore's often unpunctuated or grammatically faulty correspondence uncorrected, for I believe that the excited, rushed tenor of her writing in these letters is otherwise somewhat sacrificed. Although Moore is notorious for the grammatical fastidiousness of her published work, it is important to note that her private correspondence with her family reveals a consistent disregard for such exactitude.

7. Letter home from Moore, February 22, 1906 (photocopy, Bryn Mawr, Family Correspondence, 1906).

8. Letter home from Moore, February 14, 1909 (photocopy, Bryn Mawr, Excerpts).

9. Elizabeth Bishop, trans., *The Diary of "Helena Morley,"* by Alice (Dayrell) Brant (New York: Farrar, Straus, & Giroux, 1957). In a review of this text, Marianne Moore wrote: "The personality of Helena Morley would be hard to match. Besides an ardor synonymous with affection, she 'steps in and out of superstition' as Miss Bishop says, 'Reason, belief and disbelief, without much adolescent worrying. She would never for a moment doubt that the church is a good thing.' 'I admire good and holy people,' she says 'but I can't possibly stop being the way I am.' A main part of being the way she was, was compassion."

See Marianne Moore, "Senhora Helena," in Schwartz and Estes, *Elizabeth Bishop and Her Art*, 195.

10. Miller, *Marianne Moore*, 32.

11. Letter home from Moore, February 20, 1908, MMC, VI.14.03.

12. Bonnie Costello, "The Feminine Language of Marianne Moore," in *Women and Language in Literature and Society*, ed. Ruth Borker, Nelly Furman, and Sally McConnell-Ginnet (New York: Praeger, 1980), 222–38. In both this essay and her book on Moore, Costello provides what remains the most illuminating and subtle reading of Moore's complicated relationship to the lyric "I." Nevertheless, Martin has noted that Costello does seem to encourage the myth of Moore as modest and retiring, that Costello's analysis of this technique "removes any hint of passion and rebellion from Moore's creativity" (Martin, *Marianne Moore*, 121). Although I agree in part with Martin's commentary, I also believe that Costello's overall analysis of Moore's technique implies the rebellious nature that Martin sees here as circumscribed.

13. Costello, "Feminine Language of Moore," 227.

14. Letter from Moore to T. S. Eliot, quoted in Goodridge, *Hints and Disguises*, 105. Other critics in addition to Costello and Molesworth who have argued that Moore's "armoring" is a means of exploration, not withdrawal, are Miller, *Marianne Moore*; Martin, *Marianne Moore*; Margaret Holley, *The Poetry of Marianne Moore: A Study in Voice and Value* (Cambridge: Cambridge University Press, 1987), especially chap. 4; and Laurence Stapleton, *Marianne Moore: The Poet's Advance* (Princeton, N.J.: Princeton University Press, 1978).

15. Richard Howard, "Marianne Moore and the Monkey Business of Modernism," in *Marianne Moore: The Art of a Modernist*, ed. Joseph Parisi (Ann Arbor: University of Michigan Press, 1990), 3.

16. Michael Levenson, *A Genealogy of Modernism: A Study of English Literary Doctrine, 1908–1922* (Cambridge: Cambridge University Press, 1984). See especially chapters 1 and 2.

17. William Carlos Williams, quoted in Miller, *Marianne Moore*, 16.

18. Gilbert and Gubar, *No Man's Land*, vol. 3.

19. See Goodridge, *Hints and Disguises*.

20. Holley, *Poetry of Marianne Moore*, 96.

21. "He Made This Screen," *Egoist* 3 (August 1916): 118–19 and *Poems*, 9. Because several of Moore's earlier collections are now out of print, I will draw when possible from the versions of Moore's poems in *The Complete Poems of Marianne Moore*, so that readers may have easy access to the verses from which I am working. However, given Moore's lifelong devotion to (sometimes extreme) revisions, and the fact that many (sixty-nine) of her published poems are not included in *The Complete Poems*, I often will be reading from earlier collections, especially her first book, *Poems*, and her second, *Observations*. When a poem appears in both an early collection and *The Complete Poems*, I will be working from the first version unless otherwise noted, because of my focus on her early years (1907–25). At such times, I often will give the page number for *The Complete Poems* version as well.

22. The draft of this poem appears in a letter from Moore to her family, December 12, 1908, about a month before it first appeared in a revised form in Bryn Mawr's *Tipyn O'Bob*, January 1909, 2–3. The title of the first section, "To An Artificer," never appeared in print (photocopy, Bryn Mawr, Uncollected Poems). The poem is published in *SL*, 52–53.

23. John Ashbery, "The Painter," in *Selected Poems* (New York: Penguin, 1985), 20.

24. Martin, *Marianne Moore*, 4.

25. T. S. Eliot, "Introduction to Selected Poems," in Marianne Moore, *Selected Poems* (New York: Macmillan, 1935), vii–xiv, reprinted in *Marianne Moore: A Collection of Critical Essays*, ed. Charles Tomlinson (Englewood Cliffs, N.J.: Prentice-Hall, 1969), 60–65; Elizabeth Bishop, "A Memoir of Marianne Moore: Efforts of Affection," in *Prose*, 121–58; Jeanne Garrigue, *Marianne Moore*, University of Minnesota Pamphlets on American Writers, no. 50 (Minneapolis: University of Minneapolis Press, 1965), 8. For a detailed analysis of the influence of the visual arts on Moore's work, see Linda Leavell, *Marianne Moore and the Visual Arts: Prismatic Color* (Oklahoma: Oklahoma University Press, 1995). For a comparison of the feminisms of O'Keefe and Moore, see Leavell, "Marianne Moore and Georgia O'Keefe: 'The Feelings of a Mother—a Woman or a Cat,'" in Willis, *Marianne Moore*, 297–319.

26. Miller, *Marianne Moore*, 47.

27. "The Art of Poetry: Marianne Moore," interview by Donald Hall, in Tomlinson, *Marianne Moore*, 20–45.

28. See Pound's "The Serious Artist," in *Literary Essays*, ed. T. S. Eliot (New York: New Directions, 1954), 41–57, and Eliot's "Tradition and the Individual Talent," in *The Sacred Wood* (New York: Methuen/Routledge, Chapman and Hall, 1960), 37–44.

29. Wallace Stevens, "About One of Marianne Moore's Poems," *Quarterly Review of Literature* 2, no. 4 (1948): 145.

30. Donna Haraway, "Situated Knowledges: The Science Question in Feminism and the Privilege of Partial Perspective," in *Simians, Cyborgs, and Women*, 191 and 195, respectively.

31. Haraway, "Simians, Cyborgs, & Women," 190.

32. Haraway, "Simians, Cyborgs, & Women," 193.

33. Christopher J. Knight, "Marianne Moore: Appreciating Both the Trope of the Imagination and Wallace Stevens' Handling of the Same," in Willis, *Marianne Moore*, 426.

34. Haraway, *Simians, Cyborgs, & Women*, 193.

35. Haraway, *Simians, Cyborgs, & Women*, 196.

36. Haraway, *Simians, Cyborgs, & Women*, 196.

37. "The Fish" (*Poems*, 14–15). I read from this version rather than the slightly revised *CP* version (32) because the fluid stanzaic form of the earlier draft more clearly adduces the connection between poem and sea. First published in the *Egoist* 5 (August 1918): 95.

38. See Michel Foucault's "Repressive Hypothesis," in *The History of Sexuality*, vol. 1, *An Introduction* (New York: Vintage Books, 1980), part 2.

39. Quoted in Tambimuttu, *Festschrift for Moore's Birthday*, 32.

40. At the age of twelve, Moore announced that she had "a new riddle" in a letter to the Shoemakers, family friends of the Moore's. It went like this: "A knight started out for London, from Liverpool; he had colic; when and where?" The answer is "In the middle of the knight." Letter from Moore to Ira and Mary Shoemaker, November 15, 1899 (photocopy, Bryn Mawr, Excerpts).

41. Goodridge, *Hints and Disguises*, 92.

42. Miller, *Marianne Moore*, 38. Martin gives an excellent interpretation of Moore's love of challenge as it appears in her poetry, suggesting that "Moore's poems frequently glorify passionate intensity and seek out chaos and danger" (*Marianne Moore*, 7); see especially chap. 1. Martin also invokes Lacan's mirror stage to show that Moore resisted wholeness in favor of fragmentation; see chapter 3.

43. Marianne Moore, "In the Days of Prismatic Color," in *O*, 49. In addition to a few minor revisions in form, this earlier version differs from the final one (*CP*, 41) in one word only: "fineness" in line 3 is later changed to "refinement." This poem was first published in the *Lantern* 27 (1919): 35.

44. Charles Baudelaire, "Any Where Out of This World," trans. unknown, copied from *Vanity Fair*, March 16, 1916, 54, into Moore's Notebook 1250/2, 1916–21, MMC, VI.01.02. While the original version of the poem is written in French, Baudelaire culled his English title from a poem he translated by Thomas Hoods in 1865, "Bridge of Sighs." An English translation of "Any Where Out of This World" and this explanatory note can be found in *Charles Baudelaire: The Prose Poems and La Fan Farlow*, ed. and trans. Rosemary Lloyd (Oxford: Oxford University Press, 1991), 126.

45. Miller, *Marianne Moore*, 82.

46. Letter home from Moore, January 17, 1906 (photocopy, Bryn Mawr, Family Correspondence, 1906).

47. Haraway, *Simians, Cyborgs, and Women*, 151, 181. See chapter 8, "A Cyborg Manifesto: Science, Technology, and Socialist-Feminism in the Late Twentieth-Century," 149–81.

48. Haraway, *Simians, Cyborgs, and Women*, 151. Holley makes a similar observation about Moore's work:

> [T]he literature of material actuality either senses the world by remaining in some sense secondary and outside of things in an attempt to reproduce and represent the world, or it repudiates that imitative status in order to take its own primary place as an object in the world like any other with its own structure and texts. This either/or, however, is actually the logical clarification of both/and. We make the distinction in order to see more clearly the multiple facets of verbal art, just as we divide it up into speech in order to amplify its heard and its seen virtues, its evanescence and its derivation. Likewise we divide the inside from the outside of the poem, the signifier from the signified, the text from the world. (*Poetry of Marianne Moore*, 177)

49. "Black Earth," later titled "Melancthon" (*Poems*, 10–11). First published in the *Egoist* 5 (spring 1918): 55–56, and later in *O*, 45.

50. Martin, *Marianne Moore*, 19.

51. In her analysis of "Black Earth," Miller turns to Hortense Spillers's read-ing of the slave's body as "primary narrative," a body that is historically inscribed but unmetaphorically (actually) lived:

> [Unlike] Spiller's essay, which argues for the acknowledgment of the cru-cial experience of (black) flesh, Moore repeatedly tests the relation of flesh to metaphorical body to soul, thereby repeatedly erasing then revivifying the particulars of the flesh which determine and live its experience. In their utterly different formats, both conclude that the "I" who acts with "open[ness]" can do so only by maintaining (in Moore's words) external and internal power and "poise"; for both there is no such thing as freedom that is only of the soul, or in the realm of interpretation. (*Marianne Moore*, 146)

Miller offers the most thorough reading of Moore's poetic treatment of race that exists to date. She believes that "while in her personal life gender may be the most decisive factor in Moore's attempts to redefine relationships of power, gender is not the focus of Moore's most important or most frequent discussion of prejudice or assumed inequality, particularly as that discussion affects ques-tions of subject positioning, truth claims, perspective, and history." Rather, Moore addresses these issues most thoroughly in poems concerning race and nationality (128). See chapter 5.

52. Butler, *Gender Trouble*, 134.

53. Butler, *Gender Trouble*, 136.

54. Margueritte Young approaches this characteristic of Moore's poetry when she writes that Moore "speaks in quick, enigmatic sentences which trip away the flesh of thought and leave the bones bare and shining, so that sud-denly you feel that you are seeing into the secret heart of things. You are mis-taken, however, for soon you realize a further complexity—there is no secret heart, no simple solution but another problem, fastidious and strange" ("An Afternoon with Marianne Moore," in Tambimuttu, *Festschrift for Moore's Birth-day*, 64).

55. Though no gendered pronouns are used in this poem to denote its fig-ure's sex, Mary Warner Moore wrote a letter to Mary Shoemaker on April 21, 1925, in which she briefly described the part of "the lady's" hair in "Those Var-ious Scalpels." I thank Dr. Evelyn Feldman for drawing my attention to this let-ter (a portion of which I read transcribed from Feldman's own notes). For this reason, along with what I consider to be Moore's appropriation of the Renais-sance convention in which a female beloved is named through the itemization of her body parts, I take the figure of this poem to be a woman. I have chosen to work from the *Poems* (7) version of "Scalpels" because the original wording of the phrase "tissues of destiny" (penultimate line of the poem) underlines my reading more clearly than does the revised "components of destiny" (*CP*, 51–52).

56. Holley, *Poetry of Marianne Moore*, 33.

57. Jeanne Heuving, *Omissions Are Not Accidents: Gender in the Art of Mari-anne Moore* (Detroit: Wayne State University Press, 1992), 38.

58. Butler, *Bodies That Matter*, 1.

59. Butler, *Bodies That Matter*, 1.

### CHAPTER 2

1. Cristanne Miller and Charles Molesworth provide the most detailed accounts to date of Moore's involvement with suffrage. See Molesworth, *Marianne Moore*, chaps. 2, 3, and 4, and Miller, *Marianne Moore*, chap. 4.

2. The following books explore in detail the relationship between Bishop and Moore and, in doing so, chart different tensions that fed their complicated friendship over the years: Kalstone, *Becoming a Poet*; Erkkila, *The Wicked Sisters*; and Diehl, *Women Poets*.

3. Schwartz and Estes, *Elizabeth Bishop and Her Art*, 327.

4. See, for example, Kalstone, *Becoming a Poet*; Erkkila, *The Wicked Sisters*, chap. 4; Goldensohn, *Elizabeth Bishop*, preface, plus chaps. 3 and 7; Parker, *The Unbeliever*, chap. 4; and Travisano, *Elizabeth Bishop*, chap. 3.

5. Parker, *The Unbeliever*.

6. Letter from Bishop to Moore, October 24, 1954, MMC, V.05.04. Published in Kalstone, *Becoming a Poet*, 4.

7. This quotation is drawn from an interview with Bishop by Elizabeth Spires, "The Art of Poetry XXVII: Elizabeth Bishop," *Paris Review* 22 (1981): 57–83. The full passage reads as follows: "I think no matter how modest you think you feel or how minor you think you are, there must be an awful core of ego somewhere for you to set yourself up to write poetry. I've never *felt* it, but it must be there" (79).

8. Elizabeth Bishop, "A Sentimental Tribute," *Bryn Mawr Alumnae Bulletin*, spring 1962, 3.

9. Elizabeth Bishop, "As We Like It," special issue of *Quarterly Review of Literature* on Marianne Moore, 4, no. 2 (1948): 129–35.

10. T. S. Eliot, *The Sacred Wood* (New York: Methuen, 1920), 52–53.

11. Bishop, "As We Like It," 134.

12. Letter from Moore to Bishop, September 5, 1943, MMC, Va.01.05.

13. Bonnie Costello, "Marianne Moore and Elizabeth Bishop: Friendship and Influence," *Twentieth Century Literature* 30 (1984): 130.

14. Costello, "Moore and Bishop," 133.

15. This quotation comes from the following passage in Bishop's "Efforts of Affection":

> [Moore] once remarked, after a visit to her brother and his family, that the state of being married and having children had one enormous advantage: "One never has to worry about whether one is doing the right thing or not. There isn't time. One is always having to go to market or drive the children somewhere. There is isn't time to wonder, 'Is this *right* or isn't it?'" (*Prose*, 154)

16. Letter home from Moore, February 26, 1908, MMC, VI.14.03.

17. Kalstone, *Becoming a Poet*, 101.

18. Lynn Keller, "Words Worth a Thousand Postcards: The Bishop/Moore Correspondence," *American Literature* 55, no. 3 (1983): 405–29.

19. David Kalstone and David Bromwich offer two different, though equally thoughtful, interpretations of the "Roosters" exchange. See Kalstone, *Becoming a Poet*, 76–106; and Bromwich, "That Weapon, Self-Protectiveness," in Parisi, *Marianne Moore*, 67–80.

20. Moore's revision of Bishop's "Roosters," titled "The Cock," was enclosed in a letter from Moore to Bishop dated October 16, 1940, MMC, V.05.02. Moore's version is reprinted in its entirety in the appendix to Kalstone's *Becoming a Poet*, 265–69. All subsequent quotations of Moore's side of the "Roosters" correspondence are taken from this letter unless otherwise noted.

21. Kalstone, *Becoming a Poet*, 83.

22. Letter from Bishop to Moore in response to Moore's critique of "Roosters," October 17, 1940, MMC, V.05.02. Published in *OA*, 96. All subsequent quotations from Bishop's side of the "Roosters" correspondence are taken from this letter.

23. Kalstone, *Becoming a Poet*, 81.

24. Bromwich, "That Weapon, Self-Protectiveness," 76.

25. Herbert G. May and Bruce M. Metzger, eds., *The New Oxford Annotated Bible* (Oxford: Oxford University Press, 1973), Matt. 26:61–72.

26. Kalstone, *Becoming a Poet*, 95; emphasis added.

CHAPTER 3

1. Adrienne Rich was the first feminist to offer a revised reading of Bishop along these lines. Commenting in 1982 on her earlier view of the poet as "diffuse, elusive," and "often cryptic," Rich explained that she had "not then connected the themes of outsiderhood and marginality in her work," and that "given the times and customs of the 1940s and 1950s, Bishop's work now seems to me remarkably honest and courageous." See "The Eye of the Outsider," *Boston Review* (1982), 15. For a sampling of more recent feminist readings of Bishop, see Victoria Harrison, *Elizabeth Bishop's Poetics of Intimacy* (Cambridge: Cambridge University Press, 1993); Goldensohn, *Elizabeth Bishop*; and Lombardi, *Elizabeth Bishop*, (1993). For a diverse sampling of texts that emphasize an autobiographical tendency in Bishop's poetry, see Kalstone, *Becoming a Poet*; Goldensohn, *Elizabeth Bishop*; Travisano, *Elizabeth Bishop*; and Lombardi, "Another Way of Seeing."

2. Rich, *Blood, Bread, and Poetry*, 16.

3. Doreski, *Elizabeth Bishop*, 122.

4. Silverman, *Threshold*, 2.

5. This tension in Bishop's work is what Helen Vendler describes as the struggle between the strange and the domestic. See Helen Vendler, "Domestication, Domesticity, and the Otherwordly," in Schwartz and Estes, *Elizabeth Bishop and Her Art*, 32–48. It is also what Bonnie Costello interprets as the "grotesque" in Bishop, a poetic that works to shock, but not repulse her readers, as it "offers a challenge to fixed ways of associating beauty and nature" (*Elizabeth Bishop: Questions of Mastery* [Cambridge: Harvard University Press, 1991], 74).

6. Elizabeth Bishop, quoted in Anne Stevenson, *Elizabeth Bishop* (New York: Twayne, 1966), 66.

7. W. B. Yeats, "Ego Dominus Tuus," in *The Collected Poems of W. B. Yeats*, ed. Richard J. Finneran (New York: Macmillan, 1989), 161.

8. Elizabeth Bishop, *North & South* (Boston: Houghton Mifflin, 1946).

9. Silverman, *Threshold*, 180–81.

10. Jacques Lacan, "The Mirror Stage as Formative of the Function of the 'I' as Revealed in Psychoanalytic Experience," in *Ecrits: A Selection*, trans. Alan Sheridan (New York: Norton, 1977), 3.

11. Silverman, *Threshold*, 11. For an account of the ways in which the corporeal informs Bishop's poetic that differs from my own, see Marilyn May Lombardi, *The Body and the Song: Elizabeth Bishop's Poetics* (Carbondale: Southern Illinois University Press, 1995).

12. Alfred Tennyson, "The Lady of Shalott," in *A Collection of Poems by Alfred Tennyson*, ed. Christopher Ricks (Garden City, N.Y.: Doubleday, 1972), 90.

13. Silverman, *Threshold*, 10–11.

14. Vassar Special Collections, Elizabeth Bishop Papers, Box 72A, Folder 72A.1.

15. Costello, *Elizabeth Bishop*, 30.

16. Silverman, *Threshold*, 17.

17. Margaret Dickie, "Race and Class in Elizabeth Bishop's Poetry," *Yearbook of English Studies* 24 (1994): 48. I am indebted to Dickie for her unconventional approach to Bishop's reticence: "Bishop has seemed to critics extremely reserved and personally reticent; but her poetic interests in people that are distanced from her by class or race would appear to suggest that she was much more receptive to others, more openly involved with them, than she has appeared to be" (57–58). Moreover, my focus on the intersection of self and other in Bishop's poetry builds upon Dickie's careful consideration of the same: "On the one hand, in writing about an artist so different from herself than Jeronimo, [Bishop] was released from self-restraint into fuller form and a more open engagement with the subject. On the other hand, such a release and the habit of writing so often about people foreign to her made her afraid of losing her own identity in theirs, a fear that she both courted and held off. She needed to speak through another voice in order to hear the full ranges of her own voice, and yet she was aware of how hazardous that indirection could be" (57).

18. Kalstone, *Becoming a Poet*, 199.

19. Silverman, *Threshold*, 184.

20. Silverman, *Threshold*, 184.

21. Bonnie Costello has noted that Bishop may have identified herself with the visitor in this poem. In notes from this period Bishop wrote, "'Lying on my bed in the dark. I can look across into the bedroom of the people whose backyard adjoins ours. The blinds are up and the light bulb hanging over the double bed must be an *80 watt*, the room is so bright'" (*Elizabeth Bishop*, 71).

22. Silverman, *Threshold*, 95.

23. Costello, *Elizabeth Bishop*, 72.

24. Elizabeth Bishop, *Questions of Travel* (New York: Farrar, Straus and Giroux, 1965).

25. Vassar Special Collections, Elizabeth Bishop Papers, Box 57, Folder 57.8, and Bishop's 1955–56 notebook, Box 73, Folder 73.2.

26. Drawing on the work of Gayatri Spivak and Clifford Geertz, Victoria Harrison in *Elizabeth Bishop's Poetics of Intimacy*, chapters 5 and 6, offers an interesting reading of the ways in which Bishop's poetry identifies with the "subaltern" subject position while challenging the notion of a "centralized culture."

27. Costello, *Elizabeth Bishop*, 128.

28. Elizabeth Bishop, *Geography III* (New York: Farrar, Straus and Giroux, 1976).

29. Silverman, *Threshold*, 170.

30. Vassar Special Collections, Elizabeth Bishop Papers, Box 58, Folder 58.14.

31. *Webster's New World Dictionary*, 2d ed. (Cleveland, 1979), 98.

32. Quoted in Lombardi, *Elizabeth Bishop*, 104.

33. Silverman, *Threshold*, 190.

34. Elizabeth Bishop, "Dimensions for a Novel," *Vassar Journal of Undergraduate Studies* 8 (May 1934): 98.

## CHAPTER 4

1. Goldensohn, *Elizabeth Bishop*, 62.

2. Between their first meeting at Yaddo in the fall of 1950 and Bishop's death in 1979, Bishop and Swenson exchanged over 260 letters. Like Marianne Moore, Swenson kept carbon copies of nearly every letter she wrote to Bishop, and for this reason the majority of their correspondence is extant. Swenson's carbons and Bishop's letters to Swenson are housed in the Special Collections of Olin Library at Washington University, St. Louis. A handful of original letters from Swenson to Bishop may be found in the Bishop Papers at Vassar College. Approximately 160 of the 260 letters between Bishop and Swenson were from Bishop, 14 of which have been published in *OA*. Forty-one of Swenson's letters to Bishop appear in *MWW*.

3. May Swenson, "Introduction for Elizabeth Bishop at Bishop's Reading at the 92nd Street Poetry Center, October 10, 1977." Transcribed from tape by Rozanne Knudson.

4. May Swenson, "The Experience of Poetry in a Scientific Age," in *Poets on Poetry*, ed. Howard Nemerov (New York: Basic Books, 1966), 147.

5. Swenson, "Experience of Poetry," 148.

6. Because it was Swenson who, for the most part, kept the correspondence intact, the majority of the letters have been available to scholars only since Swenson's death in 1989. Kathleen C. Johnson presented an unpublished paper, "Two Poets: The Correspondence of Elizabeth Bishop and May Swenson," at the Elizabeth Bishop Poetry Festival and Scholarly Conference in

Worcester, Mass., October, 1997. Gardner McFall gives a brief commentary on their correspondence in her introduction to *MWW*. See also Richard Howard, "Elizabeth Bishop–May Swenson Correspondence," *Paris Review* 131 (1994): 171–86. Rozanne Knudson provides details of their meeting and ensuing friendship in *The Wonderful Pen of May Swenson* (New York: Macmillan, 1993), chaps. 7 and 8, and, with Suzzanne Bigelow, *May Swenson: A Poet's Life in Photos* (Logan: Utah State University Press, 1996), chap. 4. In her critical biography of Bishop, Brett Millier gives a brief account of the relationship (*Elizabeth Bishop*, chaps. 9 and 11). Victoria Harrison mentions the correspondence, claiming that Bishop "played the role of mentor in this relationship" (*Elizabeth Bishop's Poetics of Intimacy*, 26). And finally, I offer a brief analysis of the correspondence between Swenson and Bishop (parts of which are reprinted here) in "Urged by the Unknown You: May Swenson and Elizabeth Bishop," my afterword to *Dear Elizabeth: Five Poems and Three Letters to Elizabeth Bishop* (Logan: Utah State University Press, 2001).

7. In a letter of June 4, 1958, Bishop offers a critical commentary on Moore's poem, "Something Goes By." Bishop titled the letter "NASTY REMARKS ABOUT 'SOMETHING GOES BY' BY MAY SWENSON." MSP, Series 1.1, Box 6.

8. Swenson to Bishop, October 3, 1961, MSP, Series 1.1, Box 7.

9. "An Interview with May Swenson: July 14, 1978," interview by Karla Hammond, *Parnassus* 7 (fall–winter 1978): 61.

10. MS to EB, October 21, 1970. Series 1.1, Box 7.

11. Bishop to Swenson, September 19, 1953, MSP, Series 1.1, Box 6.

12. Swenson would have seen this poem in *Partisan Review* 18 (January 1951): 41–42, when it was published as part of a three-part poem titled "Rain towards Morning."

13. Bishop to Swenson, September 6, 1955, MSP, Series 1.1, Box 6.

14. This poem appears in full under the title "Somebody Who's Somebody" (taken from the first line of the poem) in *Dear Elizabeth: Five Poems and Three Letters to Elizabeth Bishop*. I offer an extended analysis of this poem in "Urged by the Unknown You," 25–31.

15. May Swenson, *A Cage of Spines* (New York: Rinehart, 1958).

16. Bishop to Swenson, June 4, 1958, MSP, Series 1.1, Box 6. Robert Giroux decided not to include this rather telling letter in Bishop's selected letters, though he did include the much less explicit letter of July 3, 1958 (*OA*, 360–61).

17. Bishop to Swenson, September 6, 1955, MSP, Series 1.1, Box 6.

18. Bishop to Swenson, undated (between November 7 and 14, 1962), MSP, Series 1.1, Box 7.

19. Reprinted in Candace W. MacMahon, *Elizabeth Bishop: A Bibliography, 1927–1979* (Charlottesville: University Press of Virginia, 1980), 137.

20. Marianne Moore, "Archaically New," in *Trial Balances*, ed. Ann Winslow (New York: Macmillan, 1935), 82–83.

21. Bishop to Swenson, September 19, 1953, MSP, Series 1.1, Box 6.

22. Longenbach, *Modern Poetry after Modernism*, 47.

23. Bishop to Swenson, August 27, 1963, MSP, Series 1.1, Box 7.

24. Howard, "Bishop-Swenson Correspondence," 171. Swenson's "Dear Elizabeth" was first published in the *New Yorker*, October 9, 1965, 56, and reprinted in *N*, 133.

25. Swenson to Bishop, September 25, 1963, MSP, Series 1.1, Box 7.

26. Drafts of "Dear Elizabeth," MSP, Series 2.3, Box 48E, Folder 9 (Oversized).

27. Bishop to Swenson, October 12, 1963, MSP, Series 1.1, Box 7.

28. Swenson to Bishop, October 31, 1963, MSP, Series 1.1, Box 7.

29. Drafts of "Her Early Work," MSP, Series 2.3.7, Box 52, Folder 319.

30. "A Word with You" was first published in *Con Spirito* 1 (April 1933): 2.

31. Swenson, "Introduction at Bishop's Reading."

CHAPTER 5

1. Swenson, "A Matter of Diction," 44.

2. Swenson, "A Matter of Diction," 45.

3. Swenson, "A Matter of Diction," 46–48.

4. Of the four published interviews with Swenson, three (Lazarus and Knudson; Draves and Fortunato; Hammond) contain questions about influences. See "Conversation with May Swenson," interview by Arnold Lazarus and Rozanne Knudson, *Quartet* 4 (winter 1969): 9–27; "Craft Interview with May Swenson," interview by Cornelia Draves and Mary Jane Fortunato, *New York Quarterly* 19 (fall 1977): 14–25; Hammond, "Interview with May Swenson"; and "A Conversation with May Swenson," interview by Lee Hudson, *Literature in Performance* 3, no. 2 (1983): 55–66. In each case Swenson denies direct influences, as when she claims, "My earliest poetry wasn't influenced by anyone because I didn't read poetry when I first began writing" (Hammond, 61). Nevertheless, Swenson goes on to reveal her "favorite" poets (Lazarus and Knudson, 19), or those she finds "healthy to read" (Draves and Fortunato, 20), and Moore always tops the list: "First of all, I like Marianne Moore. I think she's really original. . . . I think also that she's very daring. . . . I like the character or person she portrays in her poetry" (Lazarus and Knudson, 19); "When I discovered Marianne Moore's and Cummings' work, I was intrigued. I was interested in Marianne Moore's subject-matter, her objectivity; she wasn't writing about her emotions" (Hammond, 61); and simply, "When I started to write . . . Marianne Moore interested me" (Draves and Fortunato, 20).

5. Swenson, "A Matter of Diction," 45.

6. Swenson, "A Matter of Diction," 48.

7. In 1972, Swenson's poetry appeared in *Women Poets in English: An Anthology*, ed. Ann Stanford (New York: McGraw-Hill, 1972), and in 1973 Swenson's poetry was anthologized in the women's poetry collections *No More Masks! An Anthology of Poems by Women*, ed. Florence Howe and Ellen Bass (New York: Anchor Press, 1973), and *Rising Tides: Twentieth Century American Women Poets*, ed. Laura Chester (New York: Washington Square Press, 1973). In the coming years Swenson also allowed her poems to be published in the following same-sex anthologies: Elly Bulkin and Joan Larkin, eds., *Amazon Poetry:*

*An Anthology of Lesbian Poetry* (New York: Out and Out Books, 1975); Anca Vrbovska (a good friend of Swenson's), Alfred Dorn, and Mildred Wiackley, eds., *From Deborah and Sappho to the Present: An Anthology of Women Poets*, New Orlando Poetry Anthology, vol. 4 (New York: New Orlando, 1976); Carol Konek and Dorothy Walters, eds., *I Hear My Sisters Saying: Poems by Twentieth Century Women* (New York: Thomas Y. Crowell, 1976); Aliki Barnstone and Willis Barnstone, eds., *A Book of Women Poets from Antiquity to Now* (New York: Schocken, 1980); and Carl Morse and Joan Larkin, eds., *Gay and Lesbian Poetry in Our Time* (New York: St. Martin's Press, 1988). In 1976 a close correspondence between Ostriker and Swenson began that was to last until the end of Swenson's life. While both women recognized the important differences between their politics and poetic projects, each respected the other and promoted the other's work. Though Swenson declined Ostriker's request for a dust-jacket blurb about a collection of Ostriker's poems in 1981, claiming that she wasn't the right person to endorse her book (that it should be someone more overtly committed to a women's movement readership), she also continued to recommend the younger woman for various grants and prizes. See Ostriker, "The Nerves of a Midwife" and "May Swenson and The Shapes of Speculation," *American Poetry Review*, March–April 1978, 35–38, reprinted in Ostriker's *Writing Like a Woman*, 86–101; and Sandra Gilbert and Susan Gubar, eds., *Shakespeare's Sisters* (Bloomington: Indiana University Press, 1979), 221–32. Ostriker's *Stealing the Language* also contains brief but adulatory readings of Swenson.

8. Letter from May Swenson to Louise Bogan, April 30, 1963, Amherst College, Robert Frost Library, Louise Bogan Papers, Box VIII, Folder 9.

9. May Swenson, *Iconographs: Poems* (New York: Scribner's, 1970), 87.

10. Swenson, "Experience of Poetry," 148.

11. Schulman, "Life's Miracle," 10.

12. Although the fairly recent publications of *Made with Words, Nature, May Out West: Poems of May Swenson* (Logan: Utah State University Press, 1996), and Knudson and Bigelow's biographical project *(May Swenson)* suggest (or hope to inspire) a revival of interest in Swenson's work, critical commentary is still relatively sparse, particularly with reference to her erotic imagery and sexual orientation. One exception to this claim is Sue Russell's "Mysterious and Lavish Power." Russell reads Swenson's poetry within the context of her lesbianism, suggesting the ways in which her work is reflective of her sexual orientation. See also Grace Schulman's essay "Life's Miracle." The most thorough article that centrally examines Swenson's sensuality is Stanford's "May Swenson."

13. Hammond, "Interview with May Swenson," 62.

14. Russell, "Mysterious and Lavish Power," 131.

15. Russell, "Mysterious and Lavish Power," 132.

16. This and the following excerpts of correspondence between Swenson and Larkin are quoted from Russell, "Mysterious and Lavish Power," 132.

17. Howard, *Alone with America*, 517.

18. Howard, *Alone with America*, 517.

19. Howard, *Alone with America,* 518.

20. MSP, Box 68 (no folders in this box).

21. Foucault, *The History of Sexuality,* 15–17.

22. Drawing mainly from her previous collections, Swenson published a "children's" book made up entirely of riddle-poems called *Poems to Solve* (New York: Scribner's, 1966), as well as the later *More Poems to Solve* (New York: Scribner's, 1971) and *The Guess and Spell Coloring Book* (New York: Scribner's, 1976).

23. Richard Wilbur, memorial tribute to May Swenson at the American Academy of Arts and Letters Dinner Meeting, November 8, 1990, reprinted in Knudson and Bigelow, *May Swenson,* 26.

24. Butler, *Bodies That Matter,* 239.

25. MSP, Series 2.1, Box 44, Folder 184.

26. Russell, "Mysterious and Lavish Power."

27. Russell, "Mysterious and Lavish Power," 134.

28. Phone conversation with Rozanne Knudson, June 14, 1997.

29. MSP, Series 2.3.10, Box 57, Folder 339.

30. Butler, *Bodies That Matter,* 237.

31. Butler, *Bodies That Matter,* 241.

32. Butler, *Excitable Speech,* 8.

33. Hammond, "Interview with May Swenson," 66.

34. Hudson, "Conversation with May Swenson," 55.

35. Swenson, "Experience of Poetry," 149.

36. May Swenson, *The Floor: A Play in One Act,* in *First Stage* 6 (1967): 112–18.

37. Knudson and Bigelow, *May Swenson,* 81.

38. "To Make a Play" was first published in *Theatre: The Annual of the Repertory Theatre of Lincoln Center,* ed. Barry Hyams, vol. 2 (New York: Hill and Wang, 1965), 74. It was reprinted in *HS,* 106.

39. MSP, Series 2.3, Box 48G, Folder 24.

40. Butler, *Excitable Speech,* 51, 145.

41. Butler, *Bodies That Matter,* 231.

42. Although quite diverse, this body of work shares, for the most part, Laura Mulvey's seminal 1975 essay, "Visual Pleasure and Narrative Cinema," *Screen* 16 (Autumn, 1975): 198–209, as a starting point, in which her explication of the gaze as male seeks to expose the ways in which film reflects and encourages contemporary heterosexist constructions of sexual difference. Although it is beyond the scope of this chapter to directly interrogate the subsequent evolution of feminist film theories, I do think it is relevant to this discussion of Swenson to note the ways in which this evolution still tends to refigure the equation of the gaze as male to mean that *only males can gaze*—thus leading to the inadvertent reification of gender codes in which women are figured as the passive victims of an inherently active male subjectivity. Swenson's work provides many possibilities for an interesting comparison of methodologies. For a sampling of the different theoretical projects that are nevertheless commonly determined by this perspective, see Mary Ann Doane, *Femmes Fatale: Feminism,*

*Film Theory, Psychoanalysis* (New York: Routledge, 1991); and Bad Object Choices, eds., *How Do I Look? Queer Film and Video* (Seattle: Bay Press, 1991). For an excellent analysis of the ways in which particular films have worked to contest this equation of the gaze as male, see Kaja Silverman's *Male Subjectivity at the Margins*, chap. 3, and *Threshold of the Visible World*.

43. "Untitled" is reprinted in *LP* (63) and *N* (4) without the hand-drawn lines.

44. Lazarus and Knudson, "Conversation with May Swenson," 18.

45. Walt Whitman, *Leaves of Grass* (New York: Signet, 1980), 71–72.

46. Swenson, "Experience of Poetry," 147.

# Bibliography

PRIMARY SOURCES

Bishop, Elizabeth. *North & South*. Boston: Houghton Mifflin, 1946.

———. "As We Like It." *Quarterly Review of Literature* 4, no. 2 (1948): 129–35.

———. *Poems: North & South—A Cold Spring*. Boston: Houghton Mifflin, 1955.

———. "A Sentimental Tribute." *Bryn Mawr Alumni Bulletin*, spring 1962, 2–3.

———. *Questions of Travel*. New York: Farrar, Straus and Giroux, 1965.

———. "An Interview with Elizabeth Bishop." Interview by Ashley Brown. *Shenandoah* 17 (1966): 3–19.

———. *Selected Poems*. London: Chatto and Windus, 1967.

———. *The Collected Poems*. New York: Farrar, Straus and Giroux, 1969.

———. *Geography III*. New York: Farrar, Straus and Giroux, 1976.

———. "The Work! A Conversation with Elizabeth Bishop." Interview by George Starbuck. *Ploughshares* 3 (1977): 11–29.

———. "The Art of Poetry XXVII: Elizabeth Bishop." Interview by Elizabeth Spires. *Paris Review* 22 (1981): 57–83.

———. *The Complete Poems, 1927–1979*. New York: Farrar, Straus and Giroux, 1983.

———. *The Collected Prose*. Ed. Robert Giroux. New York: Farrar, Straus and Giroux, 1984.

———. "Influences." *American Poetry Review*, January–February 1985, 11–16.

———. *One Art: Letters*. Ed. Robert Giroux. New York: Farrar, Straus and Giroux, 1994.

———. "Interview with Elizabeth Bishop." Interview by Candace W. MacMahon. N.d. Vassar Special Collections, Box 79, Folder 79.14.

———, trans. *The Diary of "Helena Morley,"* by Alice Brant. New York: Farrar, Straus and Giroux, 1957.

Bishop, Elizabeth, with the editors of *Life*. *Brazil*. New York: Time-Life Books, 1962.

Moore, Marianne. *Poems*. New York: Egoist Press, 1921.

———. *Observations*. New York: Dial Press, 1924.

———. "Archaically New." In *Trial Balances*. Ed. Ann Winslow. New York: Macmillan, 1935.

———. *Selected Poems*. New York: Macmillan, 1935.

———. *The Pangolin and Other Verse*. London: Brendin, 1936.

———. *What Are Years?* New York: Macmillan, 1941.

———. *Nevertheless*. New York: Macmillan, 1944.

———. "A Modest Expert." *The Nation*, September 28, 1946, 354.

———. *Collected Poems*. New York: Macmillan, 1951.

———. *Predilections*. New York: Viking, 1955.

———. *Like a Bulwark*. New York: Viking, 1956.

———. *O to Be a Dragon*. New York: Viking, 1956.

———. *A Marianne Moore Reader*. New York: Viking, 1961.

———. *Tell Me, Tell Me: Granite, Steel, and Other Topics*. New York: Viking, 1966.

———. "The Art of Poetry: Marianne Moore." Interview by Donald Hall. In *Marianne Moore: A Collection of Critical Essays*, ed. Charles Tomlinson. Englewood Cliffs, N.J.: Prentice-Hall, 1969.

———. *Unfinished Poems by Marianne Moore*. Philadelphia: Rosenbach Museum and Library, 1972.

———. *The Complete Poems of Marianne Moore*. New York: Macmillan, Viking, 1982.

———. *The Complete Prose of Marianne Moore*. Ed. Patricia C. Willis. New York: Viking Penguin, 1986.

———. *The Selected Letters of Marianne Moore*. Ed. Bonnie Costello, Cristanne Miller, and Celeste Goodridge. New York: Knopf, 1997.

———, trans. *The Fables of La Fontaine*. London: Faber and Faber, 1954.

Swenson, May. *Another Animal: Poems*. In *Poets of Today I*. Ed. John Wheelock. New York: Scribner's, 1954.

———. "Eclogue." *Paris Review* 10 (1955): 97–103.

———. *A Cage of Spines*. New York: Rinehart, 1958.

———. "A Trio of Poets." Rev. of *The Dark Sister*, by Winfield Townley Scott, *The Open Sea and Other Poems*, by William Meredith, and *Time without Number*, by Daniel Berrigan. *Prairie Schooner* 32 (winter 1958–59): 331–35.

———. "Milton Avery." *Arts Yearbook 3: Paris/New York* (1959): 108–14.

———. Introduction to *Spoon River Anthology*, by Edgar Lee Masters. New York: Macmillan, 1962.

———. *To Mix with Time: New and Selected Poems*. New York: Scribner's, 1963.

———. "Poetry of Three Women." Review of *Helen in Egypt*, by H.D., *Waterlilly Fire*, by Muriel Rukeyser, and *All My Pretty Ones* by Anne Sexton. *Nation*, February 23, 1963, 163–66.

———. "On Richard Wilbur's 'Love Calls Us to the Things of This World.'" *Berkeley Review* 1 (1964): 12–16.

———. "May Swenson Replies." Letter, *Harper's*, July 1964, 10.

———. *Poems to Solve*. New York: Scribner's, 1966.

———. *Half Sun Half Sleep*. New York: Scribner's, 1967.

———. "A Conversation with May Swenson." Interview by Arnold Lazarus and Rozanne Knudson. *Quartet* 4 (winter 1969): 9–27.

———. *Iconographs: Poems*. New York: Scribner's, 1970.

———. *More Poems to Solve*. New York: Scribner's, 1971.

———. "Cheek by Jowl, Eight Poets." Review of *After Experience*, by W. D. Snodgrass, *Shifts of Being*, by Richard Eberhart, *The Descent*, by Ann Sanford, *A Bed by the Sea*, by Arthur Gregor, *Pretending to Be Asleep*, by Peter

Davidson, *The Way of the World*, by Charles Tomlinson, *Scattered Light*, by Christopher Brookhouse, and *Watch Us Pass*, by Robert Canzoneri. *Southern Review* 7 (July 1971): 954–61.

———. *The Guess and Spell Coloring Book*. New York: Scribner's, 1976.

———. "Art as Cure, Pomegranate as Grenade." Rev. of *The Book of Folly*, by Anne Sexton and *Monster*, by Robin Morgan. *New York Times Book Review*, November 19, 1976, 7, 26.

———. "Craft Interview with May Swenson." Interview by Cornelia Draves and Mary Jane Fortunato. *New York Quarterly* 19 (autumn 1977): 14–27.

———. *New and Selected Things Taking Place*. Boston: Little, Brown, 1978.

———. "An Interview with May Swenson: July 14, 1978." Interview by Karla Hammond. *Parnassus* 7 (fall–winter 1978): 60–75.

———. "May Swenson on Becoming a Poet, and on Form." *Envoy* 1 (spring–summer 1979): 1–2.

———. [Untitled.] In "A Symposium on the Theory and Practice of the Line in Contemporary Poetry." Ed. Rory Holscher and Robert Schultz. *Epoch* 29 (winter 1980): 222–24.

———. "A Conversation with May Swenson." Interview by Lee Hudson. *Literature in Performance* 3 (April 1983): 55–66.

———. *In Other Words*. New York: Alfred Knopf, 1987.

———. *The Love Poems of May Swenson*. Boston: Houghton Mifflin, 1991.

———. *Nature: Poems Old and New*. Boston: Houghton Mifflin, 1994.

———. *May Out West: Poems of May Swenson*. Logan: University of Utah Press, 1996.

———. *Made with Words*. Ed. Gardner McFall. Ann Arbor: University of Michigan Press, 1998.

———. *Dear Elizabeth: Five Poems and Three Letters to Elizabeth Bishop*. Ed. Kirstin Hotelling Zona. Logan: Utah State University Press, 2001.

Swenson, May, and Leif Sjoberg, trans. *Windows and Stone: Selected Poems*, by Thomas Transtromer. Pittsburgh: University of Pittsburgh Press, 1972.

### SECONDARY SOURCES

Aaron, Daniel. *Writers on the Left: Episodes in American Literary Communism*. New York: Columbia University Press, 1992.

Abbot, Craig. *Marianne Moore: A Descriptive Bibliography*: Pittsburgh: University of Pittsburgh Press, 1977.

———. *Marianne Moore: A Reference Guide*. Boston: G. K. Hall, 1978.

Abel, Elizabeth. *Writing and Sexual Difference*. Chicago: University of Chicago Press, 1982.

Altieri, Charles. *Self and Sensibility in Contemporary American Poetry*. Cambridge: Cambridge University Press, 1984.

Ashbery, John. "Elizabeth Bishop." Introduction to Elizabeth Bishop for the Books Abroad/Neustadt International Prize Ceremony, n.d. Vassar Special Collections, Box 79, Folder 79.6.

———. *Selected Poems*. New York: Penguin, 1985.

Baker, Houston A., Jr., *Afro-American Poetics: Revisions of Harlem and the Black Aesthetic*. Madison: University of Wisconsin Press, 1988.

Benjamin, Jessica. *The Bonds of Love: Psychoanalysis, Feminism, and the Problem of Domination*. New York: Pantheon, 1988.

Bennett, Paula. *My Life a Loaded Gun: Female Creativity and Feminist Poetics*. Boston: Beacon Press, 1986.

Berg, Temma F., Anna Shannon Elfenbein, Jeanne Larsen, and Elisa Kay Sparks, eds. *Engendering the Word: Feminist Essays in Psychosexual Poetics*. Urbana: University of Illinois Press, 1989.

Bloom, Harold. *The Anxiety of Influence: A Theory of Poetry*. Oxford: Oxford University Press, 1973.

———, ed. *Elizabeth Bishop*. New York: Chelsea House, 1985.

———, ed. *Marianne Moore*. New York: Chelsea House, 1987.

Bogan, Louise. *Achievement in American Poetry, 1900–1950*. Chicago: Henry Regnery, 1951.

Borroff, Marie. *Language and the Poet: Verbal Artistry in Frost, Stevens, and Moore*. Chicago: University of Chicago Press, 1979.

Brazeau, Peter, and Gary Fountain. *Remembering Elizabeth Bishop: An Oral Biography*. Amherst: University of Massachusetts Press, 1994.

Bromwich, David. "Elizabeth Bishop's Dream Houses." *Raritan* 4, no. 1 (1984): 77–91.

———. *A Choice of Inheritance: Self and Community from Edmund Burke to Robert Frost*. Cambridge: Harvard University Press, 1989.

Brownstein, Marilyn. "The Archaic Mother and Mother and Mother: The Postmodern Poetry of Marianne Moore." *Contemporary Literature* 30, no. 1 (1989): 13–32.

Burke, Carolyn. "Supposed Persons: Modernist Poetry and the Female Subject." *Feminist Studies* 2, no. 1 (1985): 131–48.

———. "Getting Spliced: Modernism and Sexual Difference." *American Quarterly* 39, no. 1 (1987): 98–121.

Butler, Judith. *Gender Trouble: Feminism and the Subversion of Identity*. New York: Routledge, 1990.

———. *Bodies That Matter: On the Discursive Limits of "Sex."* New York: Routledge, 1993.

———. *Excitable Speech: A Politics of the Performative*. New York: Routledge, 1997.

———. *The Psychic Life of Power: Theories in Subjection*. Stanford: Stanford University Press, 1997.

Cameron, Sharon. *Lyric Time: Dickinson and the Limits of Genre*. Baltimore: Johns Hopkins University Press, 1979.

Chester, Laura, and Sharon Barba, eds. *Rising Tides: Twentieth Century American Women Poets*. New York: Washington Square Press, 1973.

Chodorow, Nancy. *The Reproduction of Mothering: Psychoanalysis and the Sociology of Gender*. Berkeley and Los Angeles: University of California Press, 1978.

————. *Feminism and Psychoanalytic Theory.* New Haven: Yale University Press, 1989.

Cixous, Hélène. *The Hélène Cixous Reader.* Ed. Susan Sellers. New York: Routledge, 1994.

Clark, Suzanne. *Sentimental Modernism: Women Writers and the Revolution of the Word.* Bloomington: Indiana University Press, 1991.

Clausen, Jan. *A Movement of Poets: Thoughts on Feminism and Poetry.* New York: Long Haul Press, 1982.

Costello, Bonnie. "Marianne Moore's Wild Decorum." *American Poetry Review,* March–April 1978, 43–54.

————. "The 'Feminine' Language of Marianne Moore." In *Women and Language in Literature and Society,* ed. Sally McConnell-Ginet, Ruth Borker, and Nelly Furman. New York: Praeger, 1980.

————. *Marianne Moore: Imaginary Possessions.* Cambridge: Harvard University Press, 1981.

————. "Vision and Mastery in Elizabeth Bishop." *Twentieth Century Literature* 28 (1982): 351–70.

————. "Marianne Moore and Elizabeth Bishop: Friendship and Influence." *Twentieth Century Literature* 30 (1984): 130–49.

————. *Elizabeth Bishop: Questions of Mastery.* Cambridge: Harvard University Press, 1991.

Cuculla, Louis. "Trompe L'Oeil: Elizabeth Bishop's Radical 'I.'" *Texas Studies in Literature and Language* 30, no. 2 (1988): 246–71.

de Lauretis, Teresa. *Feminist Studies/Critical Studies.* Bloomington: Indiana University Press, 1986.

————. "Eccentric Subjects: Feminist Theory and Historical Consciousness." *Feminist Studies* 16 (1990): 115–50.

D'Emilio, John. *Sexual Politics, Sexual Communities: The Making of a Homosexual Minority in the United States, 1940–1970.* Chicago: University of Chicago Press, 1983.

Deutsch, Babette. "Poems Generous and Quiet." Review of *Cage of Spines,* by May Swenson. *New York Herald Tribune Book Review,* October 15, 1958, 6.

————. *Poetry in Our Time: A Critical Survey of Poetry in the English-Speaking World, 1900–1960.* 2d ed. Garden City, N.Y.: Doubleday, 1963.

Dickie, Margaret. "Race and Class in Elizabeth Bishop's Poetry." *Yearbook of English Studies* 24 (1994): 44–58.

Diehl, Joanne Feit. "At Home with Loss: Elizabeth Bishop and the American Sublime." In *Coming to Light: American Woman Poets in the Twentieth Century,* ed. Dianne Wood Middlebrook and Marilyn Yalom. Ann Arbor: Michigan University Press, 1985.

————. *Women Poets and the American Sublime.* Bloomington: Indiana University Press, 1990.

————. *Elizabeth Bishop and Marianne Moore: The Psychodynamics of Creativity.* Princeton, N.J.: Princeton University Press, 1993.

Dorenkamp, Angela, and Laura J. Menides, eds. *"In Worcester, Massachusetts":
Essays on Elizabeth Bishop.* New York: Peter Lang, 1999.

Doreski, C. K. *Elizabeth Bishop: The Restraints of Language.* Oxford: Oxford University Press, 1993.

Douglas, Anne. *The Feminization of American Culture.* New York: Knopf, 1977.

Drake, William. *The First Wave: Women Poets in America, 1915–1945.* New York: Macmillan, 1987.

DuPlessis, Rachel Blau. *Writing Beyond the Ending: Narrative Strategies of Twentieth Century Women Writers.* Bloomington: Indiana University Press, 1985.

———. "No Moore of the Same: The Feminist Poetics of Marianne Moore." *William Carlos Williams Review* 14, no. 1 (1988): 6–32.

Edelman, Lee. "The Geography of Gender: Elizabeth Bishop's 'In the Waiting Room.'" *Contemporary Literature* 26, no. 2 (1985): 179–86. Reprinted in Marilyn May Lombardi, ed., *Elizabeth Bishop: The Geography of Gender* (Charlottsville: University Press of Virginia, 1993): 97–104.

Eichwald, Richard A. "May Swenson." In *Critical Survey of Poetry: English Language Series,* ed. Frank N. Magill, vol. 7. Englewood Cliffs, N.J.: Salem Press, 1982.

Eliot, T. S. *The Sacred Wood.* New York: Methuen, 1920.

Elkins, Mary J. "Elizabeth Bishop and the Art of Seeing." *South Atlantic Review* 48, no. 4 (1983): 43–57.

Engel, Bernard F. *Marianne Moore.* New York: Twayne, 1964.

Epstein, Stephen. "Gay Politics, Ethnic Identity: The Limits of Social Constructionism." *Socialist Review* 17 (May–August): 9–54.

Erickson, Darlene. *Illusion Is More Precise Than Precision: The Poetry of Marianne Moore.* Tuscaloosa: University of Alabama Press, 1992.

Erkkila, Betsy. *The Wicked Sisters: Women Poets, Literary History, and Discord.* Oxford: Oxford University Press, 1992.

Estes, Sybil. "Elizabeth Bishop: The Delicate Art of Map-Making." *Southern Review* 13 (October 1977): 705–27.

Faderman, Lillian. *Odd Girls and Twilight Lovers: A History of Lesbian Life in Twentieth Century America.* New Haven: Yale University Press, 1985.

Felski, Rita. *Beyond Feminist Aesthetics: Feminist Literature and Social Change.* Cambridge: Harvard University Press, 1989.

Foucault, Michel. *The History of Sexuality.* Vol. 1, *An Introduction.* Trans. Robert Hurley. New York: Vintage, 1980.

Frankenburg, Lloyd. *Pleasure Dome: On Reading Modern Poetry.* Boston: Houghton Mifflin, 1949.

———. "Poetry's Bright New Star." Review of Elizabeth Bishop's *North & South,* n.d. Vassar Special Collections, Box 79, Folder 79.9.

Fraser, Kathleen. "On Being a West Coast Woman Poet." *Women's Studies* 5 (1977): 153–60.

Freedman, Estelle B., Barbara C. Gelpi, Susan L. Johnson, and Kathleen M. Weston, eds. *The Lesbian Issue: Essays from "Signs."* Chicago: University of Chicago Press, 1985.

Freud, Sigmund. *The Standard Edition of the Complete Psychological Works of Sigmund Freud*. Trans. James Strachey in collaboration with Anna Freud, assisted by Alix Strachey and Alan Tyson. London: Hogarth Press, 1953–74.

Fuss, Diana. *Essentially Speaking: Feminism, Nature, and Difference*. New York: Routledge, 1989.

———. *Identification Papers*. New York: Routledge, 1995.

Gadomski, Kenneth. "May Swenson: A Bibliography of Primary and Secondary Sources." *Bulletin of Bibliography* 44 (December 1984): 255–80.

Garcia, Jose, ed. Special issue of *Quarterly Review of Literature* on Marianne Moore, 4, no. 2 (1948).

Garrigue, Jean. *Marianne Moore*. University of Minnesota Pamphlets on American Writers, no. 50. Minneapolis: University of Minneapolis Press, 1965.

Gelpi, Barbara Charlesworth. "The Politics of Androgyny." *Women's Studies* 2 (1974): 151–60.

George, Diana Hume. "Who Is the Double Ghost Whose Head Is Smoke? Women Poets on Aging." In *Memory and Desire: Aging—Literature—Psychoanalysis*, ed. Kathleen Woodward and Murray Schwartz. Bloomington: University of Indiana Press, 1986.

Gilbert, Sandra, and Susan Gubar. *Shakespeare's Sisters: Feminist Essays on Women Poets*. Bloomington: Indiana University Press, 1979.

———. *No Man's Land: The Place of the Woman Writer in the Twentieth Century*. 3 vols. New Haven: Yale University Press, 1988–94.

Goldensohn, Lorrie. *Elizabeth Bishop: The Biography of a Poetry*. New York: Columbia University Press, 1992.

Goodridge, Celeste, ed. Special issue of *Sagetribe* on Marianne Moore, 6, no. 3 (1987).

———. *Hints and Disguises: Marianne Moore and Her Contemporaries*. Iowa City: University of Iowa Press, 1989.

Gould, Jean. *American Women Poets: Pioneers of Modern Poetry*. New York: Dodd, Mead, 1980.

———. *Modern American Women Poets*. New York: Dodd, Mead, 1984.

Graham, Vickie. "Whetted to Brilliance." *Sagetribe* 6, no. 3 (1987): 127–46.

Griffin, Gabriele. *Heavenly Love? Lesbian Images in Twentieth Century Women's Writing*. Manchester: Manchester University Press, 1993.

Hadas, Pamela White. *Marianne Moore: Poet of Affection*. Syracuse, N.Y.: Syracuse University, 1977.

Hall, Donald. *Marianne Moore: The Cage and the Animal*. New York: Western, 1970.

Hammer, Langdon. "The New Elizabeth Bishop." *Yale Review* 82 (1994): 135–49.

Haraway, Donna. *Simians, Cyborgs, and Women: The Reinvention of Nature*. New York: Routledge, 1991.

Harrison, Victoria. *Elizabeth Bishop's Poetics of Intimacy*. Cambridge: Cambridge University Press, 1993.

H.D. "Marianne Moore." *Egoist* 3 (1916): 118–19.

Heuving, Jeanne. *Omissions Are Not Accidents: Gender in the Art of Marianne Moore.* Detroit: Wayne State University Press, 1992.

Heyman, Harriet. "Eleven American Poets." *Life,* April 1981, 86–102.

Higonet, Margaret Randolph, ed. *Behind the Lines: Gender and the Two World Wars.* New Haven: Yale University Press, 1987.

Hollander, John. *The Work of Poetry.* New York: Columbia University Press, 1997.

Holley, Margaret. "The Model Stanza: The Organic Origin of Moore's Syllabic Verse." *Twentieth Century Literature* 30 (summer–fall 1984): 181–91.

———. *The Poetry of Marianne Moore: A Study in Voice and Value.* Cambridge: Cambridge University Press, 1987.

Homans, Margaret. *Bearing the Word: Language and Experience in Nineteenth-Century Women's Writing.* Chicago: University of Chicago Press, 1968.

———. *Women Writers and Poetic Identity: Dorothy Wordsworth, Emily Bronte, and Emily Dickinson.* Princeton, N.J.: Princeton University Press, 1980.

Honey, Maureen. *Shadowed Dreams: Women's Poetry of the Harlem Renaissance.* New York: Rutgers University Press, 1989.

Howard, Richard. "May Swenson: 'Turned Back to the Wild by Love." In *Alone with America: Essays on the Art of Poetry in the United States since 1950.* New York: Atheneum, 1969.

———, ed. *Preferences: Fifty-one American Poets Choose Poems from Their Own Work and from the Past.* New York: Viking, 1974.

———. "Elizabeth Bishop–May Swenson Correspondence." *Paris Review* 131 (summer 1994): 171–86.

Hutcheon, Linda. *The Poetics of Postmodernism: History, Theory, Fiction.* New York: Routledge, 1988.

Jackson, Thomas H., ed. Special issue of *Poesis* on H.D. and Marianne Moore, 6, nos. 3–4 (1985).

Jardine, Alice. *Gynesis: Configurations of Women and Modernity.* Ithaca, N.Y.: Cornell University Press, 1985.

Jarrell, Randall. *Poetry and the Age.* New York: Knopf, 1953.

———. "Her Shield." *Poetry and the Age.* New York: Ecco Press, 1980.

Jay, Carla, and Joanne Glascow, eds. *Lesbian Texts and Contexts: Radical Revisions.* New York: New York University Press, 1990.

Johns, H. E. S. "Belling the Cat." *Harper's,* July 1964, 8, 10.

Johnson, Kathleen. "Two Poets: The Correspondence between Elizabeth Bishop and May Swenson." Paper presented at the Elizabeth Bishop Conference and Poetry Festival, Worcester Polytechnic Institution, Worcester, Mass., October 11, 1997.

Joyce, Elisabeth. *Cultural Critique and Abstraction: Marianne Moore and the Avant-garde.* Lewisburg, Pa.: Bucknell University Press, 1999.

Juhasz, Suzanne. *Naked and Fiery Forms: Modern American Poetry by Women.* New York: Harper and Row, 1976.

Kadlec, David. "Marianne Moore, Immigration, and Eugenics." *Modernism/Modernity* 1, no. 2 (1994): 21–49.

Kalstone, David. *Five Temperaments*. Oxford: Oxford University Press, 1977.

———. "Trial Balances: Elizabeth Bishop and Marianne Moore." *Grand Street* 3, no. 1 (1983): 115–35.

———. "Prodigal Years: Elizabeth Bishop and Robert Lowell, 1947–1949." *Grand Street* 4, no. 4 (1985): 170–93.

———. *Becoming a Poet: Elizabeth Bishop with Marianne Moore and Robert Lowell*. Ed. Robert Hemenway. New York: Farrar, Straus and Giroux, 1989.

Kappel, Andrew J., ed. Special issue of *Twentieth Century Literature* on Marianne Moore, 30 nos. 2–3 (1984).

Keller, Lynn. "Words Worth a Thousand Postcards: The Bishop/Moore Correspondence." *American Literature* 55, no. 3 (1983): 405–29.

———. *Re-making It New: Contemporary American Poetry and the Modernist Tradition*. Cambridge: Cambridge University Press, 1987.

Keller, Lynn, and Christane Miller. "Emily Dickinson, Elizabeth Bishop, and the Rewards of Indirection." *New England Quarterly* 57, no. 4 (1984): 533–55.

———. "'The Tooth of Disputation': Marianne Moore's 'Marriage.'" *Sagetribe* 6, no. 3 (1987): 99–116.

———, eds. *Feminist Measures: Soundings in Poetry and Theory*. Ann Arbor: University of Michigan Press, 1994.

Kenner, Hugh. *The Pound Era*. Berkeley and Los Angeles: University of California Press, 1971.

———. *A Homemade World: The American Modernist Writers*. New York: Knopf, 1975.

Knudson, Rozanne. "Two Poets." *American Libraries* 2 (November 1971): 1046.

———. *The Wonderful Pen of May Swenson*. New York: Macmillan, 1993.

Knudson, Rozanne, and Suzzanne Bigelow. *May Swenson: A Poet's Life in Photos*. Logan: Utah State University Press, 1996.

Kristeva, Julia. *Desire in Language: A Semiotic Approach to Literature and Art*. Ed. Leon S. Roudiez. Trans. Thomas Gora, Alice Jardine, and Leon S. Roudiez. New York: Columbia University Press, 1980.

———. *Revolution in Poetic Language*. Trans. Margaret Waller. New York: Columbia University Press, 1984.

Lacan, Jacques. *Ecrits: A Selection*. Trans. Alan Sheridan. New York: Norton, 1977.

Lears, T. Jackson. *No Place of Grace: Antimodernism and the Transformation of American Culture, 1880–1912*. New York: Random House, 1981.

Leavell, Linda. *Marianne Moore and the Visual Arts: Prismatic Color*. Oklahoma City: University of Oklahoma Press, 1995.

Levenson, Michael H. *A Genealogy of Modernism: A Study of English Literary Doctrine, 1908–1922*. Cambridge: Cambridge University Press, 1984.

Lipking, Lawrence. *Abandoned Women and Poetic Tradition*. Chicago: University of Chicago Press, 1988.

Lombardi, Marilyn May. *The Body and the Song: Elizabeth Bishop's Poetics*. Carbondale: Southern Illinois University Press, 1995.

———, ed. *Elizabeth Bishop: The Geography of Gender*. Charlottesville: University Press of Virginia, 1993.

Longenbach, James. *Modernist Poetics of History: Pound, Eliot, and the Sense of the Past.* Princeton, N.J.: Princeton University Press, 1987.

———. *Stone Cottage: Pound, Yeats, and Modernism.* Oxford: Oxford University Press, 1988.

———. *Wallace Stevens: The Plain Sense of Things.* Oxford: Oxford University Press, 1991.

———. "Elizabeth Bishop's Social Consciousness." *English Literary History* 62 (1995): 467–86.

———. *Modern Poetry after Modernism.* Oxford: Oxford University Press, 1997.

Lowell, Robert. "Thomas, Bishop, and Williams." *Sewanee Review* 55 (1947): 497–99.

MacKay, Anne. *Wolf Girls at Vassar: Lesbian and Gay Experiences, 1930–1990.* New York: St. Martin's Press, 1993.

MacMahon, Candace W. *Elizabeth Bishop: A Bibliography, 1927–1979.* Charlottesville: University Press of Virginia, 1980.

Malkoff, Carl. "May Swenson." In *Crowell's Handbook of American Poetry.* Ed. Carl Malkoff. New York: Thomas Y. Crowell, 1973.

———. *Escape from the Self: A Study in Contemporary American Poetry and Poetics.* New York: Columbia University Press, 1977.

Martin, Taffy. *Marianne Moore: Subversive Modernist.* Austin: University of Texas Press, 1986.

Mazzacco, Robert. "A Poet of Landscape." Review of *Questions of Travel,* by Elizabeth Bishop. *New York Review of Books,* October 12, 1967, 4–6.

Mazzaro, Jerome. "Elizabeth Bishop and the Poetics of Impediment." *Salmagundi* 27 (summer–fall 1974): 118–44.

McCabe, Susan. *Elizabeth Bishop: Her Poetics of Loss.* University Park: Pennsylvania State University Press, 1994.

McConnell-Ginet, Sally, Ruth Borker, and Nelly Furman, eds. *Women and Language in Literature and Society.* New York: Praeger, 1980.

Mellor, Anne K. *Romanticism and Feminism.* Bloomington: Indiana University press, 1988.

Merrin, Jeredith. *An Enabling Humility: Marianne Moore, Elizabeth Bishop, and the Uses of Tradition.* New Brunswick, N.J.: Rutgers University Press, 1990.

Middlebrook, Dianne, and Marilyn Yalom, eds. *Coming to Light: American Women Poets in the Twentieth Century.* Ann Arbor: University of Michigan Press, 1985.

Miller, Cristanne. *Marianne Moore: Questions of Authority.* Cambridge: Harvard University Press, 1995.

Miller, J. Hillis. *Poets of Reality: Six Twentieth Century Writers.* New York: Atheneum, 1969.

Miller, Nancy K, ed. *The Poetics of Gender.* New York: Columbia University Press, 1986.

Millier, Brett C. *Elizabeth Bishop: Life and the Memory of It.* Berkeley and Los Angeles: University of California Press, 1993.

Mitchell, Juliet, and Jacqueline Rose. *Feminine Sexuality: Jacques Lacan and the Ecole Freudienne.* Trans. Jacqueline Rose. New York: Norton, Pantheon Books, 1982.

Mizener, Arthur. "Elizabeth Bishop: *North & South.*" Review of *North & South,* Vassar Special Collections, Box 80, Folder 80.1.

Moi, Toril. *Sexual/Textual Politics: Feminist Literary Theory.* London: Methuen, 1985.

Molesworth, Charles. *Marianne Moore: A Literary Life.* New York: Atheneum, 1990.

Montefiore, Jan. *Feminism and Poetry: Language, Experience, and Identity in Women's Writing.* New York: Pandora, 1987.

Moran, Eileen G. "Portrait of the Artist: Marianne Moore's Letters to Hildegarde Watson." *Poesis* 6 (1985): 124–36.

Nemerov, Howard, ed. *Poets on Poetry.* New York: Basic Books, 1966.

Newlin, Margaret. "'Unhelpful Hymen!' Marianne Moore and Hilda Doolittle." *Essays in Criticism* 27, no. 2 (1977): 225.

Nielson, Aldon L. *Reading Race: White American Poets and the Racial Discourse in the Twentieth Century.* Atlanta: University of Georgia Press, 1988.

Nims, John Frederick. Comment on "R.F. at Bread Loaf—His Hand against a Tree.'" *Western Wind: An Introduction to Poetry.* New York: Random House, 1974.

Nitchie, George. *Marianne Moore: An Introduction to the Poetry.* New York: Columbia University Press, 1969.

———. "Condescension and Affection: Some Observations on Marianne Moore." *Poesis* 6 (1985): 35–39.

Ostriker, Alicia. "The Nerves of a Midwife: Contemporary American Women's Poetry." *Parnassus* 6 (fall–winter 1977): 69–87.

———. "May Swenson and the Shapes of Speculation." *American Poetry Review,* March–April 1978, 35–38.

———. *Stealing the Language: Emergence of Women's Poetry in America.* Boston: Beacon Press, 1986.

———. "What Do Women Poets Want? H.D. and Marianne Moore as Poetic Ancestresses." *Contemporary Literature* 27 (1986): 475–92.

Page, Barbara. "Shifting Islands: Elizabeth Bishop's Manuscripts." *Shenandoah* 33, no. 1 (1981–82): 51–62.

———. "Nature, History, and Art in Elizabeth Bishop's 'Brazil, January 1, 1502.'" *Perspectives on Contemporary Literature* 14 (1988).

Parisi, Joseph, ed. *Marianne Moore: The Art of a Modernist.* Ann Arbor: University of Michigan Press, 1990.

Parker, Robert Dale. *The Unbeliever: The Poetry of Elizabeth Bishop.* Urbana: University of Illinois Press, 1988.

Paz, Octavio. Essay on Elizabeth Bishop, n.d.. Vassar Special Collections, Box 80, Folder 80.3.

Perloff, Marjorie. "Elizabeth Bishop: The Course of a Particular." *Modern Poetry Studies* 8, no. 3 (1977): 177–91.

———. "Recharging the Canon: Some Reflections on Feminist Poetics and the Avant Garde." *American Poetry Review*, July–August 1986, 13.

Phillips, Elizabeth. *Marianne Moore*. New York: Frederick Ungar, 1982.

Pinsky, Robert. *The Situation of Poetry*. Princeton, N.J.: Princeton University Press, 1976.

———. *Poetry and the World*. New York: Echo Press, 1988.

Plimpton, George, ed. *Poets at Work: The Paris Review Interviews*. New York: Viking Penguin, 1989.

Plummer, Kenneth, ed. *The Making of the Modern Homosexual*. London: Hutchinson, 1981.

Procopiow, Norma. "Survival Kit: The Poetry of Elizabeth Bishop." *Centennial Review* 25 (1981): 1–19.

Ransom, John Crowe. *The World's Body*. New York: Scribner's, 1938.

Rich, Adrienne. *Of Woman Born: Motherhood as Experience and Institution*. New York: Norton, 1976.

———. *On Lies, Secrets, and Silence: Selected Prose, 1966–1978*. New York: Norton, 1979.

———. *Blood, Bread, and Poetry: Selected Prose, 1979–85*. New York: Norton, 1986.

———. *Your Native Land, Your Life*. New York: Norton, 1986.

———. *What Is Found There: Notebooks on Poetry and Politics*. New York: Norton, 1993.

Riley, Denise. *"Am I That Name?": Feminism and the Category of "Women" in History*. Minneapolis: University of Minnesota Press, 1988.

Rodowick, David. *The Difficulty of Difference: Psychoanalysis, Sexual Difference, and Film Theory*. New York: Routledge, 1991.

Ross, Marlon B. *The Contours of Masculine Desire: Romanticism and the Rise of Women's Poetry*. Oxford: Oxford University Press, 1989.

Sanders, Charles. "Swenson's 'Snow in New York.'" *Explicator* 38 (fall 1979): 41–42.

Sargeant, Winthrop. "Humility, Concentration. and Gusto." *New Yorker*, February 16, 1957, 38–73.

Schrodes, Caroline, Henry Finestone, and Michael Shugrue, eds. "Questions and Exercises on 'Women Should Be Pedestals.'" In *The Conscious Reader: Readings Past and Present*. New York: Macmillan, 1975.

Schulman, Grace. *Marianne Moore: The Poetry of Engagement*. Urbana: University of Illinois Press, 1986.

Schwartz, Lloyd, and Sybil Estes, eds. *Elizabeth Bishop and Her Art*. Ann Arbor: University of Michigan Press, 1983.

Schwartz, Sanford. *The Matrix of Modernism: Pound, Eliot, and Early Twentieth-Century Thought*. Princeton, N.J.: Princeton University Press, 1985.

Schweik, Susan. "Writing War Poetry Like a Woman." *Critical Inquiry* 13, no. 3 (1987): 532–56.

———. *A Gulf So Deeply Cut: American Woman Poets and the Second World War*. Madison: University of Wisconsin Press, 1991.

Scott, Bonnie Kime, ed. *The Gender of Modernism: A Critical Anthology*. Bloomington: Indiana University Press, 1990.

Segnitz, Barbara, and Carol Rainey, eds. *Psyche: The Feminine Poetic Consciousness: An Anthology of Modern American Women Poets*. New York: Dell, 1973.

Shapiro, Alan. *In Praise of the Impure: Poetry and the Ethical Imagination*. Evanston, Ill.: Northwestern University Press, 1993.

Sheehy, Eugene P., and K. A. Lohfs, comps. *The Achievement of Marianne Moore: A Bibliography, 1907–57*. New York: New York Public Library, 1958.

Shore, Jan. "Elizabeth Bishop: The Art of Changing Your Mind." *Ploughshares* 5 (1979): 178–91.

Showalter, Elaine. *The New Feminist Criticism: Essays on Women, Literature, and Theory*. New York: Pantheon, 1985.

Sielke, Sabine. *Fashioning the Female Subject: The Intertextual Networking of Dickinson, Moore, and Rich*. Ann Arbor: University of Michigan Press, 1997.

Silverman, Kaja. *The Subject of Semiotics*. Oxford: Oxford University Press, 1983.

———. *The Acoustic Mirror: The Female Voice in Psychoanalysis and Cinema*. Bloomington: Indiana University Press, 1988.

———. *Male Subjectivity at the Margins*. New York: Routledge, 1992.

———. *The Threshold of the Visible World*. New York: Routledge, 1996.

Slatin, John M. *The Savage's Romance: The Poetry of Marianne Moore*. University Park: Pennsylvania State University Press, 1986.

———. "Something Inescapably Typical: Questions about Gender in the Late Work of Moore and Williams." *William Carlos Williams Review* 14, no. 1 (1988): 86–103.

Smith, Dave. "Perpetual Worlds Taking Place." *Poetry* 135 (February 1980): 291–96.

Snitow, Ann, Christine Stansell, and Sharon Thompson, eds. *Powers of Desire: The Politics of Sexuality*. New York: Monthly Review Press, 1983.

Spires, Elizabeth. "An Afternoon with Elizabeth Bishop." *Vassar Quarterly* 55 (1979): 4–9.

———. "Elizabeth Bishop." In *Poets at Work*, ed. George Plimpton. New York: Viking, 1989.

Spivak, Gayatri Chakravorty. *In Other Words: Essays in Cultural Politics*. New York: Routledge, 1988.

Stanford, Ann. "May Swenson." In *American Women Writers: A Critical Reference Guide from Colonial Times to the Present*, ed. Linda Mainiero. New York: Frederick Ungar, 1982.

———. "May Swenson: The Art of Perceiving." *Southern Review* 5 (winter 1969): 58–75.

Stapleton, Laurence. *Marianne Moore: The Poet's Advance*. Princeton, N.J.: Princeton University Press, 1978.

Stevens, Wallace. *The Necessary Angel: Essays on Reality and the Imagination*. New York: Vintage, 1951.

Stevenson, Anne. *Elizabeth Bishop*. New York: Twayne, 1966.

Summers, Joseph H. "Elizabeth Bishop." Lecture presented at Oxford University in the 1960s, Vassar Special Collections, Box 80, Folder 80.8.

Sweetkind, Morris. Discussion of "Lion" and "Landing on the Moon," by May Swenson. In *Getting into Poetry*. Boston: Holbrook, 1972.

Tambimuttu, ed. *Festschrift for Marianne Moore's Seventy-Seventh Birthday by Various Hands*. New York: Tambimuttu and Mass, 1964.

Therese, M. *Marianne Moore: A Critical Essay*. Grand Rapids, Mich.: William Eerdmans, 1969.

Thomas, Edward. *Feminine Influence on the Poets*. New York: John Lane, 1911.

Todd, Janet. *Feminist Literary History*. New York: Routledge, 1988.

Tomlinson, Charles, ed. *Marianne Moore: A Collection of Critical Essays*. Englewood Cliffs, N.J.: Prentice-Hall, 1969.

Travisano, Thomas J. *Elizabeth Bishop: Her Artistic Development*. Charlottesville: University Press of Virginia, 1988.

Untermeyer, Louis. "May Swenson." *Fifty Modern and American and British Poets, 1920–1970*. New York: McKay, 1973.

Van Doren, Mark. "Women and Wit." *Nation*, October 26, 1921, 481–82.

Vance, Carole S., ed. *Pleasure and Danger: Exploring Female Sexuality*. London: Pandora Press, 1992.

Vendler, Helen. *Part of Nature, Part of Us: Modern American Poets*. Cambridge: Harvard University Press, 1980.

Voigt, Ellen Bryant. *The Flexible Lyric*. Athens: University of Georgia Press, 1999.

Wallace, Patricia. "The Wildness of Elizabeth Bishop." *Sewanee Review* 93 (1985): 95–115.

Walker, Cheryl. *The Nightingale's Burden: Women Poets and American Culture before 1900*. Bloomington: Indiana University Press, 1982.

———. *Masks Outrageous and Austere: Culture, Psyche, and Persona in Modern American Women Poets*. Bloomington: Indiana University Press, 1991.

Watts, Emily. *The Poetry of American Women from 1632 to 1945*. Austin: University of Texas Press, 1977.

Weatherhead, A. Kingsley. *The Edge of the Image: Marianne Moore, William Carlos Williams, and Some Other Poets*. Seattle: University of Washington Press, 1967.

Wheelock, John Hall. "A Critical Introduction." In *Poets of Today 1*. New York: Scribner's, 1954.

———. "The Poet as Patron." *Wilson Library Bulletin* 36 (January 1962): 371–72.

Wher, Wesley. "Elizabeth Bishop: Conversations and Class Notes." *Antioch Review* 39 (1981): 319–28.

Whitman, Walt. *Leaves of Grass*. New York: Signet, 1980.

Wicks, Sammie Anne. "Music, Meaning, and the Adaptation of Literature." *Literature in Performance* 2 (November 1981): 89–97.

Wilbur, Richard. "May Swenson: A Memorial Tribute." *Gettysburg Review* 5 (1992): 81–85.

Williams, William Carlos. *The Autobiography of William Carlos Williams*. New York: Random House, 1951.

————. *Selected Essays of William Carlos Williams*. New York: New Directions, 1954.

Willis, Patricia. "The Owl and the Lantern: Marianne Moore at Bryn Mawr." *Poesis* 6 (1985): 84–97.

————. *Marianne Moore: Vision into Verse*. Philadelphia: Rosenbach Museum and Library, 1987.

————, ed. *Marianne Moore: Newsletter* (Rosenbach Museum and Library, Philadelphia), spring 1977–fall 1983.

————, ed. *Marianne Moore: Woman and Poet*. Orono, Maine: National Poetry Foundation, 1990.

Wylie, Diane E. *Elizabeth Bishop and Howard Nemerov: A Reference Guide*. Boston: G. K. Hall, 1983.

Yeats, William Butler. *The Collected Poems of W. B. Yeats*. Ed. Richard J. Finneran. New York: Macmillan, 1989.

Zona, Kirstin Hotelling. "A 'Dangerous Game of Change': Images of Desire in the Love Poems of May Swenson." *Twentieth Century Literature* 44, no. 2 (1998): 219–41.

————. "'The I of Each Is to the I of Each, a Kind of Fretful Speech Which Sets a Limit on Itself': Marianne Moore's Strategic Selfhood." *Modernism/Modernity* 5, no. 1 (1998): 75–96.

————. "Elizabeth Bishop's Productive Look." In *"In Worcester, Massachusetts": Essays on Elizabeth Bishop*, ed. Angela Dorenkamp and Laura J. Menides. New York: Peter Lang, 1999.

————. "Urged by the Unknown You: May Swenson & Elizabeth Bishop." In *Dear Elizabeth: Five Poems & Three Letters to Elizabeth Bishop*, by May Swenson. Ed. Kirstin Hotelling Zona. Logan, Utah: Utah State University Press, 2000. 25–31.

# Index